I0813307

IN THE AMERICAN WEST

ANDY WILKINSON, SERIES EDITOR

ALSO IN THIS SERIES:

Bad Smoke, Good Smoke: A Rancher's View of Texas Wildfire
by John R. Erickson

Cowboy's Lament: A Life on the Open Range
by Frank Maynard; edited by Jim Hoy

The Hell-Bound Train: A Cowboy Songbook, Second Edition
by Glenn Ohrlin; edited by Charlie Seemann

If I Was a Highway
by Michael Ventura

In My Father's House: A Memoir of Polygamy
by Dorothy Allred Solomon

Llano Estacado: An Island in the Sky
Stephen Bogener and William Tydeman, editors

Light in the Trees
by Gail Folkins

On Becoming Apache
by Harry Mithlo and Conger Beasley Jr.

Ordinary Skin: Essays from Willow Springs
by Amy Hale Auker

Rightful Place
by Amy Hale Auker

Small Town Author
by John R. Erickson

A Sweet Separate Intimacy: Women Writers of the American Frontier, 1800–1922
Susan Cummins Miller, editor

Texas Dance Halls: A Two-Step Circuit
by Gail Folkins and J. Marcus Weekley

Texas Red
by Red Steagall, with Jim Jennings

Gypsy Alibi

A Gonzo Memoir

Bob Livingston

TEXAS TECH UNIVERSITY PRESS

This book is typeset in Adobe Caslon Pro. The paper used in this book meets the minimum requirements of ANSI/NISO Z39.48-1992 (R1997). ♾

Designed by Hannah Gaskamp
Cover design by Hannah Gaskamp
Cover photo by Robbyn Dodd

Library of Congress Cataloging-in-Publication Data

Names: Livingston, Bob, author. Title: Gypsy Alibi: A Gonzo Memoir / Bob Livingston. Description: Lubbock: Texas Tech University Press, 2025. | Series: Voice in the American West | Includes index. | Summary: "The autobiography of Bob Livingston, bass player for the Lost Gonzo Band and contributor to the Cosmic Cowboy movement."—Provided by publisher.
Identifiers: LCCN 2025012707 (print) | LCCN 2025012708 (ebook) | ISBN 978-1-68283-268-4 (cloth) | ISBN 978-1-68283-269-1 (ebook)
Subjects: LCSH: Livingston, Bob. | Country musicians—United States—Biography. | Bass guitarists—United States—Biography. | Lost Gonzo Band. | LCGFT: Autobiographies. Classification: LCC ML419.L555 A3 2025 (print) | LCC ML419.L555 (ebook) | DDC 782.421642092 [B]—dc23/eng/20250328
LC record available at https://lccn.loc.gov/2025012707
LC ebook record available at https://lccn.loc.gov/2025012708

Printed in the United States of America
25 26 27 28 29 30 31 32 33 / 9 8 7 6 5 4 3 2 1

Texas Tech University Press
Box 41037
Lubbock, Texas 79409-1037 USA
800.832.4042
ttup@ttu.edu
www.ttupress.org

To Iris, Tucker, and Trevor—and to Donald,
who lived the life.

Contents

Illustrations

Gypsy Alibi

CHAPTER 1

Knock-down Drag-out

1972

He charged at me. Snarling and spitting and cussing and slobbering. I'd already hit him a few times and had smashed him into my pickup door like a rag doll. We wrestled around to the side yard, asses and elbows, all dusty and bleeding, our bodies scraping on the limestone rocks poking like dull knives out of the hard Hill Country ground. I hit him hard with an almost virgin fist and he fell back for a few moments then came after me again. He whacked me a good one on my left ear, the one that still rings. Some primal memory took over and I actually got into a three-point stance, the one my high school football coach Freddy Akers drilled into me at Lubbock High. It was all instinct now and I didn't have to think. I whipped my glasses off and crouched. Here he comes! I sprang up hard, my fists together under my chin, elbows out, a perfect battering ram, up and out, smashing my forehead just under his chin. It's a wonder it didn't take his head off. Though I tried. He fell back in a heap, and I was on him.

He turned the tables and got the better of me, but I ended up on top. In his face. Everything I grabbed was sweaty, slippery, and greasy, and I couldn't get any traction. I tried to pull his hair out from the roots, but it just slipped through my fingers. No matter how hard I tried to do real damage and rip his ears off or gouge his eyeballs out, I couldn't get ahold of much of anything, and all my efforts were for naught.

Then, with my hands around his throat and looking into his eyes, I saw a staggering sight. He was grinning like a gargoyle, laughing through the spit and the blood, his breath reeking of whisky, cigarettes, and beer. And he was loving this; he wasn't taking it seriously at all. I was beating the crap out of him and he was laughing at me. Laughing at us both. It was surreal and demonic in a funny sort of way. I'd only had one other fight in my life, with Greg Cobb in the fifth grade, and here I was about to strangle Jerry Jeff Walker.

And the day had started out so promising . . .

CHAPTER 2

Indian Summer

1981

It felt as though there were two suns in the yellow afternoon sky. The air was so hot I was in a crouch, trying to find some coolness low to the ground as I scuttered along the dusty road towards the railway station in South India. I was fighting to breathe.

In front of me walked a bearer, a man in a dingy red turban carrying my heavy bags and even my guitar piled on top of his head. He was quite tall and thin, sure of step and grinning wildly, showing his perfectly decayed teeth as we marched through the oppressive heat. I was drenched with sweat and as thirsty as the dry road before me. Even so, I was happier than I had been in a long while. Ten thousand miles from Texas and happy as a clam. It was April 1981. John Lennon had been shot four months before.

Back in Austin, nothing much was happening. Without much notice, Jerry Jeff had decided to go on a solo tour, and for us in the band that meant no work and no money right before Christmas. Scramble and improvise was the name of the working man's music business I knew. Nothing was for certain, and you had to have the right temperament and a thick skin to deal with this sort of gypsy-ness. But I had played and recorded some folk-rock-country classics with two of the most iconic and colorful singer-songwriter characters in the country, Jerry Jeff Walker and Michael Martin Murphey. *Geronimo's Cadillac*, *¡Viva Terlingua!*, *Cosmic Cowboy Souvenir*, *Ridin' High*. So far so good.

But now? Now I'm following my turbaned bearer around a pool of tepid monsoon water. I was overwhelmed by fatigue and jet lag, in awe of the crowd and the pressing of bodies. I fell into step behind, trying to keep up, wiping my face with a bandanna and putting up a good front as if I did this every day of my life. "Onward!" I shouted for effect. I really did. "Ah, yes, yes," the red turban said as he spat some foul-looking red goop on the road. It looked like blood but was most likely betel juice. Maybe mixed with blood.

As we ambled along the noisy street towards the railway station, I pictured myself as an international vagabond, Ramar of the Jungle, a one-man corps of discovery on the loose. I know it sounds like a daydream, but this was high adventure and hard traveling like I had never known before. On pilgrimages such as these, times are supposed to be tough and your mettle tested. I was on a mission to visit my wife Iris and my equally adventuresome boys, Tucker and Trevor. They had been staying in India for four months now, living in a village near a river. With every step, no matter how purposeful, halting, or unsteady as it might be, I was getting closer to seeing their happy faces.

There were at least four lanes of traffic on the one-lane road, and we were walking through it. Cars, lorries, taxis, motorcycles, scooters, and jeeps. Oxcarts, cows, water buffalo, and, yes, elephants. We wove past auto rickshaws, bicycles, army and police vehicles, still more taxis, and a swirling mass of humanity close up. It was a game of chicken to the death, darting in and out of traffic every which way, head-on. And all of it was done good-naturedly to the tune of thousands of chattering, smiling, laughing, shouting, hurrying people. They were dodging traffic, running a mile a minute, yelling orders, eating a variety of odoriferous foods,

Just off a plane from India with massive jet lag, wearing a juba shirt and beads at the Kerrville Folk Festival. (Photo courtesy of Bob Livingston.)

performing bodily functions, smoking, chewing, talking, and spitting. Red, yellow, brown on the street to the railway station at high noon.

Still on Austin time, I was wilting down to nothing in this cacophony of sound and time. Magical India was spread out before me in all her wonder. It was exotic and loud. Colorful, ancient, confounding, and crowded like I'd never seen before. It was awe-inspiring, smoky, smelly, devastatingly beautiful, polluted, and important. For me India was the farthest out . . . and sometimes the furthest in. Once, in the steam room at the Austin YMCA, a voice rang out from deep within the clouds—disembodied, mysterious, like it came from another world—*He whose heart in the dust of India has lain shall find peace in no other land.* It was a bolt of lightning.

So what was I doing here on the other side of the earth in such an exotic and mysterious neighborhood? How did a boy from San Antonio and Lubbock end up on this trek in the wilds of Indian summer? I'll try to make some sense of it for you soon enough. Maybe I should start at the beginning. Can I tell you a story?

CHAPTER 3

Where the Cow Ate the Cabbage

1948

I was born redheaded just around the corner from the Alamo. My mother was a Georgia peach and my dad had been a professional baseball player who gave up the game when my older brother Donald was born. "It's either baseball or us," Mama said. "You can't have both." A father being away on the road all the time is too tough on a family. I'd learn this the hard way later on.

It wasn't long before I was playing a big wooden kitchen spoon left-handed like a guitar trying to be like my older brother Donald, who had just won the Starkist Amateur Hour singing "Round-up Time in Texas." Donald was going places, and I wanted to go there too.

They called me Robert Lynn, and I was baptized into the Methodist Church. For me, the only meaningful thing at church was the powerful organ music and the singing of the hymns. That's what touched me. The powerful chords of "A Mighty Fortress Is Our God" played on a magnificent pipe organ that took up the whole wall behind the choir and the preacher. My mom worked hard on me being a good Christian and I reckon I spent the next fourteen years at church, but it didn't really take.

CHAPTER 3

When I came along, Mama and Daddy had to pick up the tempo a few notches. Everyone said I was spoiled rotten, though I don't recall. My sister Judy treated me like a wind-up doll and took care of me. Judy liked me all right until I hit her in the head with a tomahawk because she broke Uncle Lorin's miniature chair in a bottle. Donald teased me unmercifully and he and his friends used me for target practice with their BB guns. I can still hear them laughing.

Within a few months after I was born, my mother went back to work as a secretary at the AAA building downtown. She could type 95 words a minute in her sleep and quickly rose to become executive secretary to a vice president. She hired a maid who also doubled as my nanny. Her name was Ruby, and she was from Central America. She spoke pretty good English and she was black as night. Ruby cleaned the house, cooked dinner, and took care of me during the day. She was my best friend, and I loved her dearly. She had a funny way of talking and said things like "telewision" and "Let's go on a wacation." If the family went out to eat on Sunday after church, I'd bring home to Ruby greasy French fries smashed in my tiny dirty fist and she would eat every bite. If Mama had thought ahead, she would have told Ruby to speak only Spanish to me. Then perhaps I would be playing that tour in South America that the State Department offered me a few years ago—only if I could speak Spanish.

In my own world most of the time, I played by myself, making weird noises, acting out whole plays, singing at the top of my lungs, and preaching sermons. Donald and Judy walked in on me a few times and were convinced I was crazy. I still go there from time to time.

Donald played ukulele and guitar, and I watched and listened. When I turned two, I started singing. The first song I performed for an audience was "How Much Is That Doggie in the Window." My mother sat me on the indoor window box, and I played it on the wooden spoon for her two friends and Aunt Pete.

Daddy had four sisters: Anna, Dolly, Mae, and Adeline, whom everyone called Pete. Aunt Mae lived out on a farm with Uncle Jessie (a crusty old bird) and an unclear number of cattle. I used to love going out to the farm and running wild until the day Uncle Jessie and Aunt Mae gathered us around the corral. I saw my friend the calf was there too. As we watched, unaware of the horror to come, in one motion Uncle Jessie hoisted the calf in the air, shot him in the head, took a butcher's knife, plunged it into its stomach, and ripped his guts out right in front of us. After a second of total disbelief, I started screaming and Uncle Jessie shouted, "Get that kid outta here!" After that I became a vegetarian.

Our family lived in a sprawling ramshackle house on Louise Street. The front yard went down forever and ended at a dirt road. Across that road, that line of demarcation, there lived several Mexican families, their houses hidden by large trees down in a ravine. My brother Donald, who was the ringleader of our gang, directed the building of forts made out of giant appliance boxes stacked three and four high, complete with windows, trap doors, and lookout towers. The Mexican boys would regularly attack our forts and we would attack theirs. Our weapons of choice were dirt clods and rocks thrown by hand and by rather large slingshots.

There were nine of us in the house, and everyone was family except for the mysterious and mostly silent Miss Symroth, the nurse and caregiver for my mother's parents who lived in a big room at the front of the house. Our immediate family of five was scattered about in rooms I can't remember. Where did I sleep? In a room in the back was Uncle Lynn, my middle namesake. He was a collector of many whatnots, and his hoard was beginning to take up a lot of room. It was always a circus in that big house, and we constantly fought over the one bathroom. I can still see the black-and-white tile floor—how, if you stared at it long enough, it would twist into an optical illusion, shifting and rising like a 3D puzzle right beneath your feet.

Uncle Lynn worked at Kelly Field fixing bombers for the Air Force and had a girlfriend named Alice who broke his heart and plunged him into a depression that lasted the rest of his life. He had a coop of chickens out back and on Sundays it was not unusual to see a chicken running here and there with his head cut off, blood shooting to the sky. Uncle Lynn was gruff and called me "Half-Pint" and said it would take a long time before I would become a "Full Pint." He called Donald "Mutt Head" or just "Mutt" and my sister "Bo." Don't ask me where these nicknames came from.

After my grandparents passed on, our family moved into a house across town near Jefferson High School, leaving Uncle Lynn behind to fend for himself. He became a hermit and a tenacious collector of electric trains, tools, tabletop fans, doodads, and geegaws—anything he could buy at an auction. The rooms of the old Louise Street house became piled to the ceilings with his collection. He had saved a million Wheaties box tops and stashed them in cardboard boxes and stacked them up rickety. If they had survived the coming fire, I could have cashed them all in for a new bed or car. Later, when I would go visit Uncle Lynn, I had to navigate a trail through the piles of magazines, newspapers, car parts, rocks, pots of old keys, and mousetraps with their mummified victims months old. It was fantastic!

After we moved to Lubbock, Uncle Lynn died alone on a bed that hadn't seen a sheet in years. It was sad and uncomprehending and the smell of death pierced the neighborhood. His entire treasure, including hundreds of antique pinball machines and one-armed bandits that my grandfather had run at carnivals and at Playland Park, was piled in a heap in the backyard and set afire. All the neighbors came around and stared. Mama gave the whole house and land to "the church." Donald and I are still singing the blues about that one.

Our new house was a red brick two-story on a corner across the street from a vacant lot that I made into a jungle where I fought creatures both imagined and real. We were able to spread out. The second floor was one colossal room that ran the length of the house with a bathroom at one end and a dark mysterious cedar closet at the other. Oh, my god, I had to share the room with Donald. He was seven years older than me and he scared me to death like big brothers do. He told me ghosts were out there in the dark. I didn't want to stay up there with Donald and the ghosts. Taking pity on my situation, my parents forced Judy to take me into her room downstairs, much to her complete disgust. She was pissed at having to share her nice new room with her scaredy-cat little brother.

I never heard my parents argue or talk crossly to each other, much less have a fight. Ever. I thought this was the way it was in all families, like *Fathers Knows Bes*t and *Leave It to Beaver*.

Donald drove a Cushman Eagle motor scooter, secretly smoked cigarettes, and had a solid group of friends. He played in a couple of bands in San Antonio. One of them was the Melody Mustangs who played sock hops at our church. I was getting more and more interested in the music I was hearing on the radio and from Donald practicing. He knew all the hits and would practice and play all the time. When he wasn't trying to shoot me, he was a pretty decent guy and a good guitar player and singer and knew hundreds of songs. And he played the blues, cross harp. Still can.

I was four when I took Donald's ukulele and turned it around and played on the back with no strings to throw me off. I was born left-handed; my mother made me learn to write with my right hand. Donald wouldn't abide me playing left-handed either and told me it would always mess me up in the future. He said I would never be able to play well because the strings would be

Cowboy Robert in 1953. (Photo by Reeva Livingston.)

upside down. Paul McCartney, Jimi Hendrix, and Shake Russell, all lefties, hadn't come along by then. I still eat and brush my teeth with my left hand and if I get a chance to kick a football or soccer ball, I'll do it with my left foot. I shoot pool left-handed and just the other day I shot bows and arrows in Arkansas with my old friend Bill Walker and his Ozark crew and I hit a bullseye in front of a crowd. Left-handed.

Mama forced Donald and Judy to take piano lessons, but by the time I was old enough to play I think it was too much trouble and too much money so I was left out of the loop. I was glad at the time but have always lamented that I can't read music or *really* play the piano. But we always had a piano in the house and everyone took a turn at playing it from time to time. Mama had a sweet voice, and I remember sitting next to her at church and listening to her sing those great hymns. I still play "A Mighty Fortress Is Our God," "It Is No Secret," and "Just As I Am" now and again, just to raise the hackles on my neck.

Both Mama and Daddy worked at Laurel Heights Methodist Church. Back then, church was big business, and my dad was the activities director and coached all the softball and basketball teams and won city championships and state titles. He also found time to teach ceramics and pottery classes and a lot of other crafty stuff. All the kids wanted to hang out with him on Sunday and not go to church as would be the case for some time to come. Daddy treated me lovingly and was fair and square. He never spanked me or even got angry with me.

Mama was the executive secretary of the church and editor of the church news bulletin, which everybody read. She took black-and-white photographs of the congregation's activities and developed the photos herself in a darkroom in the basement of the church that smelled weird from the solutions she used. She let me come watch as the images mysteriously appeared on the photo paper in the low amber light. I was impressed. Mama was always creative and taking pictures and making things. She made wreaths and painted faces on eggs for Easter. Mama had a few dozen colloquialisms she would scatter around: "Mr. 'I Can't' never did anything, Robert." "Oh, ye gods and little fishes!" "Lord help the wicked and preserve the saints!" "I'll tell you where the cow ate the cabbage."

In my family, everything centered around the church. It was business as much as praying. I'd take a city bus from Woodlawn Elementary and get dropped off across the street from the church and go immediately to the gym. I'd see my father for a while, shoot baskets and pool, and then run like a wild Indian through the church's neighborhood with my best friend, Tommy Talcott. We would go into Piggly Wiggly for a cherry Coke and a Mounds bar before running down back alleys, climbing trees and on garages, and skipping across roofs from house to house.

♪

One fine day in 1958 towards the end of the school year a Livingston Family meeting was called. This was highly unusual, even weird, and I knew something big was about to go down. My mother said that she and my father had been offered jobs at the First Methodist Church in a place called Lubbock, far, far away north of San Antonio. They had accepted the offer and we were moving there in a few months.

There was a profound silence. *What do you mean we're moving?* Donald, Judy, and I didn't want any part of it. We did a little research, asked around, and discovered that Lubbock was in West Texas, was flat, hot, and dry, a desert with no trees, and no telephone poles 'cause all the lines are buried in the ground! We heard Lubbock was full of rednecks, farmers, and cowboys and the home of a college named Texas Tech . . . and then there was Buddy Holly.

Buddy Holly was from Lubbock? Well, then maybe it wasn't all so bad. I loved Buddy's music. The beat was funky and he sang simple, accessible songs and they played him regularly on KTSA, the only radio station I listened to. *Maybe we could meet Buddy*, I thought. He might even be a Methodist and go to our church! I had never met anyone who was played on the radio; I had never been to a real concert. But before we had a chance to get to Lubbock and meet Buddy Holly, we heard the news that he had died in a fiery plane crash in Iowa on February 3, 1959. So much for high hopes.

My parents waited till the end of the school year and then we all packed up and moved out to West Texas, lock, stock, and barrel. I was ten and noticed that the price of gas on the way north was 23 cents a gallon.

CHAPTER 4

The Hub City

1959

Lubbock was flat as a flitter and the wind "they call Mariah" would blow and scream at you and you could see the dust clouds roaring up in the distance like freight trains swallowing Lubbock and the vast cotton fields whole. Butch Hancock would say that it is so flat in Lubbock you can see fifty miles in any direction. And if you stand on a tuna-fish can, you can see a hundred miles. After further research on this, it was discovered that if you stand on a Campbell's Soup can and stare real hard, you can see the back of your head. Yes, it was flat, flat and brown. Like my mood. I was a kid uprooted.

We arrived in the Hub City as a storm was blowing in. Dusty dawn, brown, desolate, devoid of green, downtown brick streets, all right angles. Soon it was raining mud, and I think even my mom and dad were having second thoughts. Earlier that day, crammed into the back seat with Judy and the bags, on the way to a new uncertain life, I changed my name from Robert to Bob. "Call me Bob," I said to everyone. It went over like a lead balloon. But this was a big step of independence for me and somehow I thought that Bob would fit me better. The way I saw it, Robert was too proper or something. I wish I'd never changed it. These days, only my brother and sister and sometimes Iris and Gary Nunn still call me Robert.

My family in Lubbock, 1960. (Standing): Dad (Harry) and Mom (Reeva); (seated): Robert, Judy, and Donald. (Photo courtesy of Bob Livingston.)

We moved into a house in west Lubbock across the street from cotton fields that stretched into the distance past Reese Air Force Base and onward to the New Mexico line. We were on the frontier and when the dust storms came roaring up out of the west they turned the sky brown-purple and the dust seeped up through the windows and on to the windowsills, into my bed, food, eyes, ears, and lungs. The city would send bulldozers and trucks to haul away the sand dunes in the driveway. In the cotton fields, tornados would dance with lightning bolts and we would watch from the roof. I was a redheaded stranger and overnight I started wearing glasses right before the start of fifth grade at Rush Elementary. I enrolled as Bob Livingston.

My first day of school was action-packed. The first guy who actually spoke to me in a friendly way was Ronny DeShirley. At the first recess, a load of boys were playing a game with a kickball and everyone was running in packs. I joined in. There were loose teams trying to make a goal, kind of like rugby. I didn't even know what team I was on; I just went for the ball. At the bottom of the pile, I grabbed the ball and held onto it for dear life. I heard a voice shout out, "Hey, Red, Red!" This kid was yelling, "Red, give it to me!" Something made me trust him, so I threw him the ball and he roared off down the field. At some point in the game, he threw it back. I made some more friends and tried to settle in, but I never really felt settled in. For the time being I was the redheaded, freckle-faced, four-eyed new kid in town. I started looking for a way out from these troubling tribulations.

The *world itself* was having real troubling tribulations. The Cold War was being fought in the halls of Congress and in the Kremlin. We had air raid drills, everybody going into halls and putting their heads between their knees. If the bombs came raining down and you didn't have time to get out in the hall, you practiced hiding under your desk. We would get under tables or in stairwells. That was kinda fun and got us out of class. We were told the Russians were coming to get us. I never thought they would bother to come to Lubbock. Even though we were told our lives were on the line, it never seemed real to me. I had no scope of the way the world really worked. I had far more pressing problems. Even so, and covering my bases, I built a pint-sized fallout shelter in my backyard. I'd get in with barely enough room to breathe. My emergency supplies were a bottle of water and a peanut butter and jelly sandwich and my red transistor radio. I waited . . .

I found the way out down the street from First Methodist Church at the S&H Green Stamp Store. Stamps were given at the checkouts at Piggly Wiggly based on how much you bought. You pasted the Green Stamps in books and you could exchange them for goods: toasters, blankets, golf clubs, doodads. One historic day I was browsing the aisles at the S&H and saw a ukulele. A Uke. It cost three and a half books of stamps and I really, really, *really* wanted it. Desperate for this ukulele, I began collecting Green

Stamps. I stole stamps from my mother's purse and begged others from friends and their mothers. The books filled up slowly that summer, but at last I had the three and a half books. I went to S&H and traded for the ukulele with a soft case, a book of chords, and extra strings. I brought my new ukulele home and in a couple of days, I was playing.

Donald showed me how to tune it, "my dog has fleas" (G, C, E, A) The first song I learned in the book was "Carolina in the Morning." I played it over and over and then learned another song and then another. I played the uke for a year and cut my first teeth as a working musician on the ukulele when I was given a free meal at a church picnic if I'd sit on a chair and sing two songs. Eventually I bought a Stella guitar at Sears and Roebucks. Donald loaned me the money and became an investor.

At first, I kept the low strings (the E and the A) off my guitar and just played it with four strings. You could play chords on a guitar just like on a ukulele, but in reality a G on a uke was a C on the guitar. Still, you could play those chord inversions and get the feel of it. Donald kept telling me to put the other two strings back on. Finally I did and I was playing all six strings in no time.

My two best friends at church were Max Addison and Robbie Gamble. We played church basketball together and none of us were very good, so we had a sort of camaraderie there. Max was brilliant and later went to Yale and became a corporate lawyer in Houston. We're still best friends and I produced a few tracks for Max AKA Lubbock Johnson, "Don't Wait for Santa Claus" and "She's Just Too Wild to Be Country." Robbie was just picking up the guitar too. Because of our mutual interests, we would play songs together at his house or mine. We decided to get a third guy and form a trio for a gig already on the books. We chose Johnny Tull, who had run a hit squad against me a couple of years earlier walking home from school. But this was the music business, and it was already rougher than any hit squad Johnny could get together. Johnny was in the band.

Johnny played an instrument I invented, a bamboo pole with coffee-can lids attached that would rattle and clank together. You banged it on the floor and hit it with a stick. It was called a *bamboozaphone*. He was the best in the world at it because no one else had ever played it before. I played my ukulele and Robbie played guitar. We began to practice and worked up a few songs, "You Gotta Quit Kickin' My Dog Around," "Sink the Bismarck," and "Bye Bye Love." We came up with a crazy name, the New Grutchly Gofasties. In retrospect, I guess we were a jug band without the jug. Our first gig was in the basement of the First Methodist Church. We painted our faces up and I can't recall why but maybe it was a carnival. We didn't get paid, but the reviews were solid.

Robbie later turned out to be a good blues player and went on to be a music entrepreneur in Lubbock. He became known as Pappa Jelly Belly and opened a rhythm & blues club called Belly's. Years later, Robbie went to Las Vegas and ended up going to the Big Blues Club in the Sky while he was there. What is it about Lubbock dudes and Vegas?

♪

Church camp! Every summer, I would get to go off into the woods with all my friends to Ceta Canyon Methodist Church camp on a river surrounded by cabins and trees. It was a great retreat and got me out of the clutches of Lubbock and my parents. These were great days, and I got to meet new kids and play my guitar around campfires and think about flirting with girls. The songs at the campfire sing-alongs were songs that everyone knew like "Jacob's Ladder," "Hole in the Bottom of the Sea," "If I Had a Hammer," and of course the international hit, "Kumbaya." I admit I loved the melodies, and I could play the chords. It came naturally, even if it was the first time I had ever played a song. Playing around these campfires I was learning about music, testing out new rhythms and chords, and could play in several keys. As if by magic I knew the one, four, five, and relative minor chords in most keys. Somehow, I could just do it. I played other songs that I heard on the radio; I could pick most anything out by ear. There was the brilliant simplicity of the Everly Brothers, Buddy Holly, and some traditional folk songs.

My first paying gig was for a youth group at a Jewish synagogue. A school friend, Mike Levinson, hired me and paid me five dollars for a thirty-minute show. This was groundbreaking and earth-shattering. Up to then, the only ground I had broken had been chopping weeds out of long rows of cotton that went on forever. I had my little red transistor radio and during these eternal hot days of work, that red radio was my only bridge to sanity. "Not Fade Away," "Breaking Up Is Hard to Do," "Sukiyaki," "Hey Paula." Radio stations KLLL and KDAV played them all over and over. Sunburned, with blisters on my shoulders and neck, I picked out stickers from my cracked and freckled hands. But now, I had made five bucks for singing a few songs. And it was a blast. Staring at the $5 bill I knew I needed to explore this further. That night, by the light of the moon, I worked on the callouses of my left hand and committed to the life of a wandering minstrel.

KOMA was a 50,000-watt clear-channel radio station out of Oklahoma City that could reach all the way to my little red radio. I listened to local stations like KDAV and KLLL during the day, but it was KOMA when the sun went down. KOMA played the hits, but it also played Black music, soul, and rhythm & blues. The local stations shied away from music like that. I remember listening late at night to B. B. King, Freddie King, Otis Redding, and Chuck Berry. We'd tune in Wolfman Jack on XERF broadcasting from a 250,000-watt transmitter out of Ciudad Acuña. He had a low scratchy voice and would howl at the start of the show. You could get the signal everywhere in the US. The Wolfman played Howlin' Wolf, T-Bone Walker, Screamin' Jay Hawkins, and all the rock 'n' roll you could stand. It was great music, and I somehow felt I was doing something sinful to even be listening to it. I didn't understand what they were talking about but it made me feel good. What was real was B. B. King singing Willie Nelson's "Nightlife" and Otis Redding singing "Fa-fa-fa, your turn" and Hank Williams "Your Cheatin' Heart" and Buddy Holly yodeling "pretty pretty pretty pretty Peggy Sue." The world made a lot more sense when all that would burst out of my little red transistor.

A fellow classmate at Mackenzie Middle School was David Halley. We had discovered that we both liked guitars and the Beatles. He came over to my house a few times and we talked guitars and KOMA and played all afternoon in my room. We only got together once or twice more in Lubbock, but we became pretty good friends much later on when we all moved to Austin. David went on to become the writer of a great many well-crafted songs like "Rain Just Falls" and "Hard Livin.'" Jerry Jeff would record both of them. Later, I would record one of David's songs called "Month of Somedays" on my 2018 album *Up the Flatland Stairs*.

I went to Lubbock High School and had Miss Honey for English. She was an elderly woman and at the beginning of her career she had taught Buddy Holly honors English. I pestered her with questions: "Where did he sit?" The chairs were bolted to the floor. Miss Honey looked askance at me. She knew I wasn't applying myself and wanted me to do better. Miss Honey forced us all to memorize the prologue to *The Canterbury Tales* by Geoffrey Chaucer. Then she had us write an original tale of our own, and I wrote about a motorcycle gang on a road trip. I made an A and Miss Honey started to like me a bit more. And I started to appreciate and love writing like never before and it was an important milestone for me even though I was finding my way in the back alleys of the concept.

President John F. Kennedy was shot in the back in Dallas on November 22, 1963, and the dark ages began. It was a wake-up call with the alarm still going off. I was in the ninth grade, lived a block away from Mackenzie Middle School and had gone home for lunch, flipped on the TV, and Walter Cronkite was crying. You don't see Walter crying every day so something big was up. It was an unreal lightning bolt and it hit me hard. "President Kennedy died . . ." The world went black and white and for days and days after all you could see on TV was the funeral cortège, crowds of sobbing people, sadness everywhere, and they replayed it over and over. Then Oswald was shot on live television and we learned about Jack Ruby and gangsters and strippers in Dallas. It was a new, violent, seedy world we'd never thought about before. Assassinations, politics, Democrats vs. Republicans, communists. All that was suddenly part of the stories we told as we tried to grasp the full meaning. That attempt at grasping has not found any more understanding to this day.

A month later things were still dark. But that December, we all got a big Christmas present. I was listening to one of the local radio stations when "I Want to Hold Your Hand" came blasting out of the speaker creating a shockwave and getting my attention like nothing ever before. My little redheaded four-eyed Bob world suddenly became a galaxy and exploded into technicolor! It was the greatest moment, the greatest song, the greatest harmonies, the greatest band, the greatest feeling of abandon. Balls-to-the-wall, the happiest moment of my life. I couldn't believe what I was hearing. Who is *that*?? The news spread like wildfire on the High Plains, and everyone was talking about the Beatles. "Did you hear them?" I finally saw some grainy photos of the band on the news and then a video of them on Walter Cronkite singing and playing in a dingy club in Liverpool. They looked like they were from another planet. Long hair and skinny gray suits. They were like four Davy Crocketts that could sing and rock! They weren't the namby-pamby Beach Boys, that was for sure. I'd heard rock 'n' roll all my young life, but nothing like this.

The news came that the Beatles were going to be on *The Ed Sullivan Show*, the holy grail of Sunday night. It was February 9, 1964. I got ready. I went to evening church as usual but slipped out around seven forty-five and went into the basement where there was a big Zenith console that you could turn up loud. I was alone when Ed shouted, "Here they are, the Beatles!" and a million screams started and hearts leapt and skipped beats and created a vibration, and the excitement was more than the universe, and everything suddenly made sense, and life became more important and special. I fought hard to never have another haircut. Cassius Clay hung out with the Beatles. The Queen. They were "bigger than Jesus" and that was fine with me. Because they were.

Some of the best American television and music followed. The Beatles had raised the bar, and everyone seemed to be doing better and laughing harder. Brian Wilson and the Beach Boys put out amazing albums. We were an *I Love Lucy* family. Milton Berle, Jack Benny, and Ozzie and Harriet with Ricky Nelson. At the end of each episode, Ricky would sing in front of an audience of dreamy-eyed girls and boys with James Burton on guitar. "Poor Little Fool," "Travelin' Man," "Lonesome Town." All great songs. I never missed a show.

One of my best friends was Busty Underwood. He was the quarterback from Rush Elementary to Mackenzie Middle School to Lubbock High to TCU and finally the Buffalo Bills. Busty liked that I played guitar. I showed him a few chords and he was hooked. One day we strolled into Harrod Music Co. on Ave Q and both of us bought a brand-new Gibson J-45 red sunburst guitar. It was my first real guitar. I wish I still had that Gibson and so many other guitars, amps, and toys that I turned loose and now they're gone from my grasp forever. Busty, of course, still has his.

My song list at the time included such heady material as "Ode to the Little Brown Shack Out Back," "Big Bad John," "You Gotta Quit Kickin' My Dog Around," "Rocky Raccoon," "Don't Think Twice, It's All Right," and a few Jimmy Reed blues numbers. The Jimmy Reed songs were almost all the same and always in E and were easy to play and you could arrange them in a medley. I also got a harmonica and learned straight-harp right off and then cross-harp.

Busty and I worked out some songs and played high school assemblies and the occasional teen party with our twin J-45's. It wasn't long before I started writing my own songs, lame as they were. I had a girlfriend named Penni Pearson who was the sister of Tony Pearson who played mandolin with Lubbock's hippie and ultra-hip jug band The Flatlanders. I'll get to those boys in a bit. The first song I wrote funnily enough was an instrumental. It was about Penni called "Small Change Only" with the prophetic line, "The moon is high and so am I / It's a summer's night." How would I know anything about that?

We were all in the throes of Beatlemania, and the British Invasion had come in a fever pitch with a lot of fresh blood. The Rolling Stones, the Yardbirds, the Kinks, the Zombies, the Dave Clark Five, the Animals. It was all great stuff, and I learned many of their songs. "Girl, I want to be with you . . . all of *the* time."

A bumpy detour from my happy-go-lucky musical life suddenly separated me from the amazing music scene that was bursting forth in Lubbock. Football. In those days in Texas, high school football was the only important activity in the world. Nothing else held a candle to it, especially in West Texas. I played in junior high and then at Lubbock High School where the head coach was a young superstar go-getter named Freddy Akers. He made us understand that not much outside the arena of football was important. You had to make your grades all right, but nothing but football, family (sometimes), and girlfriends . . . if it didn't

The Livingston Brothers (Don on the left) pose at Harrod Music in Lubbock, 1968 or '69. This was a promo shot for our short-lived duo. (Photo courtesy of Bob Livingston.)

get in the way of his program. Girlfriends were okay with Coach Akers but not smoking, or drinking, or hanging out late at night, or having weird musician friends. And there was not going to be any sneaking into the Cotton Club with those other musician types. Most of these *good boy* rules had already been pounded into me by my parents. I was almost a preacher's kid, and you know how they are. But rebelling against the prevailing wisdom of Coach Akers was not a consideration. Going gonzo and gatoring on a beer-soaked floor would come soon enough, I suppose. But for the time being, football was my world.

I still played the occasional school assembly, but I didn't seek out the musicians that I knew were out there in the wilds of Lubbock. My songwriting, singing, and music ambitions were held in suspended animation while I went about the business of two-a-day workouts and bustin' heads in the dust, mud, blood, and snow.

My brother Donald was making himself at home in Lubbock and started playing in bands and making a good living playing fraternity parties and at the Officers' Clubs at Air Force bases. He also taught guitar lessons at Harrod Music to the aspiring rockers that probably bought their guitars at the store. One exception was Jesse Taylor, later to become a driving force in the Joe Ely Band. Jesse told me that Donald had given him the greatest single piece of music-related advice he'd ever had: "You don't need any more lessons. Just go out and play what you feel."

There were bands springing up everywhere, and the best gigs were the frat parties. Lubbock was a dry county and that meant none of the bars served booze, not even beer. Some places got around this and invented private clubs, and the booze was kept in a locker in the back and you could drink it if you were over 21. The Sparkles, the Velveteens, the Rhythm Masters, the Raiders (my brother's band), the Shucks, the Night Owls, the Ravens: all were great bands that made good money and played all the time. Mostly they did cover songs, rock 'n' roll, and rhythm & blues. But these guys were older than me; I had never played with a drummer yet or at a dance. I was a folkie, 17 or so.

The Music Box and the Village Swinger were the two main teenage music clubs in Lubbock. They had great bands playing most nights. They were close to each other out on the Brownfield

Highway. Every good band in town played both clubs. The Fabulous Sparkles were at the top of the heap. They started out as a four-piece with Lucky Floyd on drums, Bobby Smith on bass, Stanley Smith on guitar, and Donny Roberts on rhythm guitar. They were the greatest band I had ever seen live, and I would go whenever they played. My brother, Donald, said, "The Sparkles were more than musicians, they were showmen." Spot on. That's what made them a cut above. Lucky could sound exactly like James Brown or anybody else he wanted to. They dressed up and had moves. Steps. These clubs served no alcohol and you didn't have to be 21 to get in, so they were packed with sweaty teenagers very close together.

One night at the Music Box the Sparkles were playing and I was there in the front row and they started "Get Off of My Cloud" by the Rolling Stones. It was packed to the rafters, hot and sweaty, and I imagine this was exactly what The Cavern in Liverpool was like. Someone in the band, maybe Bobby Smith, grabbed my hand and pulled me onto the stage. I got to sing two verses. The charge from the live crowd entered my body electric and into my consciousness.

Nationally known bands came to Lubbock and played the Music Box, the Village Swinger, and the Municipal Auditorium. I saw Paul Revere and the Raiders, Gary Lewis & the Playboys, the Chessmen from Dallas (Jimmie Vaughan was the lead guitar), Jimmy Gilmer and the Fireballs, and the Bobby Fuller Four. Buffalo Springfield played the Music Box and the Turtles played the Village Swinger.

♪

It was the Rubik's Cube of nights, lightbulbs, and cameras flashing. The power of rock 'n' roll was in the house. I took my girlfriend Penni Pearson to see the Turtles. "It Ain't Me Babe," "Happy Together," and "You Baby." Amazing harmonies. The bass player was smiling and making eyes at Penni. Literal eyes. Penni was blushing and smiling back. I had no option but to watch it all happen. I saw the *real* power of music that night and in another world that bass player would have taken Penni out the door and down the road in a gypsy caravan. It was eye-opening.

The Cotton Club was a dance joint out on the Slaton Highway. It was owned by Tommy Hancock, a rangy, spacey, hippie fiddle player and singer. Later in the game Tommy's band would be a traveling Ken Kesey–type outfit called the Supernatural Family Band but for now they were the Roadside Playboys. Tommy and his wife Charlene played fun, country-tinged, good-time music and folks danced like mad.

There were a lot of national acts that came through the Cotton Club. Roy Orbison, Little Richard, Buddy Holly, Fats Domino, George Jones, and even Elvis. All the Lubbock boys I was to meet later on—Joe Ely, Butch Hancock, R. C. Banks, Jimmie Gilmore, and Terry Allen—they were hanging out on the fringes of the Cotton Club, some of them too young to get in.

All the while I was at Lubbock High and playing football and world-changing events in music and culture were transforming American society. Bob Dylan had appeared in a flash of brilliance and folk groups like the Kingston Trio and Peter, Paul and Mary became a big part of my musical direction. Folk music, and rock 'n' roll. Hootenanny on Saturday night TV was big. Radical song ideas. Opposition to the war in Vietnam by boys and girls was in the air, people were protesting, and the Summer of Love was here.

The Beatles released *Rubber Soul* and "Norwegian Wood" with a twangy drone instrument on it that froze me in my tracks. What is *that*? George Harrison's sitar. He'd learned from a man from India named Ravi Shankar. I didn't know much about India or Indian music, but it wasn't too long before I was one of the first guys in Lubbock with a Ravi Shankar album. This interest in Indian music and certain other premonitions that I would encounter would later thrust me to a lifelong fascination with India and all things Indian.

At Lubbock High, we won a lot of football games and were arguably the best team Lubbock High had seen since the '50s. We beat our crosstown rivals Monterey High 14–13 at Jones Stadium for the Silver Spurs in 1965. It was the biggest high school game of the century around there. My junior year, I had a couple of scholarship offers, but they dwindled when I came down with mononucleosis. I lost weight and strength, and any interest in football was once and for all blown to the West Texas winds. What now? Texas Tech looked pretty good to keep me alive because the Vietnam War was raging and a draft lottery was being threatened. If you went to school, you were exempt from the draft as long as you made your grades. Texas Tech was right there in town, so that was it. My best friend Max went off to Yale and I wouldn't see him much for years.

Then, out of the blue came a lightning bolt of grace. Abruptly, my parents moved back to San Antonio and returned to their old church to work. I think the assumption was that I'd go to Texas Tech and become a fifth-grade schoolteacher or something safe like that. But when my folks moved back to San Antone, it opened the door for me to chart my own course. I stayed in Lubbock—375 miles and a whole world away from them. It was monumental. My brother Donald and I rented a little house on 26th Street. Donald was told to watch over me for Mama and Daddy, but I was left pretty much on my own. Donald had plenty to do himself and he was fairly loose as a monitor. But this little house was still an arm of the Livingston family and it was a base of operations. The Livingstons were spreading out.

I enrolled at Texas Tech and became an art major even though I had never painted or drawn much other than comic characters. It was hip to be an art major, I thought. Penni went to Tech, joined a sorority, and dumped me in a New York minute when those junior and senior frat boys started paying quite a bit of attention to her. “You need some college polish,” she told me. The only thing I could do in response was to join a fraternity, too. I’d show her. One of my best friends of all time was Andy Kerr, who had been the president of the student body at Lubbock High. He was going to Tech too and joining up with a frat called Sigma Alpha Epsilon (SAE). He wanted me with him and told the SAE’s that he wouldn’t join if they didn’t get me in there too. Suddenly I was a *pledge brother*. I didn’t have *any* idea what I was in for.

CHAPTER 5

The Wild East!

Trivandrum, India, 1981

The plane ride from Austin with its long foreign layovers had left me with acute and all-consuming jet lag. I'd been awake for three days of constant travel and needed a second wind. Fueled by the excitement—and the potato curry and the Brooke Bond tea purchased from a street vendor—I seemed to find that elusive rejuvenation. Our walk had turned into a fast-paced romp through the constantly colorful downtown area of Trivandrum followed by an endless stream of kids surprised that a redheaded foreigner had turned up in their midst. The only English they knew was, "What is your name?"

"Bob Dylan," I said.

Two emaciated dogs followed along, perhaps hoping for a miracle. What more miserable existence is there than to be a dog in India? By the time any edible morsel reaches its table, it has been picked through and cast off by untold hordes and is usually covered with flies and maggots.

We passed by a group of onlookers that were staring at anything remotely interesting or out of the ordinary. We must have presented an astonishing sight to them with my matted hair from sweating profusely and my wide eyes, obviously a foreigner. To them, we were unusual in the extreme and they began to follow along too.

My crew in Kharagpur, India, at the railway station, 1989. We sang and yodeled and were quite the attraction. (Photo by Tucker Livingston.)

As my bearer and I continued on the crowded road, we were met with a riot of sound: conversation, high-pitched laughter, dogs barking, brakes squealing, motors racing, diesel engines spewing smoke, hammers pounding, and horns blaring. There were signs painted on the lorries, and many of the cars, that screamed, "Please honk!" And honk everyone did. At intersections, around curves, at pedestrians, on straightaways, over bridges, down alleys, and at the few stray dogs that cringed in the gutters. Any excuse to honk was a good one. But unlike in the West, where they honk angrily, in the East they honk good-naturedly. It's just to say, "I'm here too, don't forget me." You can fail your driving test in India for not honking long and loud enough. Wandering through the crowded streets, our royal ragtag procession finally reached the main railway depot.

At the station there were literally thousands of travelers, pushing and shoving to get in the queues for tickets and on board the trains. Many more were actually camped there on the platforms and in the halls appearing to have lived all their lives amidst this tumult. My football training came in handy as I fought my way with the rest of the crowd to the ticket window. I purchased a first-class ticket for the Trivandrum Mail. With a wave of his arm, the ticket agent indicated the general direction of the train. At least a dozen trains were arriving and departing at once as I searched for mine.

Wandering through the din I finally found what I thought to be the Trivandrum Mail and asked a passing conductor in his white shirt and navy pants to be sure. He said nothing, but shook his head no. It was confusing but I finally figured out an important facet of Indian culture. In India, apparently to shake one's head in that endearing way means yes, but not necessarily vice versa. To say "no," one simply flicks his hand and clucks disapprovingly. After this revelation, the conductor, laughing, said to get on any car—no reservations needed: "Go find an empty berth." I identified the newest looking car and told my bearer to follow me in. This was first class, but with no AC—only fans. In the south, only second class has an AC car—I know it's strange. In any case there were none that day.

The compartments were equipped with an upper and lower berth on each side and a small metal table that separated them. Most were full of commuters and whole families, sitting and lying down, talking rapid-fire Malayalam, playing cards, reading books and newspapers, smoking cigarettes, drinking coffee. I chose a compartment and walked to the entryway. Looking in, I saw that it contained only one passenger, a Westerner—the first I had seen since leaving Bombay. He was sitting cross-legged on the bench listening to a cassette player with earphones, singing to himself some language I did not know, tapping out some beat fiercely on the fold-down table and all the while smoking a cigarette, drinking black coffee, and preparing an Indian chew, all the while oblivious to the weary stranger standing in the doorway.

On the small fold-down table were spread dozens of cassettes, books, newspapers, and tobacco articles of various persuasions. He was dressed in what I thought to be a white sarong (which I would later find out was called a dhoti) and a white half-sleeved shirt just like the rest of the South Indian men on the train. As I stood there dripping with sweat, bags and guitar falling at my feet, I must have presented a rueful and pathetic sight. Suddenly, the busily engaged man looked up and took good a hard look at me. He slipped the earphones off, took another gander, and finally said in a heavy French accent, "Ah, you must be Iris's husband. Come in, come in!"

CHAPTER 6

God Help Me, I Become a Frat Rat

1968

The Sacred Order of Sigma Alpha Epsilon. It sounds medieval, like the Knights Templar, even as I write it. I was consumed with the rigors of fraternity pledgeship. I was a frat rat, part of a band of brothers with rituals and secret handshakes and noble codes of honor. I don't remember much of the rituals, but there were a lot of parties that made impressions. The frequent Saturday night fraternity parties were awash in beer and dancing. *Louie Lou-i-ay, oh baby, we gotta go . . .*" Then there was the terrific camaraderie of going out with my brothers, out to the far side of town, out to a cotton field of mud where we would pop kegs, get drunk as seven hundred dollars, roll around in the mud, laugh, fight, go into hysterics, and vomit. This was serious bonding business and anyone that did not partake in these rituals was considered a pussy. It was grounds for dismissal.

I made good friends in the fraternity, and I still stay in touch with some of my mystic music-loving brothers like Mike Looney, Paul Knuckley, and Jay Rigby. Paul and Looney were on either side of me in a Saturday night fraternity ritual called the "rack line" whereby you stood side by side with your pledge brothers alphabetically back at the fraternity house after all the party dates had been taken home. Like in the Marines, the full brothers would scream insults into the faces of their lowly pledges and keep them up all night. And all of this would happen after a typical rollicking Saturday night party with one of the great West Texas bands where you drank and danced and sang out loud and had photos taken with these same brothers and their dates, everyone laughing and smiling with arms around each other. Why I put myself through all of the fun only casts a dubious light on my self-esteem. Still . . .

Some of the greatest bands in Texas played at fraternity and sorority parties. The Fabulous Sparkles, the Shucks, B29 and the Bombers, the Bricks from Fort Worth, and the risqué R&B band, Hot Nuts. They were all crack musicians, singers, and, above all, showmen. The frats loved these bands and kept them working. A lot. For now, college was fun.

At one of the fraternity parties, we had a band that wasn't your typical rock or R&B band but was rather a jug band made up of Tech students. The party was more quiet and sedate than most of the beer-swilling dance-like-mad ones. The leader of the group was a clean-cut fellow named Rick Fowler, and unbeknownst to me I would run into Rick again later on that life-changing summer when I would meet a trio he was playing with.

That semester, my brother Donald and I formed a duo called The Livingston Brothers. We each had an original song or two but sang mostly covers like "Solitary Man," "Blowin' in the Wind," "Don't Think Twice," "Classical Gas," and a lot of Jimmy Reed, Kinks, and Beatles. My brother could play pretty good blues harp and taught me a few licks. But I played mainly straight harp. We played a few shows and some private parties. It was new to me and a lot of fun. I was learning a lot, no doubt about it. Donald was into "show biz" and wanted to have comedy bits with jokes and structured like the Smothers Brothers and Martin Mull. But

I wasn't interested in planned comedy bits and still am not that interested because I am so bad at it. I can be funny. I tell a lot of stories, and I may tell a lot of the same stories in my shows, but they always come out different. A different take. I try to make the story believable and I get comfortable and I put myself into the scene. The magic and flow of the story is real. Even if it is not all true. Like they say, "Never let the truth get in the way of a good story." I'm a stream-of-consciousness performer for better or worse. The Livingston Brothers disbanded one Lubbock dust-storm night after I failed to pick up on one of the lines in Donald's joke: "She was so fat she was her own buddy at camp." It was an unpardonable sin in Donald's eyes and ears, and I was out.

Meanwhile I kept searching for a major at Tech. I fell into radio and television communications. I learned how to work the board on the campus station and every so often got to fill in as a DJ. This was fun and maybe I would have ended up as another Murray the K if it hadn't been for the final exam. My professor gave us all the opportunity to do a one-hour radio show for the final. Anything we wanted to do: spin records, do the news, whatever. He was home on his radio listening to our exam in real time. I had been into the blues and so I did a blues show set starting out with Muddy Waters followed by the Rolling Stones. I screwed everything up trying to operate the equipment and punch the right cartridge. I got flustered and said "fuck" under my breath but on the air, and I was given a stern reprimand by my professor and if he hadn't thought it was sorta funny, I would most likely have failed the course.

CHAPTER 7

Lubbock Influences: Joey Ely, My Brother, and The Attic

1968–69

The room was dark and smoky and the tousled and unkempt fellow on the makeshift stage was playing "Baby, Let Me Follow You Down." He was sitting on a Fender Super Reverb amp playing a beat-up Gibson J-45 and he had a hi-hat cymbal that he worked with his right foot to keep the backbeat. Later he said he had bought the guitar off of a bum on Venice Beach in California. It had seashells glued all over it with glitter in the glue. He had taken the shells off, but the glittery glue was still there in the outline of the shells. It was magnificently funky. He was using a Barcus Berry pickup, one of the first acoustic guitar pickups, and the first one I'd ever seen. He accompanied himself, like Dylan, with a harmonica in a holder and played in a sort of a dreamy, detached way, not really caring to put on a show. He would fidget with something and look uncomfortable and rarely spoke between songs and looked down a lot and mumbled. But he sang soulfully and chose obscure songs, at least obscure to me. It was an intriguing and fascinating performance, and I'd never heard anyone live do songs like this before: alone, fingerpicking with long nails, irreverent and free.

Joey Ely (as he was called back then) was playing in an almost invisible bar in the Altura Towers, an apartment building on Avenue Q. I'd heard a lot about him: he was an artist, played some rock 'n' roll. There was a rumor he had one red leg and one blue. Well, that's what I heard. Ely was Lubbock's Dylan and there were a lot of stories about him. He hung out with disreputable characters like Lance Copeland who was the meanest guy in Lubbock. Lance was always beating somebody up bad. Real bad.

Ely's unusual and blasé performance that night had a profound effect on me, and the next day I went to a pawnshop and bought myself a hi-hat. Then I begged my brother Donald to borrow his Fender Twin amp and a Gibson electric guitar he had stashed in a closet. I was already playing with a harmonica holder. I started practicing with this new set-up into the new semester.

One way to explain the impact Ely had on me is similar to the way the Beatles affected me. The Beatles had distilled American R&B, blues, and original rock 'n' roll and spit it back out in a palpable way that was easily accessible. I learned a lot about American music from the Beatles. Ely was, in a way, doing the same thing. He did old country blues and country stuff that I had never really heard or considered, but coming from him it sounded fresh and accessible. The thing is, it was all new to me and I started exploring those types of music for the first time. Dave Van Ronk, Howlin' Wolf, Mississippi John Hurt.

Everything was thrown at me from the radio and television speakers. I couldn't duck out of the way even if I wanted to. The Beatles; Bob Dylan; the Kingston Trio; Peter, Paul and Mary. I also watched a lot of the country music TV shows on Saturday morning, especially *The Porter Wagoner Show*. Porter, Speck Rhodes, Norma Jean, and . . . Dolly Parton. There was a show called *Hullabaloo* and one called *Hootenanny* where I first saw Pete

Seeger sing "If I Had a Hammer." Then there was Dick Clark's *American Bandstand* every Saturday where girls danced in front of your eyes.

My brother's band was called the Raiders. Earl Hatchett, Gary Blakley, and Donald. He was the bass player, and they were a hot little trio that played a lot of frat parties and Air Force bases. Every so often they had more gigs than they could handle, so they would actually triple-book dates. Each of the three would hire two other players and play as the Raiders.

In the summer of 1968 Donald asked me to play bass in a trio called the Rhythm Masters. A real band. The gig was a residency every Friday and Saturday night in Plainview, Texas. It was about an hour away, so we went on the road. I had to remind Donald I had never played bass before. He said not to worry, he would show me the basics on his Gibson bass, a double-cutaway that looked like a bass version of an ES-335. My brother played and sang lead and Joe Schreiber played the drums. Joe was the original drummer for the Rhythm Masters and that's why we could use that name, which I've always thought was the coolest.

Donald gave me a quick bass lesson. "The root is 1, then there's the 4, the 5, and the relative minor. You can play almost any song we're going to play with that. Got it?"

"Not really, but . . ."

"You'll get it, let's go!"

So, I used his bass and amp and we got Nehru jackets and played the shows and I made some money and learned on the job. It was an education, and it was the first time I had ever played with a drummer. I was still unaware of what the kick drum was doing, but I played whatever felt right and it seemed to work out. We must have been fairly decent sounding, because we didn't get fired.

♪

All this time I was living in a garage apartment near the Texas Tech campus. My interests in the fraternity and in school were waning, and not much other than music attracted me. I went looking for gigs, but there weren't enough folk clubs in Lubbock to go around, so I decided to open one myself. My idea was to open a little joint and get all the frat guys to pay to get in. There was an ice cream shop on University Ave. called Ron's. Ron and I became friendly and he told me that there was a basement down there that I could use if I cleaned it up. He provided some tables and chairs, and The Attic was born.

I had stickers printed up to advertise the grand opening and hired a friend from Tech named Jeanette Scott to help me run things and heat up frozen pizza in two small ovens that Ron brought down. I stopped going to most of the frat parties and played almost every Friday and Saturday at The Attic, my own place. Many of my fraternity brothers and their dates would show up and other fraternities got wind of it and would bring beer in coolers and eat cheap pizza. It was a happening place for the sort of riffraff I was attracting. I would sit on my amp with my Joey Ely–like hi-hat and play "Baby, Let Me Follow You Down" and "Candy Man" and rockers like "Proud Mary," "Memphis, Tennessee," "You Got Me Runnin,'" and Willie Dixon's "Little Red Rooster." The last one I'd learned from my brother Donald. "Red Rooster" would make my wild frat-rat audiences hoot and holler. Everybody was sweaty and had a great time and Jeanette and I would sweep up the broken beer bottles at the end of the night. We charged 50 cents at the door and we usually had a packed house and made a little money. Of course the place would only hold twenty-five or thirty. But we were packed!

Across the alley from The Attic was another little hideaway folk club called Mesquite's. Ely was playing there regularly and I'd go see him whenever I could. I asked him if he'd like to play The Attic the next Sunday and he said okay. He showed up with his equipment and a large group of his friends. He said that he needed to put them on the guest list and introduced each one, "This is my sound man, this is my lighting director, these are my background singers, and these three are my moral support." He stacked the deck with half the audience getting in free, but that was all right with me. Some frat rats and other college folks showed up and the place was packed. Ely started playing a slow blues number and the frat guys started talking and seemed to hate it. I was still a pretty big guy and I threatened these slobs with imminent bodily harm if they didn't shut up and listen. Things got quiet fast. Quiet enough to hear the bells ringing at the Catholic church down the street. Joey Ely was always fascinating and had picked authentic bluesy material though, as far as I knew, he still wasn't playing much of his own stuff. Joey, Butch Hancock, and Jimmie Dale Gilmore, along with Tony Pearson and a fellow who played a crosscut saw, were putting together a funky acoustic group called the Flatlanders.

One night after a particularly raucous gig at The Attic, a college girl approached me and began telling me earnestly about a rustic restaurant in the little mountain town of Red River, New Mexico, called the River View Inn. She said they were in need of a solo folk singer to play there in the upcoming summer and she thought I would be perfect. The owner of the River View would take her word for it and if I wanted the job, I could have it. "It pays room and board and you can keep your tips," she said. "It starts in June and ends in August right before school starts." She said I could think about it, but she needed to know within a week. Immediately I said, "I don't need a week to think about it. I'll take it." And just like that I became a touring musician road warrior, on my own with nothing to lose and everything to gain. Just the thought of getting out of Lubbock made my hair stand up on end.

The winter semester ended with a happy bang. I had made my grades by the skin of my teeth. But if I ever had any interest in getting a college degree before, I'm sure I had lost it by then. I was just going through the motions with no plan B. I had no set career path and was clueless as to what I was going to do for the rest of my life. I owned nothing of import but a Pontiac Tempest and a Martin D-18. I was not held down by convention or by anything but my own hesitancy. Yes, yes, I'll take it. Of course. I'm going to Red River!

Reality bites, and soon I would have to confront the looming threat of being drafted into the United States Army and sent to Vietnam unless I was in school. As long as I stayed in college and got my student deferment, I was safe for the time being. But now school's out for summer. My trajectory was westward and into the mountains, diving into what, I did not know. I was looking for footing and playing a gig in New Mexico. First time for everything. The thought of it was both electrifying and daunting. My plan was to give myself three months in Red River and then head back to Lubbock, enroll in the fall semester, and stay current with my obligations. Nobody was counseling me on any of this and my parents were left in the dark.

In early June, I got up before dawn and headed west on Highway 84 through Clovis, Santa Rosa, Springer, Taos, and Questa into the Sangre de Cristo Mountains where Red River lay nestled snug as a bug in a green velvet rug. Just like Timber Jack Joe (Bobby Bridger's wild mountain man friend) used to say, "Turn me loose, I'll never be the same!"

CHAPTER 8

Back on the Trivandrum Mail

1981

I was gobsmacked. This fellow on the train had said, "Ah, you must be Iris's husband." There were thousands of people walking through the railway station and on and off the trains. For such a recognition to take place was nothing less than truly cosmic.

Struggling with my bags and guitar, I sat down opposite this wild-looking man in an Indian dhoti, his hair mussed, smoke filling the car. He was a French musician who had come to study Indian music a few years earlier and had stayed on. Iris and the boys were staying in the same general area. Iris had come here interested in the Indian arts and culture and had brought Tucker and Trevor all this way. The Frenchman heard I was coming. He had traveled to Trivandrum to take some music lessons that day and was on his way back when I appeared at the door of his compartment. It was astounding that a stranger had recognized me out of this mass of humanity. But then, there are not that many redheaded guitar players wandering around the streets of India. Nevertheless, it reinforced the enigmatic and magical quality this journey had taken on.

The stranger could speak the rapid-fire local dialect. As the train slowly moved out of the station, my new friend began to give me a rambling discourse on the customs, arts, and music of the region punctuated by wild gestures and with his eyebrows jumping up and down. He ordered more coffee and offered me a chew as he spat something red out the window. Later on I made the mistake of trying it, the incredibly strong Indian tobacco reportedly cured in camel urine. Okay, that's what I heard. I felt woozy for several days after. Just thinking about it now makes me gag.

I had arrived in India under cover of darkness and had seen two big cities in a whirlwind since early morning. But as we sped along the countryside, a real and ancient India emerged. A dense jungle of palm, banana, teak, and rubber trees surrounded by a curtain of vines and undergrowth. Rice paddies stretching into the horizon bordered by distant mountain ranges with bent-back workers toiling while the sun set. Waterwheels, oxen, and raised paths flecked the landscape. Then an endless sea of habitation, houses made of wood and piled rocks, thatch and plastic walls with flattened oil tins wired together for roofing. As the train picked up speed, we passed villages of mud and thatched huts known as pandals and lean-tos all pressed against the rail line. Then larger hamlets composed of antiquated buildings with façades of blue, green, purple, and fuchsia that resembled psychedelic Wild West towns. And there was the occasional ostentatious mansion so out of place here in this crush of color. Pedestrians walked so close to the tracks that you could literally have touched them as the train went whizzing by. How can they endure the noise that this train delivered to their ears: shrieks and whistles, rolling wheels, creaks and groans, shouts, and blasts of steam?

We banged along with a steady drumming. "Pha-pha-pha-boom, pha-pha-pha-boom." It became the rhythm track to the journey. As dusk settled in, small oil lamps were lit in the doorways of the tiny huts and houses. As the Trivandrum Mail pulled into a tiny, jam-packed railway station at the end of the line, this extraordinary day was winding down.

We drove up to the stone gates of the bungalow where Iris and the boys lived near a coconut grove. Suddenly the air seemed 20 degrees cooler as I carried my bags up the walk. They greeted me with hugs, kisses, and tears. I had brought presents for everyone along with prized American products: peanut butter, shampoo, toothpaste, granola bars, and dried soup mix, all treasures you couldn't find in the local shops. After a peanut butter sandwich and fresh cow's milk, I collapsed and slept for three days.

CHAPTER 9

Red River

Summer 1969

It's been said that timing has a lot to do with the outcome of a rain dance. I was full of excitement, wonder, apprehension, uncertainty, and relief when I pulled into Red River a couple of days before my new gig at the River View Inn. The trip up the flatland stairs with its gradual sometimes-steep climb upward to almost 9,000 feet was awe-inspiring and jaw-dropping. It was my first time away from home on my own for any extended period of time. I didn't know anybody here, not even the guy who was hiring me. I didn't know what to expect and I didn't even know it took guts to be off on my own like this. I had jumped at this chance of going on a big adventure playing and singing and getting paid for it.

The River View Inn was green-gray, a two-story wood building on Main Street just catty-corner from the biggest bar in town, the D-Bar-D. I met Jack Emory, the owner of the River View. He was thin and balding and had a weathered face. Jack had a glass eye, and I could never be sure which eye was looking at me. He told me to get my things over to the Green Mountain Lodge across the street. It was owned by Otto Barker and his wife, Bonnie, who operated a beauty parlor on the ground floor. The rooms were all on the second floor. It was sort of like a boardinghouse. Otto didn't have a hair on his head and practically the first thing he said to me was, "Bob, when you get to be a certain age, your hair starts growing down. If it hits rocks, it stops. But if it hits brains, why then it grows right on out of sight!" Otto and his wife had a son named Craig who would later become a good entertainment lawyer in Austin. The room Otto showed me was a seven-by-ten knotty pine box with walls so thin you could hear every breath, snore, and whispered secret from the other rooms. It had a bed, a desk, and a chair—just enough to suggest civilization. The bathroom was at the end of the hall, so it was basically a communal adventure—part obstacle course, part waiting game, and always good for some late-night drama and awkward encounters. It was great!

The stage of the River View Inn was tiny, big enough for one or two, with a sign over it that said "Singer's Survival Depends on Donations." The restaurant held about thirty-five to fifty starving tourists. It was pretty good food and I ate there a couple of times a day. On the second floor there were hotel rooms, all of them much better than the one I had been given across the street. I met a couple of guys who lived up there, dynamite experts at the Questa Moly Mine, and they gave demonstrations occasionally where they would blow the side of a mountain off and all of the rock would land perfectly in the world's largest truck. These two rounders would become faithful fans and come to my show every night.

At about 6 p.m. I would play a set while people were eating dinner. I mostly did cover stuff. Dylan; Peter, Paul and Mary; Kingston Trio; Beatles; Gordon Lightfoot. Jack's favorite song was Lightfoot's "Early Morning Rain," and he would prime the pump by putting a dollar into the tip jar in full view of the diners, both of us hoping they would take the hint and follow. I would take a break at about 7 and Jack would introduce me to some of the locals and other regulars who had come up from Texas for

First real gig out of Lubbock, at the River View Inn, Red River, New Mexico. Note sign at top: "Singer's survival depends on donations." Nothing has changed. (Photo by Evelyne Taylor.)

the summer. I got a 15-minute break spent roaming around the room then did another set at about until 8 and that'd be it. I was very self-conscious with this regimen for a few nights, but I got the hang of it soon enough. One night Jack said, "You should get a haircut." It would become an issue.

A couple of days later, Jack took me down the street to a jeep rental business run by Don Dossett who was a gruff, no-nonsense, barrel-chested redneck, but who gave me a job driving jeep tours into the mountains. My hair was not long by most standards, but I did have a mustache and Mr. Dossett and Jack now both agreed I needed a haircut. I got paid $4 for each jeep tour plus whatever tips I could wrangle out of the tourist customers. I'd make at least three trips a day, sometimes four, $12 to $16 a day. That, and the $10 to $15 I made in tips at the River View, added up to quite a haul—for me—especially with no expenses. It was pure fun driving jeeps with five or six passengers clinging onto the rails as we bounced along treacherous switchbacks and sharp turns to lost mines and ghost towns up the mountain's rutted and washed-out roads. If it wasn't for my amazing skill as a driver, I told my audience, we would probably be plunging into the abyss like a jeep full of tourists had done last week.

On one of the jeep trips I met a girl from Fort Worth named Evelyne Sumner, who was 16 and visiting up there with her church group. She sang and laughed and had a great brightness and innocence about her. She was also a folk singer and later started a group called The Banded Geckos in Houston with her soon-to-be-husband, Tim Taylor. Lyle Lovett opened for them at Anderson Fair, and look what happened to him. We have all remained lifelong friends and Iris and I still stay at the Taylors' adobe hacienda with them whenever we are in Santa Fe. Tim and Evelyne are the happiest people I have ever known and it's infectious to just be around them. Always laughter and music. New Mexico has that effect on some people.

One night, after my set at the River View, Jack told me, "I want to take you down the street to meet . . . *the Boys*." We walked down Main and took a right turn right after the D-Bar-D and there was a funky log cabin with a sign that read, The Outpost. It was a folk club and the group that played there were also the owners. They were called Three Faces West, and they were from Dallas. It turned out I was following in their footsteps. They had come to Red River a few years before and sang for Jack at the River View and had driven jeeps for Mr. Dossett. They loved Red River, did quite well in the bars, and had decided to open their own place.

That night, The Outpost was packed to the gills with locals and tourists and the show was about to start. Jack and I found two seats in the back.

The lights went down and three fellows walked from a side door onto a tiny stage. They were wearing outfits that I immediately wanted: leather pants and vests, bandannas, wild shirts, and Frye boots, and they had rakishly long hair. They welcomed everyone and started playing something fast. They had great voices and cool harmonies and they played their instruments well. I was surprised to see Rick Fowler from the fraternity music party back in Lubbock playing lead on a Martin and he sometimes picked up a banjo and was damn good with it. Wayne Kidd was in the middle and played a Höfner bass that was campy and amazing. Wayne was also a good singer and harmonizer. The other guitar player was a wiseass named Ray Hubbard, a sardonic, quick-witted guy with an interesting voice. He wasn't Ray Wylie yet. Just plain Ray Hubbard. Or Hubbard. They were all quick-witted and funny. They had slick comedy bits between songs that seemed spontaneous. They spoke to each other with off-the-wall stuff, like the one about dipping Ray's grandmother in creosote down at the creosote plant. I don't remember just why it was so funny, but they had great timing and everyone in the place was engaged, laughing, and clapping. It was a great show. And they were my age, sort of, and I wanted to hear them again.

I had never heard of the songwriters they were talking about in the introductions. Keith Sykes, Tom Rush, John Stewart, Johnny Vandiver, and others I can't remember. But the songs that really struck me were by someone named Mike Murphey. I later learned Wayne, Rick, and Ray had gone to high school in Dallas with Murphey and they had all gone to North Texas State in Denton, which was well known as a great music school. Mostly jazz music. They all jammed and wrote in the Folk Club along with fellows like Segle Fry and Buckwheat Stevenson and Steven Fromholz. By this time, Murphey had already written "Wildfire" but had never recorded it. Three Faces West did a great version of "Wildfire," and I thought these guys had it, whatever "it" was.

After the show, Jack and I waited around. "This is Bob Livingston, my new boy," Jack said as the three of them walked up. All three of them sniggered as one. They were not much different offstage than they were on, friendly but sarcastic and cracking jokes and making fun of everything. I looked at their instruments and wished I had a banjo.

Jack said, "Hey, one of you loan Bob a guitar. I want him to play something for you. Sit on this stool, Bob, and play . . . that 'Early Morning Rain.'" Rick handed me his Martin and I sat down and began to sing, very earnestly, "In the early morning rain, with a dollar in my hand . . ."

I got through the first verse and at some point, I looked up to see how this was going over. Jack was grinning like a possum, egging me on. But the other three were looking at each other and rolling their eyes and putting their hands over their mouths. It dawned on me that I was doing something tragically unhip, though I didn't quite know what it was. Some cosmic lesson was being taught. But I couldn't stop to analyze it, so I plowed right through feeling weird and unsure of myself but singing in tune and with gusto, ". . . with an aching in my heart and a pocketful of sand."

I sang the last chorus and looked up hoping to have some acceptance, or something. Jack was still grinning and the other guys were still looking snippy. Afterwards Wayne and Rick just sort of melted away into the night saying nothing more.

But Ray Hubbard said to me, "Come over here, I want to give you two pieces of advice." He looked at me hard and I had no idea what he was about to say. "Number one." he said. "Don't ever sit down when you play. You command the room when you're standing up. You're engaged and have a lot more energy, the audience will pay more attention. Don't sit down, okay? And number two . . . don't *ever* sing 'Early Morning Rain' again!" He pointed out that every folk singer does that one. "If you are going to do a Lightfoot song, do something obscure. That's the secret with doing other people's material, don't do a song that everybody else does." It was good advice, and to this day I rarely sit down when I play, and even though it's a great song I haven't done "Early Morning Rain" since.

We all became friends, and I saw Rick and Ray almost every day and they showed me the ropes. Wayne was married to Marsha and was living a more settled life. All three had driven the jeep tours before me and told me wild stories that I could tell my jeep customers. Black Jack Ketchum had been hanged right there and they put so much weight on his feet that his head popped right off and his ghost still roamed the high mountain trails that we were driving. My jeep driving tips went up considerably after I started using these valuable story suggestions.

Both Jack and Mr. Dossett kept on me about cutting my hair and finally forced the issue. They wanted Otto's wife Bonnie Barker to cut my hair and told me to "go there now" or I might lose both my jobs. It was a beauty parlor, not a barbershop. I hated haircuts in the best of circumstances. After I saw the Beatles on Ed Sullivan I never wanted to cut my hair again. I wanted to be Davy Crockett as a kid and have long hair, but my mother would always make me get a flat-top, which I hated even though all my friends had the same cut. In school, only dudes with ducktails had long hair. I had grown it out in college, but it wasn't long in the scheme of things. When I look at photos from that time I look like a guy in the Air Force with a mustache. Mrs. Barker got me in a chair. She began to rub my shoulders, saying, "You are so tense, Bob. Relax." She squeezed my neck and I closed my eyes. When I woke up, she had given me a buzz cut. Barely an inch long. It was a setup, a plot. I dragged myself into work the next day and Mr. Dossett grinned at me for the first time all summer.

Ray and I played every afternoon on the front porch of the D-Bar-D where we wrote our first song called "Life in the Pines." It later became Three Faces West's first single.

> Life in the Pines, makes it worthwhile
> With a rust hickory woman, and a blue-eyed child . . .

The odd and unusual description of a woman being "rust hickory" was Ray's line and I asked him what he meant by it. He said, "Oh, you know, a rust hickory woman is a kind of woman that when she raises her arm, a whippoorwill flies out!"

I would go see Three Faces West every night and not just because I was so interested in their show. There were songs I wanted to learn and do in my set, especially the Murphey ones: "Wildfire," "Fort Worth, I Love You," and "You Can Only Say So Much." But Ray and Rick refused to show me the chords or tell me the words. They said I had to come to the show and learn them, they weren't going to give away their secrets for nothing. I sat in the back with a notebook scribbling away.

Ray and I played a couple of duo gigs in Taos that summer. We called ourselves Speck Ellis and the New Mexico Playboy, a name Ray and Rick had kicked around using but didn't so we co-opted it. We didn't delineate which one of us was Speck or the Playboy. We did dark folkie swing songs for the hippies in a Taos bar, many of them from a commune called New Buffalo out on the vast and bitter prairie north of town.

Rick Fowler and I co-wrote a song called "Compromise" that Ray would later record on a Cowboy Twinkies album for Lone Star Records. We wrote "Head Full of Nothin'" that would later appear on Jerry Jeff's album, *It's A Good Night for Singin'* on MCA. I usually had the melody and the first verse and a piece of the chorus and Rick would plug in his sly whimsical rhyming and make it all come together:

Just high and hoboin' in the breeze with a pocket
full of hand
Head full of nothin', boots full of holes, holes full of
sand . . .

And I added:

It's gettin' on into the afternoon and the rides are
coming slow
I'd sure like to get to Texas, but I'd settle for Del Rio

It was a great summer, the best summer of all. I had joined a tribe and was starting to get comfortable in my own skin. I had made new and creative musical friends who were models for the kind of life I wanted to live. I had received valuable information about music, songwriters, and songwriting. I learned new chords and I played them and sang a lot better than I had only three months before. And just as important to the vague future before me, I had saved some money.

But my ideal life in the mountains—so full of music, creativity, and fun—was ending as the Colorado spruce began turning blue, signaling that summer is over, fall and winter are coming on. A new semester was starting at Texas Tech, and I hadn't considered for one second that whole summer long what courses I was going to take. I didn't want to train for a career—what would that be? A schoolteacher? Running a Piggly Wiggly? I had no ambition to become a businessman. All I knew is that I wanted to play music and I would find a way.

I drove back to Lubbock, down out of those beautiful green Sangre de Cristo Mountains, down past the mesas and canyons, down to the brown fields and dust of the West Texas plains. My antennae were out and opportunity was knocking. That was certain. I would return to Red River again, sooner rather than later. Red River would become a cornerstone and a mighty, if not well-advertised, footnote in Texas Music history. Jerry Jeff Walker, Michael Martin Murphey, Rusty Wier, Willis Alan Ramsey, Michael Hearne, Bill and Bonnie Hearne, Walt and Tina Wilkins, Kelley Mickwee, Jed Zimmerman, Susan Gibson, and many others all would hang out, play, and write there. Three Faces West was a big influence on all of us, even the young ones, and the vibe was still in the air. Folkies still love to hang out in Red River, now more than ever. I get to go back a few times a year to play Michael Hearne's Big Barn Dance and the Red River Folk Festival. I was lucky to have stumbled onto this magical cosmic hamlet and be part of everything that was about to happen.

CHAPTER 10

Number 309

1969

Back from the road and the ultimate experience with a newfound freedom in every step I was now a man of the world, and I walked and talked like it. I reenrolled at Tech and busied myself finding a place to live near the campus. I found a little garage apartment on the second floor, one room, iron spring bed, tiny kitchen, clawfoot bathtub. I signed up for fifteen hours—English, biology, math, art history, and PE. My favorite course was Dr. Brewer's English class. She encouraged me to write what I wanted, to think outside the box. She wrote helpful comments in the margins of my papers. I can't say I had the same feelings for any of the other professors or their courses and it wasn't long before I dropped out of math and biology and struggled with everything else, even art history. There was something about Rome that would take me years to figure out and in the end, it wouldn't matter.

I was still in the SAE fraternity and I went to parties and drank way too much. The bands at the parties were great and I would dance like a demon, even once or twice do the Gator and many times jump up onstage to sing with them. "Mustang Sally, slow your mustang down."

Playing at the Brookshire Inn on 19th Street close to downtown Lubbock was my next real gig, two or three nights a week.

It was a private club where folks could drink in otherwise-dry Lubbock. The Brookshire provided little backroom lockers for customers to stash their liquor. Folks would come in, have a steak, drink whisky, and listen to the lonesome country folk singer in the corner. That was how they got away with drinking in the city limits.

The club and bar were upstairs. I would play a couple of hours for a small fee and tips. No sound system, pure acoustic. I'd make $25 to $45 a night. It wasn't good but it wasn't bad either. I had some $50 nights. I remember playing in one room while Johnny Carson was in another. He came in after doing a show at the Municipal Auditorium. He brought his entourage and NBC Orchestra leader Doc Severinsen. They all sat around a big round table and drank scotch. The waitresses said Johnny was a cheapskate and didn't leave much of a tip.

As the semester wore on, the Vietnam War was everywhere. Television, newspapers, and the radio talked about battles and casualties and more boys were going over there to die. Walter Cronkite was showing us movies right in our living rooms of bodies and attacks and bombings with napalm. Horrible and frightening images, but still far away. Vast anti-war protest marches were held all over the country, even in Lubbock. Then the war came right through the door. They spoke of a draft lottery. We might all have to go! This was serious.

On December 1, 1969, the first lottery drawing was held. There were complicated rules. Any young man born between the years 1944 and 1950 was eligible. Unless you had some provable medical condition or mental illness or had a student deferment, you were most likely on your way to Vietnam pronto. If you were in school, you were exempt. If you got a low lottery number but were still in school, you could still stay safe until you graduated. Then, if the war was still going on, you had to report to the draft board, take a physical and, if you passed, you were gone.

All three television networks broadcast the drawing. A congressman put his hand into a glass bowl and began to draw out birthdays. The whole world watched. The men and boys, their parents, their brothers and sisters and wives and girlfriends, were all sweating bullets. Your very life was on the line. After about a hundred birthdays had been drawn, I began to breathe a little easier. At 200 I stretched out, and when my number was finally drawn, it was #309. I let out a whoop! I wasn't sure, but it seemed that the hand of fate had steered me clear. The next day I went to the draft board to ask what it all meant. I told them I was thinking about leaving school and laying out a semester. They said that they expected to draft about thirty numbers a month. At that rate, I could leave school and if it got close to my number, I could re-enroll and get my student deferment back in the spring.

Up to that point, I'd done my best to play the game—follow the rules, get an education, stay on the path: college, career, steady job. But the whole thing had always felt like I was wearing someone else's shoes. Now here I was, seriously thinking about walking away from Texas Tech altogether. Was I really about to step out of the dugout and call it quits? The only reason I was going to school at all was because of the insane Vietnam War. I had that student deferment and now I had a high lottery number which was the answer to my prayers.

I didn't know who to seek out for advice. My mom and dad would take a dim view of my quitting school, so I looked for someone I respected to talk with. That person was Dr. Mary Brewer, my creative writing professor. I scheduled a meeting and told her I had received a high draft lottery number. Thank God that pressure was off, but I was thinking about dropping out for a semester or two, and what did she think?

Now I know that what follows is pretty corny and cliché, but Dr. Brewer asked me, "Bob, what do you want to do with your life anyway?"

I really had no idea, but I told her I wanted a chance at playing music as a career path. "I want to get out of Lubbock for sure."

"Well, then you know what you want to do. You have a chance to live your dream. Most people don't get a chance like this. You might always regret it if you don't at least try. And like you said, if it doesn't work out, you can always go back to school."

It was the perfect advice. I thanked her for her insight and walked out into the cold windy Lubbock day and breathed a deep sigh of relief. The looming burden of Vietnam had been lifted off my shoulders. I had been given permission to move on with my life. Permission was what I needed, and it wasn't my parents who gave me that permission. That was a bold leap in itself. There was a dust storm kicking up in the west, and the world was whipping around in a fury. Drama everywhere!

As the semester ended, a musical light appeared at the end of the tunnel. My brother, Donald, was in Aspen playing at The Anchorage, a restaurant club at the base of the main ski run. Donald called and said I could get on at The Anchorage playing the après-ski show from 5 to 7 every day right before he went on. It wasn't much money, but room and board were thrown in, and back then room and board was *big*. Still is. Aspen was one of the most notorious and wild tourist destinations in the world. High in the Rockies; celebrities and movie stars were everywhere, a thousand skiers, professional and otherwise, and tons of snow. I told my brother to count me in.

There had to be a call to my parents telling them what I was going to do. I explained I was going to leave school "just for a semester. I really need some time off." Of course they both were upset, my mother more than my dad, who was more easygoing. I told them that I'd get back to school in the spring. I wasn't exactly lying because I really had no idea how this would all play out, but I was going to go for it.

My fraternity brothers were mystified. Mike Looney later said, "We had never heard of one of our guys just leaving school. It made no sense. We didn't think Livingston would do it." Yes, I would miss the friendship, the parties and good times, but I *wouldn't* miss the grind of studying and the stress of making my grades in what was for me a pointless enterprise. I didn't belong in Lubbock anymore and I knew it. I wanted to play music. I wasn't thinking about making a living. How long this new course would last and what path would appear would make itself known soon enough. For now, a way out had been found and, like Mac Davis sang, "Happiness was Lubbock, Texas, in my rearview mirror."

CHAPTER 11

The Aspen Connection

January 1970

The streets of downtown Lubbock are made of red brick and when it snows it's slicker than owl shit. That was such a day when I crept out of town towards Colorado. It was bleak and the road stretched out into a snowy whiteness. By the time I got to Raton there was a whiteout, and I stopped to pass the night in the back seat of the car with the motor running.

Somewhere in the high country the sun came out. It was a beautiful day with spectacular scenery and I was happy and determined and couldn't wait to get to Aspen. In Colorado they knew how to make it happen in the snow. They were used to it and they all had four-wheel-drive cars and they seemed to be able to buzz around pretty well. But I had no chains on my Tempest and I spun out several times crossing some of the passes. Loveland Pass was always a hairy proposition in winter.

It took me forever to get there and I was worn out and exhausted when I pulled into snow-drenched Aspen. I went looking for Donald's house, but the street signs were snowed over and I decided to head for the club. I finally found The Anchorage and walked in and as luck would have it, there was my brother sitting at the bar talking to a guy that looked an awful lot like John Denver. And it was John Denver.

Born John Deutschendorf, John Denver went to Texas Tech and Donald knew him there. One spring day in 1963, John told Donald he was heading out west to Los Angeles.

"We will never amount to anything here. We have to get out where the real entertainment scene is. Come with me."

"Nah," my brother said. "I'm doing okay here. Good luck."

The Anchorage was a wild place. Located at the base of one of the main runs, you'd ski right up to the outside deck, take off your skis, and order a drink. The joint was jumping and was packed from lunch to the late dinner hours. Everybody started out with hot buttered rum and brandy to warm up, talking, shouting, going through the motions of their last run down the mountain, waving their arms and laughing. I discovered how shrill drunk voices could be. Ski bunnies in sexy outfits who were also amazing athletes let their hair down once the day's skiing was over and partied like it was 1999 and it was only 1970. Many of the patrons wore casts and slings and had broken bones but still skied or in the worst cases watched longingly from the outside landing and got drunk as Texas skunks by the time 4 p.m. rolled around and the lifts closed. This was the crowd I would play for, and I was going to have to be on top of it to break through the din and reach them. It was new to me but would prove to be great training for playing in the many bars that lay ahead. Christmas came and my brother and I said Merry Christmas to each other and that was about it. It was the same as any other day and we played our sets and went home late.

One unforgettable night after my first set a man with a beard and long hair and expensive-looking ski clothes approached me. He really liked what I was doing, he said. He wanted to hear some originals, so I played five or six of mine and a couple of covers. After the set, I walked over to his table, and he stood up to introduce himself.

"My name is Randy. Randy Fred. I really liked your songs and your voice. Do you have a record deal?"

Of course I didn't have a record deal.

Randy said he lived in Los Angeles and was an agent there and he thought he could land me a record contract. I didn't really believe him, but he seemed real enough and talked a good game. He said he had been an agent for a lot of movie stars and had made a lot of money and had dropped acid, had "seen the light" and quit his job and was skiing the winter away in one of the most expensive places to live on earth. He said he was going back to LA after the season was over in a couple of weeks and if I so desired, I could meet him out there and stay at his house while he would work on getting me a record deal. I was flabbergasted and found it hard to fathom. But I said I'd be there. Meanwhile I had another two weeks on the job, and he came in most afternoons to hear me, skiing right up to the door.

Two weeks later the season was over and after my set on Friday night, Randy told me that he was serious about my coming to Los Angeles. He said he would come to my place on Sunday morning and give me the keys to his house and he would meet me there a week later. This was amazing news, and I began packing my bags that night. I bought provisions for the journey across the Mojave. I met a hippie couple hitchhiking and one thing led to another and they said if I would give them a ride to LA they would split the gas with me. I gave them my address and told them to meet me at 10 a.m. sharp on Sunday morning. Randy was to be there at the same time.

Sunday came full of anticipation. This was the last day I could stay at the Aspen house; new renters were already moving in. I got up early and walked outside. It was snowing heavily, and I cleared the snow off my windshield and started my car up to have it idling. White exhaust smoke billowed up and mixed with the curtain of white snow coming down. Everything I owned went into the car. I drank coffee and waited. My driving companions showed up at 9:45 and threw their things in the back seat. We waited for Randy.

An hour later he still hadn't come, then noon came and went and still no Randy. He was an hour and a half late. I looked at my new friends and said I didn't think he was coming. "I *may* have to change my plans right now and head back to Lubbock. I don't know what else to do or where else to go and we can't just stand out here in the blizzard." I hated the idea, but it was looking like I was going back to Tech. The greatest thing about it was that the hippie couple looked at each other and quickly said, "Okay, we'll go to Lubbock. We've never been there. No problem." They didn't even think about it and were ready to turn on a dime without so much as a look of disappointment or a groan.

My red Pontiac was still idling and the exhaust was white and billowing up in the cold. Snow was coming down hard and the driveway would soon be impassable until a snowplow came the next day. This was the moment of truth. I had to make a decision. I had just reached for the door handle and was about to get in and head south. Suddenly a dark blue-gray Buick Riviera came barreling up the driveway and slid to a halt right behind my car. Randy got out, all scarves and gloves, long hair and apologies.

"Bob. Hey, I'm sorry, man, the season has been extended because of all this snow. I had to get a few runs in this morning. There was no way to call. Are you ready?"

"Wow, I didn't think you were coming!"

"Yeah, man, I'm sorry. Here are the keys to my place. There is a guy named Brian house-sitting for me. He's expecting you."

Randy gave me his address, phone number, and keys and rough directions to his place. He lived on Beverly Glen, right next door to Beverly Hills.

"You'll find the house fine. I have to go back and get on the mountain. I'll see you there in two weeks. Allen is a good guy and he'll show you what's what. We are gonna get you a record deal. I'm going to take care of everything. Don't worry, see you there!"

We had some harrowing times on that road, especially in Utah where some folks in a diner wouldn't let us leave until I sang for my supper, all of our suppers. In Los Angeles, I dropped my new friends off, drove around, and tried to follow Randy's directions. The sun had set and there was no moon, so it was slow going. I made it to Sunset and drove past the famous Whisky a Go Go and gawked.

I found Randy's house on Beverly Glen and a lanky fellow with long straight hair and John Lennon glasses answered my knock. We introduced ourselves and Brian seemed vaguely pissed about having me show up and ruin his solitude. There was a piano in the corner and I hadn't had a chance to play one for a long time. I made a beeline to it and Brian seemed to lighten up. In the coming months, I really learned how to play on this piano, practicing and writing almost every day. The title song on my *Gypsy Alibi* album had its beginnings with the Gershwin-esque melody I wrote in Beverly Glen all those years ago.

In a few weeks Randy came back from skiing his heart out in Aspen. He said the first order of business was for me to lose weight. Aspen was all free food and beer so I had gained twenty-five pounds in two months. Randy put me on a pure protein diet—only steak, chicken, fish, and a little salad. No bread, alcohol, sweets, or carbs. I dropped all that weight and more in a couple of months. Randy kept me going—cooking healthy meals, introducing me to Hollywood types, and hustling behind the scenes to land that record deal.

CHAPTER 12

"Every Step Is Two Steps"

1970

Randy had a lawyer friend named Richard Trugman who was well known in the music business circles around town. I went with the two of them and my guitar to Capitol Records Tower on Hollywood and Vine into an immense empty recording studio and waited. This is where they said to meet them. In about fifteen minutes some men in black suits walked in and sat down in front of me. One of the suits looked straight into my eyes and said, "Okay, Dr. Livingston, I'm Sal. Whaddya got?"

Salvatore Iannucci was the president of Capitol Records. He looked like a mob boss and he was sitting there staring at me and waiting for me to play something. For the life of me, I can't remember what I played. They were things I had written back then that I have completely forgotten now. I was deeply uncomfortable in that sterile room, surrounded by suits who just stared at me, stone-faced and unreadable. After four songs, without warning, Sal suddenly stood up. In lockstep, the others followed. He glanced at Richard and Randy and said, "I think we can work with that. Send me a contract." Then he turned and walked out. Just like that. It was the first and last time I ever saw—or spoke to—Sal.

Two weeks later, Randy and I walked into Lawyer Trugman's office for the big reveal. I'd cleaned up a bit—sort of. Sporting a makeshift suit, a new beard, and a scarf slung rather rakishly (I thought) around my neck, I was leaner, scruffier, and feeling halfway like a rock star. Also going with us to the meeting was Jan Smithers, an actress friend I was around in those days. I'd first seen her on the cover of *Newsweek* when I was sixteen—a thunderbolt moment. I fell in love instantly and would stare at the cover endlessly, right alongside a few million other teenage boys. As fate would have it, Randy Fred became her agent, and Jan would later go on to star in the hit TV series *WKRP in Cincinnati*. During my time in the surreal swirl of Los Angeles, Jan showed me the ropes—and there were a lot of ropes.

Trugman said, "All right, we've got a deal. Details can wait, but here's the headline: $10,000 advance for *you* with a three-record deal. You'll earn more with each album. I'll take 10 percent of that and Randy gets 25 percent as your manager. That leaves you with $6,500." He handed me the check. "Take this straight to the Bank of America and open an account. I'll be in touch when it's time to cut the record. Congratulations, Bob—welcome to the music business."

A lot of what followed happened in slow motion. We walked across the street to the Bank of America, where I opened an account. They handed me a little cardboard card that came with a kind of superpower: At any Bank of America branch, I could flash it and walk away with at least $100 in cash. It felt like magic. And like most magic tricks, it didn't last long.

We all went out to eat and celebrate. Randy had made money, Richard had made money, and I had made the most money I had ever seen in my life. I was rich. I picked up the tab for our fancy dinner and walked back to the bank for another $100 just for the hell of it.

My Pontiac was on its last legs, so the advance money couldn't have come at a better time. First I bought a used Datsun pickup truck for $1,200. The next stop was for a new guitar. I drove over to Westwood Music near UCLA to take a look. The owner, Fred Walecki, had a rack of Martin and Gibson guitars, new and used. Fred had told me that when a new batch of Martins came into the warehouse, he would personally go and play every one of them and only bring back the good ones, the ones that met his standards. He showed me a 1967 Martin with beautiful and unusual inlay on the fretboard. I played it and decided on the spot *this was the one* and paid him $450 cash. I still have that Martin and have played it to Timbuktu and back.

While I was waiting to record, Randy thought it wise for me to get some gigs and play. The record was everything, but I hadn't played a real show since coming to Los Angeles. Randy set me up to audition with Joey Gallo, the head of entertainment for the Reuben's restaurant chain. Their eateries were everywhere on the West Coast from San Diego to Seattle, each having a lounge with a stage and sound system, and they hired solos, duos, and sometimes full bands to perform. Some of these acts were great, and many California musicians would cut their teeth in showbiz by playing in Reuben's and lounges like that. They could make a living while they bided their time and waited for something big to happen to their musical careers. A few of these soon-to-be stars included the Carpenters, Captain & Tennille, Scatman Crothers, and Michael Martin Murphey.

Joey Gallo was a pretty good musician himself, played piano and did show tunes from musicals like *Man of La Mancha* and *The Sound of Music*. I went out to Gardena where he was and played a few songs for him and he nodded his head and said, "Play something I know!" I knew some Beatles covers and the stuff I played in the bars with my brother and he nodded his head and said, "Okay, okay." He hired me on the spot and told me to start at the Gardena location the next Tuesday night. I'd play Tuesday through Saturday. It was May 1970.

In a way it was like most other gigs from hell even though the money was pretty good. I tried to connect with the audience and talk to them and do my own songs and Murphey songs and the other new cooler songs I had learned from Three Faces West. But one day Joey Gallo called me and told me to come in early, that he wanted to talk to me. He led me into his back office—a dim, moody room lit only by a single lamp glowing behind his desk.

"Bob, are you happy here at Reuben's?"

"Yes, I guess so. I'm getting into the swing of it."

"I like your voice, you can sing, ya know?"

"Thanks, Joey, and I . . . I'm going to . . ."

"Bob! I got to tell ya something. Look at me. Number one, you're talking way too much in your show. And that's what we're doing here, you know, putting on a show. Listen to me, just sing, okay, that's what we do here. Are you listening to me? And you're doing too many of your own songs, which are okay I guess, but the audience doesn't know 'em. You can do a few of your own, but not too many, okay? This isn't a folk club like the Troubadour. We don't sing *Kumbaya* and have the audience join hands and sway and sing along, okay? We sing songs that people know, up-tempo, rock 'n' roll, show tunes, the hits, whatever. I don't want these people to think too much. And you know why? Because these idiots just want to have fun and hear songs they know. It sells booze. Look at me! And here at Reuben's we put on these shows for one reason only, so our customers will buy booze. That's it! That's *all. Otherwise there is no need for the expense.* Let me tell you something, the Beatles would be nothin' if they couldn't sell booze! Nothin'! That's what the music industry is all about—selling booze. Now are you going to remember that?"

What? That the music business is all about selling booze? The Beatles were the greatest and most creative geniuses on the planet and Joey Gallo was boiling it all down to booze. This guy was crazy. Or was he? The Beatles played bars and packed them every night . . . and sold a lot of booze, true enough. But that point of view is so cold-blooded.

"Hey, Bob, are you hearing what I'm saying? Look at me. Are you going to remember all this?" I was thinking of the Mafia as he spoke with those intense eyes staring into me, hammering in the point.

So . . . I did my show that night, kept my brilliant stories to a minimum, and played every cover song I knew. I was on shaky ground now, selling myself to drinkers. This was my job now. Human jukebox. "Hey, play 'Close to You' for me!" they'd yell between shots. I was a deer in the headlights onstage. I smiled, nodded, died a little inside. I knew I couldn't do this much longer. I wished I could start my record tomorrow—or maybe just fake my own death.

Later that night, as I was driving home on the Santa Ana Freeway, I was listening to the radio when I heard a news recap that gave details about a tornado that had hit Lubbock earlier that night. It had caused a lot of damage and killed a lot of people. I was stunned and the next day I called some of my friends to see how they had fared. Nobody I knew was killed or injured, but the two places I might have been when the tornado struck were my little garage apartment and the Brookshire Inn where I played the year before. They were both totally destroyed.

I called my brother, who by then was playing at a bar on the River Walk in San Antonio. We talked about the tornado, and then I told him what happened with Joey Gallo the night before.

"He's RIGHT, Robert! You have to sell drinks. That's the name of the game. I've told you that before."

"Well, you ought to come out here then and sell booze. I can't do it anymore."

I called Joey and told him that Donald would be perfect for the job, that he knew every cover song there was, and about all

"I can't call you up, 'cause the phone would just ring, it would ring off the wall. I've thought of everything." —Bob Livingston (Photo by Gary P. Nunn.)

the bands he had played with, and he pretty much hired him right then, just on my say. Later that day, Joey Gallo and Donald talked on the phone and Joey was convinced that Donald was *the guy* and Donald made plans to come out West.

There was still no word from Capitol about the record. I was depressed about everything and needed a change of scenery. I had to get out of there. Randy agreed that I needed to leave town, go somewhere far away. I think he knew something I didn't.

Jeanette Scott, who had worked as my waitress at The Attic back in Lubbock, was going to the University of Hawaii. I called to tell her what was up with the record deal and the bad experience at Reuben's, and she said to come over. "You need to get out of there and hang ten with us." I got on a plane a few days later and flew to Honolulu.

Besides going to class, Jeanette was friends with a lot of surfers, and we hung out in the North Beach area. We went to a party at James Michener's house and ended up staying there for several days. We swam in dangerous waters and tried to surf—I nearly drowned from the powerful undertow. I shaved off my beard and almost drowned again.

Three weeks into my stay at my Hawaiian hideaway the phone rang with a menacing vibe. It was Randy calling from Los Angeles with disturbing news.

"Bob . . . they fired Sal. They fired everybody. All the A&R guys, the art department, marketing—gone. I can't get ahold of anyone at Capitol. Artie Mogull's taken over. It doesn't look good. You might as well stay put for now. When the dust settles, I'll give you a call."

It was a blow, but for some reason I took it in stride. At least then. It was a good story for the surfers who thought I was a wimp that I wouldn't continue to surf every day and night with them. At the end of the month I headed back to Los Angeles and uncertainty. *The future ain't what it used to be*, I thought.

CHAPTER 13

The Hand of Fate, Part 1

July 1970

It started out like most of my days in Los Angeles, driving around to nowhere in particular looking for something to explore. I hadn't yet quit playing the nightly Reuben's shows but my days were up for grabs. Restless, I drove aimlessly toward Sunset Beach then thought better of it and turned around and headed back to the San Fernando Valley where there was a music store. North Hollywood has bumpy streets and a hitchhiker caught my attention. As a rule I never stopped for hitchhikers but for some reason that day I did. *The Hand of Fate* had intervened again and steered my little Datsun over to the side of the road a block south of the Palomino Club where a somewhat odd but otherwise avant-garde-looking fellow in a jumpsuit stood with his thumb out.

If I hadn't stopped for that hitchhiker that day at that exact moment I wouldn't be here today telling you this story. Maybe I would have eventually run into Murphey through some other mystical circumstance, but maybe I wouldn't have. Maybe I wouldn't have met Jerry Jeff or ever met Iris and had children and grandchildren if not for this perfect stranger on the road. In any case, this was a turning point for me. Cogs clicked and I knew it.

The man jumped in my Datsun smelling of grease and smog. He said he was going a few miles up the road to his garage. He was an auto mechanic who worked on foreign cars for movie stars and musicians. We traded stories about our lives and then he said in a German accent: "Th' only otha Texan I know iss from Daalles. Hee's a moosician tooo. Hiss name iss Mike Muurphey. I verk on hiss Jagvar."

I was startled, to say the least. "You've got to be kidding! Mike Murphey, the songwriter?'

"Yes, you know heem?"

"No, I don't know him except through his songs. But there are friends of his that went to high school and college with him. We've all been looking for him." I didn't know what else to say.

We drove for a while, and the mechanic said I could drop him off a little further down Lankershim Blvd.

"Hey," I said, "let me write my name and phone number down. If you ever see Murphey again, please give it to him." I jotted my name and number on a small piece of paper and handed it to him.

"Goodbye, then, thaank you for zee riide. I vill see dat Muurphey gets thees."

As I drove off, I cussed myself out thinking I should have gotten that hitchhiker's name and number. I'd never hear from Murphey. But later that same night the phone rang.

"Hello, is Bob Livingston there?"

"That's me."

"This is Mike Murphey. What's going on, who are you, and why am I supposed to call? My *mechanic* gave me your number."

There was quite a pause on my end, but then I launched into telling Murphey about Three Faces West and Red River and how they still play his songs and how I thought they were about as good as anything I had heard since the Beatles.

"You know what? You're a genius," he laughed. "We need to meet, you've gotta come up to Wrightwood where I live."

I stammered around for an answer.

"Listen, you have *got* to come here and see. It's beautiful up here and I want to meet you. Come up Saturday."

Wrightwood is in the foothills of the San Gabriel Mountains across I-10 from Big Bear and Lake Arrowhead. The Mojave Desert is spread out far down below. Wrightwood is a ski resort in the winter but it was low key when I drove up on Saturday afternoon. Murphey lived on a back street up away from the little town. I found his house in a grove of pines and knocked on the front door. Murphey appeared, red beard, blond hair, and eyes twinkling.

"Come in, come in, Bob!"

We were immediate friends. Murphey seemed excited to meet a fellow Texan. I met his wife Diana and his son Ryan and everyone was all smiles. I told Murphey about my record deal and living in LA and about Randy and Red River and Lubbock. He told me about Dallas and playing bass in a country band called Tex in the roadhouse circuit in Southern California. He said he'd written a hit for the Monkees called "What Am I Doing Hangin' 'Round." Later on that afternoon, Murphey took me for a drive around the ski town and I saw how beautiful the place really was. I think he saw it in my eyes because he said, "You gotta move here!"

I just laughed. "I wish."

"No, really, you have to move up here, let's find you a place."

This was happening way too fast, I thought, but I went with it. We drove around town and down the end of a road on the west end. There was an A-frame house for rent. It felt like I was being carried along by some strange foretold event and we went back to his place and called the number and arranged to meet the landlord in fifteen minutes. I walked in and took a look at what was going to be my new home for the next year and a half. It was one big room with a loft overhead and the west side all glass overlooking the Mojave. Now this was a cool place. It felt good. I just looked at Murphey and he said, "This is perfect, you've got to take it."

Am I really going to do this? I thought. After a few more minutes of deliberation, I said, "Okay . . . I'll take it."

I moved in with my meager possessions in two days. There was a bed in the loft and a small kitchen table with a couple of chairs and a fireplace. That was it.

Over the next month and actually for most of my stay there in Wrightwood, I became a desert rat and drove into the Mojave and scouted the antique shops and roadside attractions looking for cool stuff and necessities. I bought a small chest of drawers, a couple of stuffed chairs, a bedside table, all worn old wood. Of course I needed cooking utensils and pots and pans and everything else one really needs to live. I hadn't done this ever. Most of the places I'd lived came equipped.

One day, on the way home from my rambles, I bought an old stand-up radio that you could dial in Radio Moscow if you wanted. And an old upright piano that played great. One of my new friends was also the piano tuner and he tuned it up on the spot. I was set.

Even though Murphey had his songs recorded by others, he still needed to pay his bills and dues and work the honky-tonks. Murphey was playing bass in a country band called Tex. They were basically a cover band, did a lot of fast country songs, plus Beatles and Top 40 hits. But they also did their own songs which were just as good. I went to see them at the Palomino in North Hollywood and I watched Murphey like a hawk. He had a unique way of playing bass, moving around it a lot. There was hardly a soul in the room, but Murphey and the guys were great. The other members of Tex were Herb Steiner on steel guitar, Owens "Boomer" Castleman on lead, and Stoney Bramith on drums.

Boomer played a guitar mounted with an invention of his called "the Boomerizer." It had the ability to bend every note like a steel guitar and he and Herb would play amazing twin steel licks lightning fast. Boomer had played with Murphey for years and co-wrote some of Murphey's best songs, including "Texas Morning" and "Fort Worth, I Love You." Great stuff.

There were many adventures living in Wrightwood. I got all moved in and we went on long hikes through the mountains with a new friend Murphey had introduced me to, Willy Matthews, a fantastic artist and banjo player from Northern California. He would later become one of America's greatest water colorists with his own gallery in Denver, painting under the name of William Matthews. He just painted the cover for my latest album *Up the Flatland Stairs*. You really should check him out.

One afternoon, Murphey, Willy, and I walked along the San Gabriel River in the middle of nowhere, got completely naked, and acted like we were cavemen or apes, jumping from boulder to boulder making ape-like sounds and scratching under our armpits like you would see in a cartoon. We really did this. It was hilarious fun!

Back in my cabin on the edge of the Mojave, I would stare out into the desert and burn all the wood I had left and drink red wine and contemplate my life. The main thing I contemplated was, when was I going to make my record? Randy had no answers, so I decided to take it upon myself and contact Artie Mogull, the new president of Capitol, writing a letter inviting him up to Wrightwood "to hear my new songs and discover some trees." I sent the letter off and wondered if it would ever reach Artie and how he would take it.

Meanwhile we would have wonderful picking parties with Murphey, Diana, and new friends Duke and Terry, Spunky, Harlan, and Jan Smithers. Duke was part Native American and knew the mountains and always carried a sharp knife and even an ax. He could play good guitar and sing interesting homemade songs about the forest and living away from the material world. And man, could he chop wood. Anywhere.

Murphey and I would play and sing late into the night. He was a *great* songwriter, player, and singer and could play guitar, piano, banjo, whatever. He was a driven man and sometimes could be sullen and make barbed comments to me. But I was learning a lot and Murph was a cut above any other singer-songwriter-musician I had known personally. A cut way above. His songs touched me in a way that none had before, especially when he sang them live. There was something about a voice and the wood and air pushed out of an acoustic guitar in a room with no microphones or amplification that bypasses your brain and goes straight into your heart. Murphey had magic about him. So I could look past his being so mercurial, warm one minute and cold the next.

Murphey's wife, Diana, was a smart and interesting woman, a Brit who used to be Brian Epstein's personal assistant. She knew the Beatles personally and had amazing stories about the '65 tour of America. Big league. Diana was a great cook and there were always lots of stray musicians from Los Angeles seated around her big dining room table.

One night Murphey was driving us down a mountain road, back from a jam at Duke's house. He was driving his red Jaguar convertible—the same Jaguar that the hitchhiker worked on. As we rounded the turns, and we were going a little faster, Murphey got in a strange, fatalistic mood.

"Have you ever wanted to just *drive off into the abyss*? To just *drive right off the edge of this mountain and see what happens*?" He would sort of steer the car towards the edge of the road when he said "*drive off this mountain.*"

"No, Mike. I never have wanted to do any of that. And you shouldn't either. Why don't you pull over and tell me about it?" I was really worried that he might actually do it. I never knew if he was serious or not, but he pulled over on a narrow outlook. It was dark and the stars were out as he rolled the top down.

"Bob, I don't know where my songs come from," he began. "I just see them floating up there, the words are just right there. I just grab them and write them down. I take dictation."

All the while Murphey was staring at the dwindling light and shadows on the mountains, somewhat glassy-eyed and unblinking. He was not there, maybe lost in the words to some song. Anyway, it was hard to tell. Jan Reid, in his book *The Improbable Rise of Redneck Rock*, described "the metallic neutrality of Murphey's eyes," and that's what I saw that night.

After we talked a bit more, Michael suddenly said he was hungry and that he needed to get home to his wife and son. The spell was broken, and we traveled down the rest of the way without incident.

♪

A few days later, Murphey and I went down to Santa Monica to the folk mecca The Troubadour. Linda Ronstadt was playing, but that wasn't who we were going to see. I had heard of Jerry Jeff Walker, and I'd heard "Mr. Bojangles" on the radio in Lubbock in 1968. Murphey had known Jerry Jeff for years on the folk circuit; they weren't in touch all that much but respected each other's work. Jerry Jeff was opening the show for Ronstadt that night and that is why we were there.

Jerry Jeff came onstage. It was the first time I had ever seen him, even in a photo. He seemed tall and was dressed in jeans and a cowboy coat and shirt and hat. He was rough and wrinkled and looked and talked like he'd had a few drinks but he was sure of himself, which was important, at least to me. He sat down to play and his jeans came up to reveal a stunning pair of cowboy boots, cut slim with embossed letters that read JJW on the tops. He had a flair and a way about him and he had a good rhythm style and overall I was impressed and liked it a lot. He did "Mr. Bojangles" and "Driftin' Way of Life," which was my favorite, and several others that I had never heard. He had an easy banter between songs, didn't say much, but he was funny and loose when he did.

After his set he met us in the bar. Glenn Frey and Don Henley were there. They were in Ronstadt's band. Jerry Jeff said that we ought to all get together later that night. I told him we could go to our house in Beverly Glen, not too far away. I gave him the address, and he said he would bring Linda and her band with him. We watched most of her set but then left to get provisions for the party. That was the biggest mistake. Out of sight, out of mind. We hit a little store on the way home and bought chips and dips and beer and wine and spread it all out on the kitchen table and waited.

And waited.

Yeah, you guessed it. Jerry Jeff and his crew never showed up. We were disappointed but Murphey got a good song out of it called "Empty Handed Compadres." Murphey could make lemonade out of lemons at the drop of a hat.

Back in Wrightwood, I made a foray down into the desert and happened upon a roadside attraction. There was a crazy old desert rat named Calvin Black who had three or four trailers full of junk and had built a city of primitive wooden dolls. Thousands of them in various odd situations but mostly just lined up all dressed in bright cloth staring out of wooden wagons. It was more than strange but Calvin Black was a fount of wisdom and spouted hundreds of old sayings and non sequiturs and many times talked for the dolls in a high-pitched screech.

I told Murphey about Calvin's roadside attraction, and he said he had to see it to believe it so the next day we spent the afternoon with Calvin, picking his brain about the desert. He was full of hundreds of stories, pearls of wisdom, and desert lore. Murphey later wrote a song about him called "Desert Rat" that appeared on his album *Blue Sky, Night Thunder*. It has a line Calvin had said to us, over and over: "Success is survival, boys." Many times in my life I have counted on that philosophy to get me through.

Murphey went back out to the desert many more times to talk to Calvin and then went further down the road to an old silver mining town called Calico that Knott's Berry Farm had bought and restored somewhat but kept it like it was and the whole town was a kind of museum. Murph sat on a hill overlooking the graveyard and the tombstones with their faded epitaphs. The poor lonely souls in their graves began to speak to him, "Write me down, don't forget my name. Write me down, don't forget my name."

So began Murphey's most ambitious project, a country rock opera about that lost silver mining town called *The Ballad of Calico*. He wrote at least twenty songs, and Kenny Rogers and the First Edition recorded the whole work. I thought it was genius. Murphey's co-writing partner on "Wildfire," Larry Cansler, helped with orchestration and wrote some of the most beautiful melodies. These were the days of *Jesus Christ Superstar* and rock operas, and Kenny Rogers wanted to cash in on that theme. But in the end, it was not to be. Cash in, that is.

My old compadres, Three Faces West, came to Los Angeles in September 1971 after their regular summer season in Red River was done. They had an opening slot at a club in Pasadena called The Ice House. I would go over to their house and take them places: the beach, a vegetarian restaurant on Sunset Blvd., the movies. One day when I came to get them there was another burly guest at the house. He was round and had long curly hair and a beard and was wearing overalls. His name was Buckwheat Stevenson and he had gone to school with the Three Faces and was a singer-songwriter trying to make connections like the rest of us. Except he didn't want to do much of anything but watch cartoons with Ray. Maybe he was writing "My Maria" for all I know, but he said his favorite cartoon was Woody Woodpecker so I know he couldn't be all that bad a guy because that was my favorite cartoon too.

From time to time, I would come down the mountain from Wrightwood and get the guys out of the house for the day and Rick and Wayne would always come with me. But Ray and Buckwheat would usually be watching cartoons and drinking beer and would almost always decline. Daytime television, and Ray was taking notes. They had a grocery sack between them to hold the empties and when we would return that evening, it would be full of empty bottles and they would still be watching cartoons and I swear they were the same ones playing when we had left that afternoon.

Murphey and I played a local Wrightwood Music Festival, with Bill Matthews on the banjo. Murphey had a friend up from LA named Charles John Quarto. He was a poet and had been hanging out with Crosby, Stills & Nash reciting his wild poems at their parties. Nash had even produced an album of his poetry for Atlantic. Quarto looked like Einstein with the deep-set eyes and the wild hair. His poems ran the gamut of emotions and many of them were remarkable and peculiar.

Later that night, Murphey gathered us around and told us that he had received a tape of the new Kenny Rogers and the First Edition's *Calico Silver* album. We were all anxious to hear it. Someone pulled out the couch bed in the living room and chairs were brought in. We got some food and drinks and as many of us as could lay down on the bed in front of the speakers and listened. The album begins with "Ballad of Calico" sung by Kenny Rogers. I had mixed emotions about the recording, mainly about the performance. I was used to the way Murphey did the songs: his versions were a lot better—they were real. But this was a big-time Hollywood production with a lot of reverb. On the other hand, it was revolutionary. I just knew it was going to be a hit record for Kenny Rogers. We all cried, it was so beautiful.

Murphey's writing inspired me and I wrote new songs and thought about others for the record. I got into that mindset, and you can write a song at a red light when you are in that zone. I was anxious to get things moving along with my record for Capitol.

About two weeks later I got a call from my manager, Randy. He was yelling at me about the letter I had written to Capitol president, Artie Mogull. "You idiot! Why did you write him of *all* people? He is totally pissed. I told you to always go through me. The artist is never supposed to talk to the record company directly. You just blew it!"

"What are you talking about? I just wanted to know what was going on. Nobody seemed to know. You didn't know. I couldn't even get anyone on the phone at Capitol so I wrote to the top."

"Bob, Bob, Bob! Artie thinks you're crazy and I think he's probably right. He was insulted! He just released you from your contract. It's over! You're out!"

What?

Capitol Records president Artie Mogull had taken over a company that had been awash with cash from the Beatles and had come in, kicked ass, and taken names. He fired everybody: the previous president, Sal Iannucci; the vice president; the art department; the publicity department; and practically everyone else including more than a hundred recording artists who were signed to the company. My name appeared in *Rolling Stone* for the first time when they published that list of fired artists. Randy said they were going to get me a settlement and a release from my contract. This part of the adventure was over. Things looked bleak. Now what?

I immediately called Murphey and asked if I could drop by. I told him something had happened to my record deal and I needed to talk. He said he'd come over instead. I told Murph my record deal was gone and they were going to tear up the contract and throw it into the dust heap of history. I didn't know what I was going to do next except I was probably going to go back to Texas . . . but I didn't know for sure.

Murphey just looked at me. He said that something would come up and walked out of the cabin. I was left to mull it all over by myself and weigh my options. There was no plan B. For whatever reason, I never even considered going to another record company. I was in shock and I couldn't comprehend what any of this meant. There was a void where the future had been. My best friend Jan had run away to Hawaii. My bubbles had burst. There was a ringing in my ears. I just stared into the fire.

The next morning, I was surprised to see Murphey at my back door with a large flat rectangular guitar case in his hand. He said he had some gigs back in Texas and Colorado. As he was opening up the case, he pulled out a Fender Precision bass and said, "Since you're going back to Texas anyway, why don't you come play this bass with me?" I was not a bass player, I told him. I'd only had that one summer of playing bass with my brother. "You'll learn," Murphey said as he handed me the instrument.

My mind was reeling at the turn of events and with nothing particularly profound to express, I simply said "Yes" and took the gig. From that moment on—and for the next forty years or so—I made my living as a roving bass player, with some piano and guitar work tossed in along the way. I kept writing songs and playing the occasional gig in one guise or another, but my dreams of making records were shelved for the time being—probably for the best in the long run. Meeting Murphey and what followed remains one of the most pivotal connections of my so-called music career. I'll always be grateful to him. Everything that came after started right there.

CHAPTER 14

The US State Department and Me

1986

I was drawn to India. Drawn and pulled, I would return often to visit. We were at the end of an ancient road. It was always profound. Far away from any main thoroughfares, the silence screamed in my ears for a few days until I could acclimate, stop the internal dialogue, and listen. I settled into Iris's and the boys' routine of getting up before sunrise and going to bed at 9 p.m. at the latest. We bathed in a river as the sun rose upstream and the moon set downstream. I have a song that talks about "the full moon leaning on the dawn." We ate with our hands the wonderful South Indian vegetarian food that was served on banana leaves. It seemed like there was always a new adventure. With my jaw hitting the floor, I listened incredulously to the boys' wild jungle stories: "And the man yelled 'Stop! You can't come here into this clearing, don't you see that this is a wild elephant trap?'"

Then I joined up with the world's greatest propaganda machine.

During one of these visits to India, I met an American professor, a Fulbright Scholar and legal aid expert, who was giving speeches at law schools for the US State Department. I asked him a million questions about what he did and how he got connected. He told me of a program whereby the US Information Service (USIS) sent visiting American scholars and artists on tours throughout India and many other countries. If you were an expert on something, whether it be law, hydroponics, or even country music, it was possible to tour, present programs, and get paid an honorarium for it. The Russians and the Americans had been duking it out for the cultural hearts and minds of Indian citizens since the fifties. The Russians sent the Bolshoi Ballet and the Americans sent the LA Philharmonic and many other artists, musicians, dancers, actors, and photographers.

I wanted in. The man said to contact the US Embassy in New Delhi, the largest embassy in the world. These were the days when there was no internet. Mail might take a month or two. The phones didn't work unless you jumped through hoops. It was so antiquated you couldn't hear anything when you tried to make a call. The British left India with a civil service, the English language, and the railroads. Everything else was chaotic, especially their phone system. For me to get a phone call through to anywhere I had to get on a train and ride three hours to a big city, book a hotel room, book a call, and then I might wait another three hours or longer for it to go through. It was another world.

A month or so earlier I had needed to know what was going on back in Austin and whether or not there was a tour planned with Jerry Jeff. Freddie Krc was our drummer at the time. He would know. The big city of Trivandrum was where we went to check into a hotel for an afternoon and book a call. Tucker was with me for the big adventure. He was about 10 or 11 at the time. After we got settled we ordered lunch and waited. A couple of hours later the phone rang in the room. "Hello?" The operators had us both on the line. Freddie answered and I heard his "Hello" sounding a million miles away, very faint and weak. I shouted "Freddie!" and he yelled "Hello?" "What?" I screamed. "Freddie, this is Bob. Can you hear me? I'm in India." "Whaaat?" he yelled. And we went back and forth like that screaming and not understanding much. Somehow I was able to get from Freddie that there were no Jerry Jeff tours afoot and I didn't need to come back just yet. After that experience any communications with the outside world were by telegram. Forget the phones. The telegraph office was located in the funkiest post office ever in the history of post offices. But it could be depended on, sort of.

So to follow up with a State Department inquiry I walked straight to a telegraph station down the road. "To Whom It May Concern, I am musician from Austin, Texas . . ." I got a response a week later that said to get to the closest US Consulate and have an audition. That would be Madras (now Chennai), a sixteen-hour train ride away.

By happenstance and great luck, John Inmon, my fellow Lost Gonzo bandmate, was also visiting India at the time. The Gonzos were following in the Beatles' footsteps. I told John about meeting the State Department fellow and the possibility of a tour. John jumped at the chance, so we began to plan the trip to Madras to see what would transpire. This was mostly an untraversed path for either of us, but I was knocking on the door and excited to see what would happen.

The trains in India were still mostly steam engines with coaches that looked to be left over from the British Raj. We boarded the Madras Mail and set off westward towards Madras and the meeting I had arranged with the State Department USIS. We were in air-conditioned second class and had a sleeping compartment, so we settled back, alternately reading books, playing our guitars, and causing a good deal of interest and conversation from our fellow travelers.

Some of the best food in India is to be found on trains, and at about 8 o'clock that evening we were served a wonderful veggie dinner. Afterwards I wandered back a world away through the second- and third-class compartments. Hundreds of passengers were jammed into each car talking, eating, laughing, playing cards and other games, sleeping on top of each other, and snoring. This was where the real life of the train was! Like steerage on a ship, entire families were crammed together with all their worldly belongings. I met a family of Gypsies who were also traveling to Madras. Gypsies originally came from India and then spread out over Eastern Europe. This family was generous with their hospitality and laughter and offered me an Indian sweet. As we talked, I explained I was a musician and had my guitar with me. They were interested and continued to ask me about it until I went forward and brought my guitar back for a song or two. They laughed, sang, and danced along as I sang, "The stars at night are big and bright / Deep in the Heart of In-di-a!" After an hour or so, we said our goodnights, though I think they wanted me to join their family and take this show on the road. "No, thank you, I *mu*st get some sleep. I have a big day tomorrow."

John and I were not prepared for the cold! We were in second class AC and didn't think to book a blanket or pillow so when we got on the train they were all taken. We were wearing short-sleeved shirts. We were also both on top berths, the worst on the train, right next to a vent that was blowing out the most frigid air. The vent couldn't be closed. It was a miserable experience, and I got very little sleep.

I awoke at dawn and looked out the window. The train was still clanking along. I had rolled into a ball trying to stay warm and needed to unwind myself. The sun was just peeking out over some mesas onto the desert floor and I swore I was in the middle of West Texas. Scrub, cactus, and bushes not unlike mesquite dotted the landscape. Then, just as I was marveling at this dream, I saw a flock of albino peacocks running as fast as the train, then we passed a caravan of camels and I was snapped back into the reality of the moment. Whoa! It looked like a surreal Texas landscape done by Salvador Dalí.

Bouncing and rolling herky-jerky all the way across South India towards Madras I was trying to come up with an idea about what we were going to tell the State Department people what the show would be like. I knew we could play the music just fine, but we needed a theme. I decided we'd do a history of American folk and country music and fake it.

When we arrived in Madras, John and I went to a hotel and sat around drinking coffee and reading the *International Herald Tribune* for news of home before we took a taxi to the US Consulate. As we were clearing security, we were met by Tim Moore, a fresh-faced Princeton grad who was a State Department public affairs officer (PAO).

We sat down in Tim's office and pulled out our guitars. I pitched the idea for the theme of the proposed tour, that we would present a unique history of American folk and country music. That was broad enough. "All these songs came over from England and Ireland and landed in the Appalachian Mountains." We played "Blue Ridge Mountain Blues" and I made up the words. John played some hot country licks and it sounded good. Moore just stared at us and didn't say a word. I kept charging. "And those same melodies and songs moved out west and the cowboys took 'em up and wrote new lyrics for them and we'll do some old cowboy songs, and prisoner songs, and work songs, and gospel." I sang "Bury Me Not on the Lone Prairie," and Tim just kept staring at me. I went into another song but I was thinking it wasn't going very well at all. I couldn't read him and his noncommittal eyes. About halfway through that third song Tim Moore put up his hand as if to stop us then said, "Do you mind?" And he reached down behind his desk and pulled out a *banjo* . . . then he said, "I've been waiting for a long time for you guys to walk through this door."

It turned out Tim was a bluegrass enthusiast, and he had no one to play with out there in the wilds of the Third World. We

Mr. Ganipati, John Inmon, me, and Public Affairs Officer Tim Moore about to head out on our *first* State Department tour, 1987. (Photo courtesy of Bob Livingston.)

were his big opportunity. He settled in and began to play "Fox on the Run" and we played along. And of course John Inmon tore it up and Tim was laughing and smiling and the whole scene changed. We gelled musically and hit it off as friends. Tim was happy as a clam to have some fellow Americans around to pick with. John was one of the most inventive and fastest pickers Tim had ever met and he liked the whole concept with the songs and stories. We passed the audition, and Tim told us he would arrange a tour for us in India the coming September. For that tour and for several other solo tours after, Tim would bring along his banjo and play some wild bluegrass picking that added to the show.

Back home a Jerry Jeff tour materialized just at the right time. Iris and the boys would come back to India again and again, but for now we all headed back to our place in Oak Hill just outside of Austin where we had a rock house on five acres. Running down the Indian Railway platform in a mad dash throwing bags and kids into the kind hands of strangers as the train pulled out of the station would test the road chops of any family. We would have the State Department tour of India later in the year, but for now, the work was back in the States with Jerry Jeff.

CHAPTER 15

Snowed in with My Top 10

1971

Murphey took Diana and Ryan back to Dallas for Christmas. I had just lost the Capitol record deal and, trying to cheer up, tagged along for a while and went back to San Antonio for the holidays. My brother Donald was somewhere in California or Hawaii—we didn't know which—and Judy and her family were living in Dallas. So it was just me and my parents for Christmas, and I was sullen and morose and Mama and Daddy probably thought the worst, maybe for good reason. Restless and not knowing anyone in San Antonio anymore, I had nothing else to do but nothing. As soon as I could get going, I drove back to Wrightwood in one shot, twenty-six hours straight. Hallucinating from road exhaustion. Every now and then I would shout out the windows "This is a plot to destroy my mind!"

As I drove up the road from the interstate it started snowing. And snowed and snowed. I hit the tiny store in town for provisions on the way in. I had about a half a cord of wood stashed just down the steps and a metal fireplace for heat. The cold wind blew and the white snow flew and I had a fire roaring at all waking times. There were four-foot snow drifts around my drive and

I couldn't go anywhere. I rationed my food and stared into the ever-present fire for five days. When the weather would break and the sun would peek out I went for walks and made it down the mountain a couple of times. But I was poorly equipped for traipsing around in snow, except for my treasured Stephen Stills mountain boots that I had bought upon seeing the cover of the first Crosby, Stills & Nash record.

My most prized possession during this time was my stereo and turntable. I only had ten or so records that I listened to over and over, maybe hundreds of times, while I continued to stare into my fire and out the front window down to the shimmering sands of the Mojave far below. I waited for someone to plow the road to my door and rescue me. The Top 10 for me in that time and place and in no particular order were:

1. *California Bloodlines* – John Stewart (Three Faces West introduced me to this classic).
2. *After the Gold Rush* – Neil Young (I pored over the album credits and wondered about Nils Lofgren).
3. Keith Sykes' first album with Vanguard Records (it was just so pure).
4. *Blue* – Joni Mitchel (her romantic loneliness stoked my fire).
5. Tom Rush (the one with "Driving Wheel").
6. Crosby, Stills & Nash's debut album (the one with Stills' boots).
7. *Workingman's Dead* – Grateful Dead (I played "Uncle John's Band" until it disintegrated).
8. *Driftin' Way of Life* – Jerry Jeff Walker (still his best).
9. *Surf's Up* – Beach Boys (Terry Williams of Kenny Rogers and the First Edition gave me the record with instructions to listen to the amazing production of Brian Wilson.

10. *Silk Purse* – Linda Ronstadt (because of the cover as much as anything else).

As the snow thought of melting and I took to creative ways to shake off the cabin fever, I could only wonder what would spring forth in the spring.

CHAPTER 16

The Hand of Fate, Part 2

1971

It was still cold as a witch in the mountains as Murphey and I went down to Los Angeles to stay at manager Randy's house for a few days. Around 6 a.m. we were sleeping soundly when the house began to shake. Violently.

"This is it!" Randy yelled. "This is it!"

"What do you mean, this is it? This is what? What's happening?"

"This is *it*!!"

We were all disoriented and scared as bookshelves crashed and glasses fell out of the cupboards. We were right in the middle of the California earthquake. February 9, 1971. The big one. It would kill a hundred people and scare millions more. *This is it!* The Three Faces West boys living up on Mulholland Drive went through the earthquake too. As soon as the world stopped shaking, Buckwheat Stevenson immediately took a taxi to LAX and flew back to Dallas that afternoon. We all got over it, but we kept thinking a lot about it. Murph was still based in California and the Texas tour was coming.

We rehearsed in my cabin for a week. When it came to the bass, I was green. A green machine. As Murphey played his unique and compelling songs, I started working out bass parts to match his sound. Since it was just the two of us—his acoustic guitar and my bass—I had the freedom to move around the neck a lot, playing some melodic lines, filling in cosmic space, and singing vocal parts right with him. Murphey liked what he heard, I guess, because he didn't call it off, and after a few rehearsals, we got ready to hit the road.

We took off for gigs in Dallas, Houston, Colorado, and back to Dallas, all in March. I can't remember all the territory we covered or how many days we were gone from California. But I was on the road now, sleeping in funky motels or by the side of the road, eating truck-stop food and playing most every night somewhere.

We drove in Murphey's rugged Ford Ranger. He had a camper on the back, and we took turns driving the extra-long miles of the West. The first show was at the Rubaiyat, a folk club in Dallas on McKinney Ave. Apart from a couple of times in Wrightwood this was the first real show I had played with Murphey. The place was packed. Murphey was from Dallas and as yet I didn't have a handle on just how well known and beloved he was in his hometown. We did songs like "You Can Only Say So Much," "Boy from the Country," "Seasons Change," "Blood Brothers," "What Am I Doing Hangin' 'Round," and many, many more. The audience loved it. Murphey was a showman and he called a great set. He was also a stern taskmaster and tolerated nothing less than complete concentration on the task at hand.

We called ourselves The Melodious Mountain Music Brothers. We both had long red-blond hair and red beards and wore old-timey long coats like Johnny Cash. I would sometimes smoke a pipe onstage, so we presented quite a unique presence. We would play Houston then come back to the Rubaiyat, then to Colorado and back around to the Rubaiyat again—our home away from home. We'd go down to Austin and play Rod Kennedy's Chequered Flag and a new club there called the Saxon Pub. The Pub was then in its original location on 38 1/2 Street on the frontage road of I-35.

Michael Murphey and me standing out front of the legendary Rubaiyat, Dallas, 1971. The folk club where it all began. (Photo courtesy of Bob Livingston.)

We'd been gigging steadily, and I was no longer the nervous greenhorn I'd been. Murphey, meanwhile, was the brightest flame in the Texas folk scene and the Rubaiyat was the place to play if you were a folkie in Texas. On any given night you might hear Mance Lipscomb, Three Faces West, Larry Groce, Lightnin' Hopkins, Buckwheat Stevenson, a 20-year-old Alan Ramsey (as he was called then), or Frummox, the best folk duo around.

One weekend, after a run down to Houston and Austin, Murphey and I drove in early for a show at the Rubaiyat in Dallas. We were dog-tired but drove straight to the club to see what there was to see. On the little marquee outside was a crude hand-lettered sign that read, "Frummox Tonite!"

"You gotta hear these guys, Bob," Murphey said. "They're old friends of mine, they're great! Wait 'til you hear 'Texas Trilogy!'"

We barged in through the standing-room-only crowd and Frummox was already onstage. Two guys with beards, Steven Fromholz and Dan McCrimmon. They had a great vocal blend and sang "Man with the Big Hat," "Texas Trilogy," and "The Rest Area Waltz." During the break, we met with Steve and Dan and talked music and laughed and told war stories and Fromholz made fun of me because I was from Lubbock. I was the new guy. I liked Steven immediately. He was a big man with blue-gray eyes who sang and talked in a sonorous baritone, a really loud baritone! There was nothing soft about him and he was very, very sure of himself and a major part of the Texas folk scene.

There was a cast of characters that frequented the Rubaiyat. There was a scruffy guy who came to see us every time we played there. His name was R. A. Caldwell. He drank beer in the beer garden and would go on and on about one thing and then another. He was a tall tale teller and there was something endearing about him. Not fake. I didn't know him well enough to really trust him or not. "You need to meet Bob Johnston!" he would say. "He's a brother, he's a *brother*." Now Bob Johnston was a Texan gone to Nashville who'd made good working with the icons of the music business, recording Nashville cats like Marty and Johnny Cash, but he'd also worked with Leonard Cohen, the Byrds, and Simon & Garfunkel. The list goes on and on. Johnston produced some of the holy grails of music: Dylan's *Blonde on Blonde* and *Nashville Skyline*, Cash's live *At Folsom Prison*, Simon & Garfunkel's *Sounds of Silence.* So to hear R. A. say that Bob was his brother seemed like bragging about a brotherhood we couldn't be sure of. Some truth was in there, but how much we didn't know. We played the Rubaiyat again a couple of weeks later and after the show R. A. was at it again: "Bob Johnston is a brother! You need to meet him." Yeah, right.

That summer I took some time away from this back-and-forth California-to-Texas loop and headed back to Red River for a month, a place that was a lodgepole for me, all mystical and magical and cosmic. I loved the misty forest and took long walks through the green. I hung out with Ray and Rick a lot and we played guitars at a variety of mountain cabins. It was rainy and cold and spooky in the mountains. I loved it and thought seriously about moving there for good.

I had heard a rumor that Jerry Jeff Walker was in town living up at the Lazy H, a dude ranch with a smattering of cabins on a mountain lake. He had landed a new record deal with MCA a couple of years after he released *Bein' Free*. We were at a party one night and guitars were out when he walked in. A woman shouted, "Jerry Jeff, do something!" Without any thought at all, JJ made a beeline to a vase of flowers and poured the whole thing on his head. *That* got the party going. He was audacious and magnetic. Almost everyone has a Jerry Jeff story. This was the second time I had ever seen him, after that first time back in LA at the Troubadour when we were Empty Handed Compadres. Jerry Jeff saw me and remembered me and came over and we talked about that night he never showed up. I told him about the song Murphey wrote about it. "Yeah," Jerry Jeff said. "Murphey just follows me around and writes it all down." We became pretty good friends in those few weeks and we played songs and would meet up at the bars or I would go up to the Lazy H to see him.

There is a story about that summer that starts back in Los Angeles before the earthquake. Ray Hubbard had an old Gibson guitar, a Roy Smeck Stage Deluxe that had a crude painting of an angel that curled around the bridge. Ray told me he had traded Jerry Jeff Walker for that guitar. I played it and really liked it. I had a Martin D-18 that Ray really liked so we agreed to trade for a while. We both said it wouldn't be a permanent thing but we would trade and see how it went. I played that Roy Smeck for half a year and had it with me when I came back to Red River that summer. I was missing my D-18 something fierce, missing how easy it played, so Hubbard and I traded back. Ironically and cosmically enough, Jerry Jeff had lost track of the Roy Smeck and was writing a song up at the Lazy H about it called "That Old Beat-up Guitar." He had two very descriptive verses about the angel painted on the guitar and how much it meant to him. He was looking for a third verse. Ray Hubbard had just got the Roy Smeck back from me and leaned it against the piano of the Last Run bar just as Jerry Jeff walked into the room and right into his third verse. Jerry Jeff ended up trading Ray a brand-new guitar that the Guild company had made for him to get that old beat-up guitar back.

That night the weather turned cold as a witch and winter was roaring up Bitter Creek Canyon. I got sick as a dog and had to weather the fever in a lonely cabin at the Lazy H. Rick Fowler came up to check on me a couple days later and he sat on a chair at the foot of the bed and played my Martin D-18 that I had traded back for the Roy Smeck. It was some of the sweetest music I'd ever heard and I fell fast asleep. When I awoke I was healed, as if by magic.

In the meantime, Murphey had tracked me down and left a message for me to call. He said to meet him in Dallas for another Texas–Colorado swing. That sounded good to me and soon I began packing up. In October 1971 we took off for a gig in Nacogdoches and swung back around to play a weekend at the Rubaiyat. There he was again, R. A. Caldwell. "You need to meet Bob Johnston," he said for the forty-eleventh time. "He's a brother!" It was getting annoying . . .

Northwards toward Denver and Pueblo, we were somewhat concerned about shelter. We'd always search for a free place to stay, of course, and Murphey knew a guy named Marty Javors who had a house up above Denver. Somehow it was okay for us to go there even though Marty was out of town. We drove around in the twilight trying to find the house before it got dark. After a few false starts knocking on wrong doors, we found the house. A skinny fellow with a funky cowboy hat answered the door. He introduced himself as Craig Hillis and yes, this was Marty's place and would we like to come in? Hillis didn't have a clue as to who we were, but he saw our guitars after we loaded in. He immediately pulled out an unconventional-looking lap steel and before long we were highly engaged in playing and singing and laughing, to such an extent that Murphey asked Craig to play with us the next night at the Café York in Denver.

Café York was Denver's best folk club and listening room, their Rubaiyat, but much larger and with a better sound system. Folk music was big in Texas but even more so in Denver. The Café York was sold out and there were a lot of interested folks waiting to see and hear Murphey's new material. The word had spread like wildfire and people came out. We went in cold with almost no rehearsal but played a great show. Craig added a lot to the sound, funky rock 'n' roll inspired leads and slide guitar against Murphey's acoustic and my bass. It went so well we asked him to play in Pueblo for a weeklong gig we were starting the next week.

After the Colorado shows, winter was coming on and we had to get back to California. Murphey had his truck and I had my Datsun Gypsy Caravan. But on our way back and just for fun we decided to go see a fortune teller, a woman someone had told us about. Murphey and I went in and met her and she did readings on us. Craig was still with us, but he didn't go in. He said he didn't want a mere human to play God and read his future. I feel the same way now and always steer clear of fortune tellers, tarot card readers, and such. The woman seemed a bit crazy to me, but Murphey was blown away when she described his dining room table at home and some other stuff that Murph was sure she couldn't possibly have known. The main thing we both got out of it was that she told us we had to get out of California, that it wasn't safe for us to be there anymore. So we headed back home to Wrightwood with new mystical thoughts in our heads.

Shortly after we got back to Wrightwood, we were paid a visit by Steven Fromholz, Travis Holland—the former bass player of both Murphey and Jerry Jeff—and Emily McKenzie, Travis's girlfriend and later his wife. Murphey called her Earthwoman Emily and wrote a song about her. Craig and his soon-to-be wife, Dana Strait, were also there. We partied and picked for a solid week and had a rather large time. This was to be our last blowout in Wrightwood.

We had more gigs in Colorado and Texas and ended up back at the Rubaiyat. There was R. A. Caldwell again, and he was still going on about Bob Johnston being his brother so I finally said to R. A., "If you are such a brother to Bob Johnston, well then, just get him here!"

So he did!

I still don't know the full extent of their relationship, but when R. A. said he would get Bob Johnston to the Rubaiyat to hear us, it turned out he wasn't talking shit. The opportunity came by way of a sad family thing for Johnston. His father had passed away and Bob came back to Fort Worth for the funeral. R. A. asked him to come to Dallas and meet us at the club. It wasn't during regular business hours; in fact, it was set up for 2 p.m. one winter afternoon in early December. Murphey and I got there around quarter to two and waited in the little club. I remember that it was dark inside, with only the stage lights on. At 2:30 we started to wonder if Johnston was really going to come. At 2:45 we were thinking it was all a bust when the front door suddenly flew open, flooding the room with the bright light of the afternoon sun. In burst a bandy rooster kind of a guy with long straight hair and energy flying out the seams.

The first thing Johnston said was, "Is there a piano in here?"

"There's one on the stage."

"I just wrote a song on the plane and I have to play it. It's a gospel song."

He bounded up on the stage, which wasn't as big as a minute, sat down at the piano, and played a chord. He took a napkin out of his coat pocket and placed it in front of him flat against the top of the piano and began to sing. It wasn't bad. In fact, he sounded good and when he finished, we told him so.

"Well, I wrote that today. Here's one I wrote a couple of days ago. I'm really into gospel these days."

While he was playing, Murphey picked up his guitar and began to play along with him. I grabbed my bass and followed Murphey's lead and started to play along too. We finished that song and he said, "Here's another one," and started going again and we were going along with him wherever he went.

Then he stopped and looked up from the keyboard and said, "Hey, I didn't come here to play the piano for you. Which one of you is Mike Murphey?"

"That's me," Murphey said.

"Well, I've been told you have some good songs and that's why I'm here. Let's hear what you got, son."

He walked into the empty club where an audience would be later that night and sat in the dark. The stage lights more or less blinded us and we couldn't see him at all.

Now I swear what happened next is completely true.

The piano was at the rear of the little stage and when you played it your back was to the audience. Murphey sat down at the piano and began to sing "Calico Silver." It was then a new song, the opening for the soon-to-be-released *The Ballad of Calico* that Kenny Rogers had recorded but hadn't released yet.

No rain and the weather got warm
Broke down and I sold my farm
Headed for the silver strike

I took my wife
Calico Silver, gave us life . . .

. . . then Murphey played a beautiful melodic hook that sets up the second half of the verse. C F A Dm G G7. It was brilliant and it sold the song.

Suddenly from out of the darkness we heard Johnston's voice: "That is the most beautiful thing I have ever heard! I don't need to hear any more and as far as I'm concerned, I'm going to make a record on you!"

Murphey stopped, and we didn't know what to do.

"Aww, keep playing. I want to hear the rest."

So Murphey finished "Calico Silver," and Johnston said, "Shoot, man, that is beautiful."

Then Murphey played "Natchez Trace" and "What Am I Doing Hangin' 'Round." After every song Johnston would say, "That was better than the one before. Man!"

Finally, after about five songs, Johnston said (again) he didn't need to hear any more. "Let's sit down here and talk."

We sat at a little table, Murphey directly across from Johnston, me catty-cornered on the side.

"I want to make a record with you, son," said Johnston looking directly into Murphey's eyes.

"Well, that . . . that is just great," Murphey said.

"I want you to come to Nashville next Wednesday. I have a George Jones session, but I'm going to reschedule it. Columbia, Studio A. Will you be there?"

Murphey was flabbergasted, and I was blown away at what I was hearing. But Johnston had not looked at me. His eyes were glued on Murphey. He had never once spoken to me or even acknowledged my presence when we sat at the table.

Murphey said that he would be there.

"Okay then, my office will get in touch with you, and you will be staying with me, at my house. Is that all right?

"That's great, Bob," said Murphey.

"Okay then," Bob said. Then he thought for a second. "What about him?" he asked, still focused on Murphey, sort of nodding my way.

"Him? You mean, Bob? What do you mean, 'What about him?'"

"Is he funky?" Bob asked.

"What was that?"

"Is he funky?" he said, still looking straight at Murphey as if I wasn't there.

"Is he funky?" Murphey said. "Well, just look at him. What do you think?"

Bob finally looked at me and said, "Okay, you come too. Next Wednesday. Be there."

We all just laughed.

Johnston sat back in his chair. No one else was in the near darkness of the Rubaiyat and Johnston pulled something out of his coat pocket and said, "This comes from the tomb of a Lebanese prince, and it was given to me by a woman I met in New York. She had a lot of tattoos and I'm sure she was a gypsy." It was a large block of hashish, very light-vanilla colored, almost white. He broke off a good-sized chunk and took out an instrument, a thin wood rod with a needle protruding out of it, and impaled the chunk on it and then whipped out a lighter and lit the hash and watched it smolder, blue and green. Murphey and I were looking at this in wonder. Suddenly Bob blew out the flame and an enormous cloud of smoke came from the embers and he immediately inhaled every stray plume into his lungs, a loud sucking and gigantic inhalation, and he held his breath for a long, long time. Then he exhaled, and used-up smoke burst out of him like a cannon shot. I had never seen anything like it before or since. That was Bob Johnston's way of sealing the deal.

CHAPTER 17

Making Tracks

1971

On Wednesday we borrowed Murphey's mother's Buick and headed out towards Nashville with Charles John Quarto in the backseat. Murphey had a new song he'd just written with Quarto called "Rainbow Man." R. A. Caldwell had played a big part in getting us here. We pulled up to Bob Johnston's house on the corner of Caldwell Ave and Rainbow Lane. It was a sign.

We stayed there that night and in the morning took off for Columbia Studios on Music Row, a collection of streets in the heart of Nashville where it all goes down. Demonbreun Street, Division Street, 16th Avenue South. There're a lot of music-related businesses one after another—record company offices, publishing companies, and recording studios—all up and down Music Row. Columbia was a standout because Studio A was immense, with high walls and a lot of space. You could record an orchestra there.

Bob introduced us to Neil Wilburn, who was to be the engineer of the session. This was really the first time I had ever been inside a big studio and I was in awe and nervous as hell. We walked from the control room to the big room, Studio A, and got right down to it. Murphey was fitted with a vocal mic and two mics on his acoustic. I plugged my bass directly into a box that sent the signal to the board. There was no bass amp, so this way Murphey and I could play in the same room and there would be no bleed. We both wore headphones, and it was weird in the extreme having no amp. I couldn't feel it. Only hear it in my ears. A disconnect that I got used to.

We had no idea how it was to go down. There were no other musicians, and Murphey and I were to do what we did in live shows, just him and me. There were bass notes required that were not in the root of the chord but for example in the third note of the chord. It was complicated and breathtaking stuff to me, but I was on the edge a lot. Not really knowing the music language and just by the very nature and construct of Murphey's songs, I was, in a way, flying blind and it's a miracle I got through it without a crash on the mountain of love. I was used to being a freewheeling freeform raw folkie going at my own pace alone. Now I was getting a rapid-fire education in music theory and counterpoint and not quite catching it all. Run that by me one more time. But I was willing and learning on the fly and making a lot of it up as I went along. These insecurities and unease were with me, but now we were about to record for real.

After about twenty minutes of sound checking, Bob Johnston walked in the room carrying an old lamp with a long extension cord. There was a horizontal crossbar at the top of the lamp and there were lightbulbs at each end, one white and one red. The white light was on. He dragged in a metal folding chair and put the lamp on it, a pretty funky setup.

Johnston just looked at us with a wistful smile on his bearded face and said, "Boys, some of the greatest music ever recorded has been played and sung right here in this room. This is a room full of magic. Bob Dylan recorded *Blonde on Blonde* and *Nashville Skyline* right where you are sitting. When this red light goes on, we are engaged in the recording process, the recording of magic. There is magic in the walls and magic in the air. I want you boys to have a great time and just have fun and make music and add to the magic and let the magic take you. I know you will because it's already here, I can feel it." With that, Bob walked back into the control room and we heard his voice in the phones say, "Anytime you want to start, just go." The red light went on.

Murphey played "Natchez Trace" first. It's a funky, swampy song about being on the Natchez Trace Trail and we had set guitar and bass parts. There was no drummer on this session, so I was allowed a lot more latitude and longitude to cover more ground than I would have normally been given if there was a drummer with a kick-drum keeping the bottom. We had played these songs a lot and we knew the parts and the arrangements were there.

When we finished "Natchez Trace," Bob shouted into the phones, "Beautiful! You can't do it any better. Let's move on!"

Move on? After just one take?

We cut "What Am I Doing Hangin' 'Round" next and Johnston again said, "Wonderful—we got it!" This was Murphey's song that The Monkees recorded, and we did it with a lot more feeling than they did for sure.

Everything was one take except for one or two that required second takes. We never did three takes on a song. We recorded for just a few hours and put down maybe fifteen songs before quitting for the day. Bob was right, there WAS magic being made and he was a big part of it. He made us feel so good and special and that the songs were "incredible" and "beautiful" and "wonderful" and my bass sounded "killer" and "perfect." "We don't need to change a thing!"

We left for Bob's house and dinner. Quarto was with us, and we all sat around the table and had a great home-cooked meal. After the last bite, Bob took me aside and said, "I want to show you something." He took me down to the basement where he had a monstrous stereo system, the biggest I had ever seen, and he pulled out drawers that were full of what they call acetates. These looked like regular record albums but were much thicker and had been cut on the spot at the recording studio and usually only the producer or artist had possession of them. One of my favorites from Dylan's *Nashville Skyline* is the duet with Johnny Cash of "Girl from the North Country." Bob Dylan loved Johnny and had been influenced by him and vice versa and they had recorded several songs together, maybe twenty, and "Girl from the North Country" ended up closing *Nashville Skyline*. Bob carefully took an acetate out of a drawer while he was telling me this story and put it on the turntable and dropped the needle on the disc. It was Dylan and Cash doing duets on songs like Dylan's "One Too Many Mornings" and Johnny Cash's "I Still Miss Someone."

At the time, none of this had been released to the world on any record but had been living in Bob's basement, so this was awesome and special. Johnny Cash and Bob Dylan were heroes to me and Bob Johnston had recorded them and was responsible for the recordings and he was sharing it all with me. I felt I was being shown a state secret.

Next Bob pulled out an acetate of Dylan's that had "Mr. Bojangles" on it. Dylan had recorded Bojangles! I'd just met Jerry Jeff a couple of months before and I felt I had some magical connection to all of this. I slept really well that night wrapped in magic and music and privilege.

The next day, we headed back to the studio and knocked out another four songs. Just as Bob said, "Ok, let's take a break," in the studio door walked Leonard Cohen. He was dressed in a dark suit, accompanied by a striking, dark-haired woman in a long coat—like they'd stepped off a film set. I was starstruck. But Leonard, with that soft, low voice of his, put us instantly at ease. He was gracious, warm, and every bit the poetic presence you'd expect.

Bob Johnston, who had produced several of Leonard's records—including *Songs from a Room* in '69 with "Bird on a Wire"—just grinned and said, "Let's go to lunch. I know a great

Chinese place." We went out for Chinese with Leonard and the dark-haired woman. Even Quarto was impressed—and that didn't happen often. Over tea and noodles, we mainly listened to Leonard. He told us he'd just come down from a Buddhist monastery on Mount Baldy in California. His head had been shaved, but the hair was starting to grow back. He spoke about his monastic life with quiet humor, including the time he asked his master a question and got a lightning-fast kick to the chest in reply—one so quick and powerful it launched him right out of the yurt and sent him rolling down the hill.

"It was the perfect answer, and I understood it completely," Leonard said.

We asked him what it was like living in such solitude that you were committed to silence.

"The fish don't have to ask each other where the water is," he said.

Lunch was great—and not just because Leonard Cohen and the dark-haired woman were at the table (though that certainly didn't hurt). When the fortune cookies arrived, we took turns reading them aloud. Leonard cracked his open and read: "Lifelong companions await where paths unexpectedly cross." He looked up, smiled, and said, "My fortune has already come true." (I swear he said this.)

Then we all headed back to the studio to listen to the tracks. The recordings were spare, honest—and Murphey's songs were great. We'd laid down twenty-four songs in two days, most of them first takes. Murphey said he'd like to cut one more song. It was a gospel song by the Happy Goodman Family called "Lights of the City." We gathered around the incredible Steinway Grand. I played bass and sang on the choruses basically into the open piano. No other vocal mic but Murphey's. Bob Johnston, Quarto, Leonard Cohen, and his woman friend all sang into the piano, "I can almost see the lights of the city . . ."

The songs had been played and sung and we were done and we went back to Bob's house. He broke another big chunk off that hashish bar, handed it to me, and said, "You better take this, it might come in handy someday." I put it in my shirt pocket.

We left Nashville in the dark of the night for the long drive to Dallas. Murphey was asleep in the back seat when police lights filled up the rearview mirror as a Tennessee State Trooper pulled us over. I was driving. The officer came up to our car and invited me into his. I sat in the passenger seat of his patrol car, the chunk of hash still in my shirt pocket.

"Where are you going so fast, sir?"

"We're going to Texas, back home to Dallas."

"Where you coming from?"

"Nashville, we just made a country record there."

"Is that right?"

"Yessir, we recorded in Studio A in Columbia for Johnny Cash's producer, Bob Johnston. He also recorded George Jones. We just cut an album with him."

"Is that right?"

"Yessir, and we just left there. We're on our way home."

The officer was staring straight ahead with his headlights on bright, blazing and lighting up Quarto's hair, who was sitting in the passenger seat. It looked like a halo. I imagine Murphey was still asleep, because I hadn't seen his head lift up yet.

"Do you know the speed limit around here?" asked the trooper.

"Well, I think it's 65."

"You were going 71 miles an hour and the speed limit is 55."

The hash in my pocket was getting really heavy and I thought he would have smelled it by now.

"Officer, I'm sorry, I really am, I didn't know. I thought it was 65 and we were coming down a hill. We're just trying to get home. I'm really sorry."

"Who'd you say you was playing with?"

"That's us, Michael Murphey and Bob Livingston. We play country music and we got a record deal. It's amazing. We recorded where all the country stars make records. You're gonna hear about us."

"Well, I'll be. You, a country singer." It wasn't a question. "You got long hair for a country singer."

"Yessir, I'm a country singer and I play bass and guitar. And I sing."

"Well . . . do you know Hank Snow?"

"Yes, I know him," I lied. "I love his music."

"I love it too. And that Johnny Cash. You meet him?"

"No, sir, not this time. But when we come back, they said we could meet him and play a show with him."

"Well . . . I love Johnny Cash."

"Yessir, me too. He's the best there is. The man in black."

"The man in black."

The trooper looked at me and then straight ahead at the Buick and Quarto's hair again. Still no Murphey.

"Okay, sir, I'm gonna let you go this time. You need to slow it down, okay?"

"Yessir, thank you so much. I'll be careful."

"Okay then, you go on . . . and be careful."

I returned to the Buick and slid back in like a grateful shark. I had just dodged a major bullet that might have changed all our life histories. Quarto looked at me with those weird deep-set eyes of his, forehead glistening, veins swelling on his temples, said something cynical, and we burst out laughing. It broke the tension. I flung the hashish as far as I could out the Buick's window into a pasture where later that morning a cow ate the cabbage and would be high as a kite for a week and whose milk would make kids start writing rock songs. We had escaped down the road by the skin of our teeth and I shudder to think what could have happened. On the long drive back to Dallas through the night I had a lot to think about and a lot to process. Thank God Murphey slept through the whole thing.

CHAPTER 18

Forth and Back

1972

It had been a whirligig of emotions and it had happened so quickly. I felt like I was being guided by an existential train that was speeding along with me in it. It could have been coincidence, but I think not. The unexpected recording opportunity had changed everything. But right then, all of it was unknown to me. For now, it was twenty-six songs cut live in a couple of days. Just Murphey and me. Guitar, piano, and bass. Bob Johnston making us feel special and important. I recall Bob saying we had cut "the basic tracks," whatever that meant.

As it turned out, many of the songs we recorded on these sessions would end up on Murphey's first record album, *Geronimo's Cadillac*. But for now, Michael and I headed to California to pack up and return to Texas once and for all. Murphey assumed I would follow him and he was right. We spent so much time in Texas and in the general central Southwest region we might as well get back there permanently. This was a giant step for me, cutting all those ties with California. A lot had happened out there and I'd learned a thing or two, but I was still operating on instinct and feel. There was opportunity knocking at the cellular level. There was no time to waste looking back into the hallways and offices of Capitol Records. Maybe this was a plan B.

CHAPTER 18

My cabin's rent in Wrightwood was paid up for another ten days and I would use the time to mull it all over as I packed up my little Datsun truck for the long trail ahead. A carpenter in town named Spunky built a wooden camper with a rounded-off roof and a stained-glass window on the back. It was a gypsy wagon. On the night I moved out of my cabin a new group of folks were moving in. I couldn't tell if it was one or twenty. They were long-haired kids and they were having a wild house-warming party and I was tiptoeing through it. They had no respect. I remember walking past them while they partied in my house, playing my piano, sitting in my chairs, dancing on my floor and balcony, rolling around in my bed upstairs. As I had no way to take anything with me I just left it all behind. They were playing loud music and I looked out at my friendly neighbors just across the mountain and they were standing on their verandah looking over at us with concern. I heard later that the police were called several times before the long-hairs moved out and gave the neighborhood some much-needed peace. In any case, I was packed up and out the door, and I drove away and never looked back as the loud music and laughter faded into the uncertain mountain night air, bringing beautiful silence.

We were going for an early start, so I slept at Murphey's house that night, a thin restless sleep. The next morning we drove out of there on I-10 towards Texas. Murphey didn't want us to follow one another, to caravan. He said it made him nervous. Even so, I followed behind him and then he disappeared into the distance in his Ford Ranger camper while my Datsun struggled in the Mojave. I picked up a hitchhiker, a young Black guy I'd met at a gas station. He was a good traveling companion, and we whiled away the hours with stories and songs sung a cappella. Suddenly, about fifty miles west of Las Cruces, there was a lot of white smoke coming from the engine and the thermostat skyrocketed. I would find out later I'd blown a head gasket. It's ironic that Craig

Hillis and Murphey had written a song called "Crack up in Las Cruces" and here I was living it out. Stranded on the side of the road, my hitchhiker buddy and I emptied out an old rusty toolbox for a vessel, crawled over bob-wire fences to a cattle watering tank, and brought water back in several trips until the radiator was full again and we could limp to the next water tank and on into town.

I called Murphey's mother in Dallas explaining my sad news and I was surprised to learn that as luck would have it, Murphey had stopped for the night and was behind me fifty miles or so. We arranged to link up. When he got there, he looked at the situation and determined that he had no choice, so he literally towed my Datsun and its wooden camper 680 miles to Dallas. Murphey was irritated and now I owed him big.

After those sessions in Nashville—and the crack-up in Las Cruces—things between Murphey and me started to feel a little rickety. Everything had moved so fast, and I still didn't have a place to live. I was bouncing from couch to couch, relying on the kindness of strangers, which kept things on edge even before I picked up an instrument. I'm sure I wasn't the easiest guy to be around either—spoiled rotten as I was, still figuring myself out. This was the *real deal*, no slacking off allowed.

Musically, I'd been tossed into the deep end, playing an instrument I barely knew on a whole set of new songs—most laced with Murphey's gorgeous, unpredictable chord changes. It was a challenge every moment. Singing harmonies? That was easy—I'd always had an ear for that. But this was something else. The pressure, the pace, the sense that something big was brewing but no one quite knew what . . . it was electric. I wasn't used to any of it. Strangely enough, most of the disquiet I was feeling didn't catch up with me until after the Nashville sessions. Up until then, I'd been riding high, caught up in the synchronicity and swirl, having the time of my life.

On tour we had no guitar tuners with us. Not even a pitch pipe. We tuned backstage and there wasn't an amp for my bass so

I couldn't hear the note. I had my bass up against my ear trying to hear and sometimes—to be honest—it wasn't precise. It was hard to be so exacting about everything and Murphey was more than exacting. I don't know where we got the note to tune from. Sometimes there was a piano onstage and we got a note and carried backstage. I was learning a lot in real time on the job, but it got to me sometimes and I felt in over my head. In hindsight I had become paranoid about making a mistake to incur Murph's wrath and there was a lot of pressure to be great, night after night.

The breaking point for me came one night at our home club in Dallas, the Rubaiyat. It had been icy between me and Murph for the past few weeks. We hadn't been talking much and didn't talk before we took the stage and started the set out with the beautiful "Calico Silver." In the arrangement the bass comes in on the third note of the C chord for the first bar, an E note. It stays in that vein and then straightens out after a few bars. I knew it perfectly; I had just played it on the session in Nashville. But when the song started and I came in with my big badass bass note, I hit the root of the chord which was a C instead of the third or E like I was supposed to. It's not the same, but it is not really out of tune. For the time being, it would have worked and no one but Murphey and I would have known. In bands you do that all the time. If someone makes a "clam" you don't stop in the middle of a song and tell everyone in the room about it. But Murphey stopped "Calico Silver" and said out loud, "You're out of tune, get that A string in tune!" It was a shock to me, especially in front of a roomful of people, and it sort of drove me into a shell. I was seething and just stared at Michael with a drum beating in my head, fumbling getting that A note just right. We finished the show and got a standing ovation *like always* and the audience didn't notice or care about the tuning incident. To them, that was part of the charm of the show.

But I cared—deeply. I brooded over it, turning it over in my mind again and again. Sure, the sessions were a breakthrough for Murphey, and things seemed to be moving. But I was upside-down, sideways, caught in the tension of it all. I needed space. For better or worse, I cast a cosmic net in search of an exit. After all, what's the point if you're not happy?

♪

Out of my comfort zone, and out of the blue, Ray Hubbard unexpectedly gave me a call. He wasn't Ray Wylie yet but in that Ray Wylie voice he asked, "What's going on?" I was elated to hear that voice. I told him I was playing with Murphey and had done some recording in Nashville but I had no idea what would come of it. Ray got straight to the point, "Listen, we've got this band, me and Rick and a *drummer*." They had never played with a drummer before and now they wanted to rock it up. "Wayne is leaving to settle down with Marsha . . . and we need a bass player and . . . well, we were wondering if you wanted to be the bass player?"

Murphey and I were in the middle of some shows around Texas and we had a show at the Saxon Pub in Austin coming up with more being planned. It would be a big move. It was crazy. Hubbard said, "Man we've got a lot of gigs coming up and we split everything four ways, and we'll be making good money."

Making good money was music to my ears and I'd be playing in a band with my buds. Yes, I had recorded in Nashville with Murphey and Bob Johnston, but strangely it didn't all sink in and truthfully I still couldn't believe it was going to be an album. The song "Geronimo's Cadillac" that would be the title track for the album hadn't even been written yet. There were no drums or other instruments on the tracks. There were a lot of unanswered questions. Murphey didn't communicate anything to me and because of the pervading tension between Murphey and me I didn't even know what questions to ask. I felt like I needed a change. I saw no light at the end of any tunnel except the one being offered by Ray Hubbard. I was going on pure feel when I said "yes, I'll be there." I'm not sure how I told Murphey that I was leaving and that the Saxon Pub show would be my last. The only thing I can recall about his reaction was that he didn't try to talk me out of it.

♪

Enter Gary Nunn. He was not yet Gary P. Nunn. Just plain old Gary Nunn. Gary was a rock and roller from Brownfield and Lubbock and had been playing in an outfit in Austin called Genesee with Richard Dean, a folk singer from Colorado. I thought they were a great band, but they were a cover band. They played all the fraternity parties and made decent money but they hardly ever got to play their own songs. It was a dead-end street for a songwriter to be in such a band and Gary was getting out. Genesee had broken up and Gary recently told me, "I was disheartened and frustrated with the music business in general and I decided to give it up and go back to my family's ranch in Oklahoma, do some manual labor and get my head together." His pickup was packed up. Richard Dean called him and told him that Michael Murphey was in town playing at the Saxon Pub and said, "You need to see this guy before you leave town. He writes all his own songs."

The original Saxon Pub was one of Austin's great listening rooms, maybe the best. There was no backstage or tune-up room, only a hallway full of people to tune up in. Murphey and I were in the hall tuning before the show, people streaming in and around us. I tuned the best I could and Murphey looked at me and said, "That A string is sharp, just jerk on it to make it come back." As he said it, he reached out and grabbed the string and pulled it so hard he jerked it right off the bass. He didn't mean to do it, I know that, but still. . . . And we were about to be introduced! Luckily, I had an extra string and got it out and started tuning up again, but it was new and I would fight with that son of a bitch the whole night. Murphey stared at me and my frantic efforts to get a new string on. Right about then the emcee introduced us.

Gary Nunn was in the front row. I barely knew him except from when he played with the Sparkles in Lubbock and I had seen Genesee play a few times in Austin and hung out at their gigs and shot the breeze. But we were at best mere acquaintances. It was surreal and a total surprise to see him there. Gary looked like a buzzard on a rusty bob-wire fence watching me, his face an unreadable mask. He was after my gig, I knew it. Gary Nunn was the guy taking my spot.

We played the Murphey greats: "Say So Much," "Texas Morning," "Fort Worth, I Love You," "Natchez Trace," "Blessing in Disguise," and "Calico Silver" . . . every song better than the last. The audience was spellbound because of the songs and Murphey's fingerpicking and that high but gritty voice with soul pouring out of it. He put on a great show. I was holding it down and singing my parts while still reeling from the ripped string incident in the hallway and seeing the Gary on the bob-wire. I saw everything through a fish-eye lens in slow motion even as my mind was racing. In hindsight, and after talking to Gary about it all these years later, I realize that Gary was not thinking about anything but the songs and how great they were and he was looking straight at Murphey. A lot of Austin rock and rollers were in the room that night and I'm pretty sure that it was an awakening for them too. These guys didn't hang around in folk clubs much but there was no denying the power of this music, whatever genre you wanted to call it. There was about to be a big change in Austin and it was being born right then and there. And I was walking away from it.

At the end of the show, I was out the door before the last note had faded. Afterward Murphey came up to Gary and said, "My bass player just quit. I hear you're a bass player, would you like to play in my band?" Gary was totally surprised but said "Sure, yes." He unpacked his pickup and his life changed forever.

What did I do? I quit Murphey and all the shows coming up and I was now disconnected from the new album I had played on.

Who else would do that? Where would that get me? Murphey was a fascinating man. He had a lot of sides to him and was purt near a genius and the power of his songs was addicting and I loved to play them. This was very important music and better than anything else out there. We had great conversations driving all those miles. I was learning the bass and laying down parts Murphey was good with. He never told me much what to play. I think my place in the success of *Geronimo's Cadillac* and later on *Cosmic Cowboy Souvenir* was that I was an unconventional and atypical bass player dancing on the edge with a lot of feel. I wasn't a studio guy. I also sang those close harmonies with Murphey, and Bob Johnston was sold on what he heard in that little Rubaiyat club. Sold enough to bring us to Nashville and make a record. He said he had heard magic.

But I needed a break. Driving through Waco, I had remorse and guilt about leaving and wondered if I had done the right thing. But I was also glad to be out of there. I needed a breath of fresh air, and those Three Faces West boys were it. I was on my way to Denver to meet up with Ray and Rick, and the new drummer, whoever he would be.

Meanwhile, Murphey still needed to finish the new record for A&M. He took Gary and a guitar player named Leonard Arnold back to Nashville to wrap it up. Leonard was a great player, he was tall and lanky, and he always had the longest hair of any of us. He wore skintight jeans, cool boots, and a big cowboy hat. I don't remember his appearance any other way.

After I left, Murphey and Charles John Quarto wrote "Geronimo's Cadillac." They saw a 1905 photograph of the Apache Geronimo sitting in an oversized black convertible automobile. It wasn't really a Cadillac, but it was a compelling image. They saw it as a natural way to describe the Native American's story. Murphey said, "There was something in Geronimo's eyes that said, 'You may have me here but you don't own me!'"

"Geronimo's Cadillac" turned out to be the keystone Bob Johnston had been searching for—the song that pulled the whole album into focus. Murphey, Gary, and Leonard headed to Nashville to record it. Kenny Buttrey—one of the greatest drummers to ever come out of Music City—played drum on *Geronimo* and then overdubbed drum parts on the rest of the tracks. I had played bass on those original sessions the same way I played live: responding to Murphey's guitar, with no thought of a kick drum or rhythm section being added later. I had no concept of four-on-the-floor; my playing was loose, instinctive, a little outside the box. But somehow, it all worked. The result was *Geronimo's Cadillac*—a groundbreaking album. But at the time? Nobody had any idea.

I met the Three Faces West guys up in Breckenridge, Colorado, to get reacquainted and choose a band name. We didn't want to be Four Faces West, so we found a novel solution. We took two cowboy hats—we really did this—and we put adjectives and adverbs (you know, modifying words) on little sheets of paper in one hat and nouns and pronouns in the other. And we would pull out combinations of words, with names like "Bloody Chimney" and "Ice-water Enema" and all this was hilarious weird fun. I pulled out the name Tucker Boots. Rick Fowler said he thought that it was kind of cool but not the right name for our band. But I remembered that name and years later when Iris's and my first son was born, we called him Tucker Boots. His name was pulled out of a hat. Don't tell him.

Hubbard and Rick came up with Texas Fever and that was that. We drove down to the Café York in Denver. Michael McGeary was the new drummer and it was fun playing with him because it was practically the first time I had ever played with a drummer except for that Rhythm Masters summer back in Lubbock. McGeary was a character. He was a good drummer and had lived a wild rock 'n' roll life in California. He fancied himself an actor, speaking in a British accent on occasion and quoting lines from movies.

Texas Fever in front of Virginia's Cafe, Austin, 1972. (L–R): Michael McGeary, Rick Fowler, Ray Wylie, and Bob Livingston. (Photo courtesy of Bob Livingston.)

We played the Midwest, the Southwest, and Texas. I felt I had been through the wringer and exhibited a little PTSD when I showed up to play. I was also intimidated by Three Faces West who were my heroes. Their show was almost like a scripted musical. They were funny, everybody had lines and punchlines. I told them up front not to expect too much from me in the way of being the funny guy that Wayne was. They said that was fine.

I would disregard Ray's earlier advice to "never sit down when you play." I sat down for the shows and was barefoot, staring straight ahead and not saying a word unless I was singing. I was also concentrating on my bass playing and working things out with McGeary the drummer, things that I would use for years. Rick and Ray took it in stride and would make fun of me in the show, and that became the shtick. They'd be telling a joke and be having some repartee and then they'd turn to me and say, "And then we've got Bob." And I would be sitting stone-faced. And for some reason the audience would laugh. This became a regular bit. I was the brunt of their jokes, but I didn't mind too much because I knew these guys and their punchy wit. If I could get a laugh by staring at the audience, then I was doing my part.

We did the great songs that Three Faces West were known for and learned and wrote new ones. Rick and I had written "Head Full of Nothin'" that Jerry Jeff would later record. Things were coming back around for me and I got to sing a few of my songs and one by Charles John Quarto called "Cross Between a River and a Cross." It was a cappella and it was unique in the set. Ray and I did our song "Life in the Pines." After a while, I got some self-assurance back and I was having a lot of fun playing music again and I started standing up . . . and wearing cowboy boots.

Texas Fever was based out of Red River and Dallas. One night in Red there was a party going on. There was a "rust hickory woman" who had a log cabin at the top of the pass and that's where we ended up. The musicians had brought their guitars and beer. Townsfolk had heard about what was going on and had dropped by with food and cases of beer. Tourists from Texas and South America were walking in like they owned the place with more beer and whisky. At about 1:45 a.m. on the third day we ran out of beer. Ray was the big man on campus and if anyone was going to be able to finagle some beer at this hour, he was the guy. He walked down the mountain dirt road and slipped into the D-Bar-D Bar, the only bar in town that would accept a scruffy hippie like him. He ordered two cases of beer to go.

Ray thought he was home free as he was walking towards the door, a case of beer on each shoulder, when a woman from Tulsa approached him in a menacing way. She took one look at him and was immediately disgusted with his long hair, leather pants, and squared-off Frye boots. She told Ray he probably wasn't a real

American looking like that. It was getting heated and it looked like a fight! Ray said he was about to take her on; if it was just him and her he could get a boot in there somewhere, claw his way through. Then a whirling ball of butcher knives and testosterone otherwise known as the woman's son came roaring up from the four corners of the earth and cold-cocked Ray with one punch. He was "face down on the barroom floor" like Murphey wrote in "Backslider's Wine."

Ray got up, dusted himself off, and to his credit came back to the party . . . with the beer.

Hubbard wrote "Redneck Mother" about the experience. I thought the song was funny and irreverent and Texas Fever should start doing it right away. But Ray was scared to sing it because those were the days of "Okie from Muskogee" and there were a ton of rednecks in our audience just like that woman and her son in Red River. The rednecks outnumbered us and seemed to be out there looking for chance to kick a hippie's ass. I couldn't get Ray to sing it for the life of me. So I learned it.

Most folks can't imagine a life on the road like this. One town after another, driving all night through any kind of weather. We played at the All American Bar in Breckenridge owned by a city boy turned mountain man, Gig Geiger. The accommodations for the bands were up in the attic, but it felt like a basement, cold and dank, frogs in the shower. There was a band that played during the week called Mullet—Chuck and Julie Joyce with a blues guitar player named Bill Campbell from Austin. Bill was famous in Austin and was the real authentic blues deal. Gig told us to go up to the attic and pick a spot to sleep. There were no beds, just shag carpet that smelled real bad. It was dark and musty. You threw some blankets down and hoped for the best. We all staked out our spots and were asleep when Bill Campbell came home from a jam session at three in the morning and found Ray in *his* spot. We awoke to the sound of a vacuum cleaner as Bill tried in vain to vacuum Hubbard up and remove him. It was just *so* weird and hilarious.

I was wide-eyed a lot. But in general things were going forward for us. Good friends, good money, and good times. Texas Fever was working out. But I got the feeling all of us were continually restless.

Suddenly snapping me away from all this fun, the phone rang with a "Bob! Bob—what are you doing?" It was Murphey.

"I'm playing with Ray and Rick."

"Bob Johnston just called and told me I've got to get you back in the band. Bob said he liked your energy and bass playing and singing." Murphey didn't say *he* wanted me back, but he said, ". . . and we are going to do an East Coast tour . . . and we need you there."

It was a major dilemma. Things were stable and going well with Texas Fever and besides that these fellows were my friends. But I felt something else was going on, a pull. Those Nashville tracks had turned into a full-on album on A&M Records. I had played on *Geronimo's Cadillac* and I felt loyalty there and a vested interest in the outcome. The Murphey band was going to embark on an East Coast tour to support the record. I had to make a decision on the spot. Maybe it was destiny or the restlessness that is always lurking inside me, but I told Murphey I would be there.

I gave Rick and Ray my notice and hoped there would be no hard feelings. But everyone was cool with it. I think Ray was wanting to go out on his own anyway. And Rick had plenty to do back in Red River. He was a great artist and there were a lot of paintings to be painted. He would go on to play in the Great American Honky Tonk Band with Michael Hearne and Mark Webernick. They would be Murphey's new band for years. For now with Texas Fever, it was every man for himself.

Bob Johnston had interceded on my behalf for whatever reason and had convinced Murphey that he needed me back in the band.

I got on the road for Austin, driving day and night until I pulled in. I was still a gypsy and lived out of my gypsy wagon for the time being, parking in driveways and sleeping on couches.

Murphey was offered a chance to open for Elton John at the Palmer Auditorium. "Whoever gets here first gets the gig." Murphey couldn't find his drummer, Donny Dolan. It was a surprise gig offer and Donny was out of pocket. Texas Fever drummer Michael McGeary had followed my lead and showed up in Austin too. Murphey had heard us play and knew McGeary was a good drummer, so he hired him for the gig never having met him. No rehearsal or sound check, just plug in and go for it. Gary was playing bass and I felt awkward not knowing how I would fit in to this band with Gary in it. Murphey and the boys did well for themselves that night, all things considered. His great songs and the warm reception of the Austin audience made it almost impossible to fail.

I watched from the wings. Elton John took the stage with his band met by a roar from the crowd. I was fifteen feet away from his incredible energy and sense of showmanship. I could hear his breath and feel his sweat. He kicked ass and took names and hammered his piano with staccato precision and slippery Jerry Lee glitzes. His voice was that of a rock god, singing and teasing the audience by taking his wild winged shoes off and placing them on his piano. The crowd knew what was coming and pressed forward. The joint was rocking and the two Palmer Auditorium balconies literally bounced up and down in waves and in rhythm to the beat when Elton threw his shoes into the audience, causing a major rock and roll melee. Now *that* was showbiz.

The next day there was a band meeting followed by a rehearsal. Murphey and Gary had rented a house together with their families at 6214 North Lamar. They had built a rehearsal studio in the garage out back. There were no windows and it had a harsh light overhead but there was an air conditioner humming in the corner and it was cool, literally. Walking into the rehearsal studio I was intimidated at first, unsure of myself. There were two bass players in the room. How would we deal with that? Right off the bat, Murphey cleared everything up by saying, "Bob, you play bass on the songs that you recorded and Gary, you play bass on *Geronimo's Cadillac* and the new stuff we've been working on. And you guys switch to the piano when you're not playing bass." For me, the way forward was clear and I found my place in the band. In Gary's great book *Home with the Armadillos*, though, he wrote that he felt he had lost control of the band when I got there. Bass players have a tendency to feel strongly that they are the foundation of the world, not just the band.

The new band was Craig Hillis on lead guitar, Gary Nunn on piano and bass, Michael McGeary on drums, myself on bass and piano, and Michael Martin Murphey—as he was now known on the *Geronimo's Cadillac* album—on acoustic guitar, banjo, and lead vocals. Gary and I sang harmonies, and switching between bass and piano became the template that would carry us forward into the Jerry Jeff and Lost Gonzo Band years. Craig Hillis was playing his great woodshedded leads and Michael McGeary kept a good solid beat with surges and some theatrics thrown in. Murphey's great soulful voice and his acoustic guitar were at the center of it all. We all had reverence for Murphey's music and played those songs and sang them knowing they were special, and we coalesced into a tight band that put on an exciting action-packed show. Folk-rock-country music. Story songs and orchestrated masterpieces. Great fun!

CHAPTER 19

The Whisky a Go Go

June 1972

Jerry Jeff Walker moved to Austin lock, stock, and barrel and was quick to buy a nice place on five acres west of town. It was a ranch-style home that was always under construction, adding rooms and remodeling everything. Much of the amazing woodwork, tabletops, and cabinets were done by Homer Wills, a harmonica-playing commando carpenter craftsman. Zebra wood, teak, pine, and oak. Homer could eyeball and cut that wood and put that refrigerator right in there perfect. He installed a Murphy bed in Jerry Jeff's man shack/office that pulled down out of the wall, the same bed that Ramblin' Jack Elliott would be caught in a few years later. Just flipped him right up there in the middle of the night. "Help! Ramblin' Jack to tower! Help! Mayday!"

Jerry Jeff had a past with Austin, coming and going, and now with a new record deal and some money, he decided to make it permanent. I had become friendly with Jerry Jeff in Red River so I called him up and invited him to a Murphey rehearsal. We were in the middle of a gospel rock song called "Harbor for My Soul" when Jerry Jeff poked his head in the door. And what Jerry Jeff saw was—instant band! When we took a break, he got us in a corner and said he wanted to record in Austin and wanted us

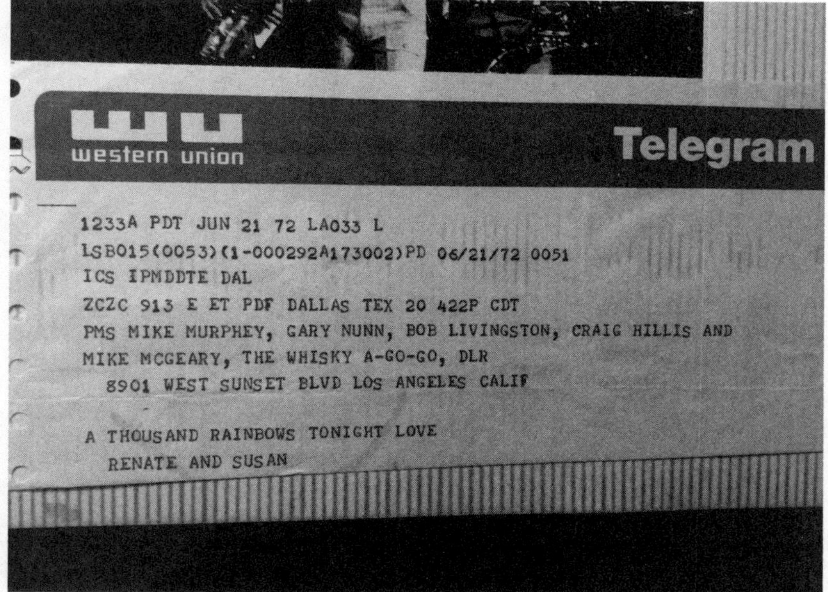
western union Telegram

1233A PDT JUN 21 72 LA033 L
LSB015(0053)(1-000292A173002)PD 06/21/72 0051
ICS IPMDDTE DAL
ZCZC 913 E ET PDF DALLAS TEX 20 422P CDT
PMS MIKE MURPHEY, GARY NUNN, BOB LIVINGSTON, CRAIG HILLIS AND
MIKE MCGEARY, THE WHISKY A-GO-GO, DLR
8901 WEST SUNSET BLVD LOS ANGELES CALIF

A THOUSAND RAINBOWS TONIGHT LOVE
RENATE AND SUSAN

Whisky telegram. (Image courtesy of Craig D. Hillis.)

to play on the record. We said we were into it, and it was left like that for a while.

The Murphey band headed for California to play the Whisky a Go Go. Gary, Craig, McGeary, and I were packed into a rented Dodge van for the long drive from Austin across West Texas and New Mexico, through Arizona, Death Valley, Needles, and San Bernardino. We were dog-tired and whipped into a frenzy from the heat and the wind blowing on us constantly. The air conditioners in cars and especially in vans didn't work all that well back in those days. The driver and the guy in the shotgun seat were okay because the AC was blowing right on them. But the two guys in the back were hot and tried to sleep, waiting for their turn to drive. We pressed forward into the mythical more-than-hip world of Los Angeles. Driving on the LA freeways, five or six lanes each way, packed with commuters, trucks, and fast motorcycles darting in and out. The trials and tribulations of that long drive were inconsequential as we were engaged in the peculiar ritual of bonding as only a band in a van can.

CHAPTER 19

The cheeky Whisky a Go Go on the Sunset Strip beckoned. Bright lights, big city. Murphey had flown into LA a couple of days earlier. He was waiting for us to rehearse in the big room at A&M Studios on La Brea Avenue. The facility had been built by Charlie Chaplin for his movies, many of which were filmed on the soundstage there. Because I'd lived in Los Angeles, I was sort of familiar with the area and the maze of streets. I had always seen the studio from the outside as I drove past. It looked like a work of art with an archway and a barrier and a guard. Now, we drove under that archway through the gate into the inner sanctum. We rehearsed on the soundstage with the vibes of old movie stars and the ghost of the Tramp peeking over the backdrop as we worked on songs like "Natchez Trace," "Geronimo's Cadillac," and "What Am I Doing Hangin' 'Round." Murphey had invited Herb Steiner, his old steel guitar player from the group Tex, for the rehearsals. Herb added a considerable country flavor, and we invented Texas progressive country music on Charlie Chaplin's soundstage.

We met Lou Adler, the president of A&M. He said he liked *Geronimo's Cadillac* and was prepared to promote it. We did lunch with Lou and a pretty secretary who was pure LA. We rehearsed for a full day and then we played our first gigs with a four-day run at the Whisky. It was exciting to play the Whisky with all its stars, starlets, musicians, and record people. In his book, Gary Nunn reported that Robert Plant of Led Zeppelin was in the audience and he spoke to him. Robert said, "Great band!" It was see and be seen in the scene like I'd never seen. We played loud and did all right for ourselves and it got people talking and suddenly there was a lot of work coming around the mountain.

Back in Austin, we prepared for our first extended tour to the eastern regions of New York, Baltimore, and Georgetown. Herb Steiner had joined the band permanently, and we played some Austin gigs to warm up.

On July 15, 1972, we played our first-ever show at the Armadillo World Headquarters, the vast, ramshackle former armory that Eddie Wilson and his company had transformed into Austin's version of the Fillmore West complete with giant armadillos crawling over the walls and into the ceiling painted by Austin artist Jim Franklin. It was a packed house and the crowd loved it. There was a lot of power up on that stage and we filled the room. It was the first of many Armadillo shows and Murphey was proclaimed a god that night. Jerry Jeff had come to the show and sang on "Geronimo's Cadillac." He got into the spirit and saw the *power of the band* and what could be had here in his new hometown and he was itching to be part of it. Meanwhile, "Harbor for My Soul" put those Austin hippie holy rollers into a frenzy. "Do you believe it? Yes I do! Do you really want it? Yes I do! Do you really need it? Yes I need it! I need a Harbor for My Soul!"

I was watching it all go down. In the center of I knew not what. Rolling on an electric current of cosmic soul into the ground we were all dancing on. It was electric in more ways than one. And to top it all off, a seismic shift in the *force* was about to come, just now . . . from a girl.

CHAPTER 20

Cosmic Flower

1972

That night after the Armadillo show, Murphey, Jerry Jeff, and I were standing in the middle of the walloping-sized room talking about the show and what might be, or might not. Around us, the roadies and their helpers were hauling equipment back into the trucks and secret spaces in the back. The stagehands were slamming tables and metal folding chairs together and stacking them up. The place was alive with noise—shouts, laughter, sweeping brooms, scattered conversations, and distant music from parts unknown.

Then something caught my eye.

From the center of the room like a spark in the chaos there was a sprite of a girl, no bigger than a minute, dressed in a piece of bright flower-print cloth that wound around her. She had long electric hair with waves, practically glowing. She was throwing a frisbee for a giant Great Dane twice as big as she was, and he was bounding back and forth in delight. It was a startling and wonderful sight. I kept staring at her. She was so cute with that dog. I was trying not to be obvious and I was thinking she was oblivious to me. I wished I could go up and talk to her, but I was too shy.

It stopped me cold—this wild, wonderful scene in the middle of the post-show mess. I couldn't take my eyes off her. She was so cute with that dog, so completely in her own world. I tried not to stare, thinking she hadn't noticed me. I wanted to talk to her. I really did. But I was too shy.

Murphey, Jerry Jeff, and I started walking towards the side door, continuing our conversation about nothing in particular. The mystery girl was walking ahead of us through the big double side doors of the Armadillo. I was paying no attention whatsoever to the conversation with the guys, their voices drowned out and a thousand miles away. This cosmic creature walking ahead of me was all I was thinking about. I wished I had the guts to go talk to her, but she was walking away and out of my life. Unless I did something. The three of us paused in the parking lot. Then Jerry Jeff peeled off toward his car and disappeared into the night—off to who knows where. Murphey and I exchanged goodnights, but I was barely there, running on autopilot. My eyes were fixed on the alchemistic young woman drifting ahead of us, walking away like a vision dissolving into the dark.

Suddenly she stopped in her tracks. She turned around, looked at us for a moment, then walked straight up to us. She told us she thought we were great and that it was "special music." She had been kinda low for a few days, she said, and "I wasn't going to come out tonight, but I'm so glad I did. You lifted my spirits."

Murphey and I both responded with our thanks, me trying to keep my mouth from hanging open. Then Murphey said, "I'd like to introduce you my bass player, Bob Livingston."

"Hello."

"Hello."

We shook hands and she said her name was Iris and then she thanked us again. There was a what-do-we-do-now moment in the silence that followed. But as they say in the movies, she had me at hello. Or at the first frisky frisbee throw. She turned to leave, walking across the parking lot. My mind was racing. *I'm really blowing it.* I was tongue-tied but couldn't let her walk away.

Suddenly my inroad came in the form of a homeless raggedy-scruffy who walked up to her and said "Hey you, hey baby, you have any change? You got a cigarette? Where you going?"

That was my cue to step in—and I didn't hesitate. I moved between them and said, "Excuse me, but I think it's time for you to go. She doesn't want to talk to you. She's with *me*." He stared at me for a second, muttered something I couldn't catch, then melted into the shadows.

I looked at this cosmic beauty—wildflowers in her hair, radiating something otherworldly—and blurted out, "Do you want to go to a party?" I know it sounds lame, but it was all I could think of. And, as Iris would later tell our kids with a smile, "*There was no party.*"

We got in her flat-red Volkswagen bug. The right front seat was missing, so I had to sit in the back like it was a tiny limo. She drove erratically and ran traffic lights and I thought I was going to die a couple times. From the back, leaning forward, I gave her directions to the furnished apartment I was temporarily staying in, such as it was. Susan Antone—the sister of Clifford Antone, the blues kingmaker of Austin—managed the apartment among other side hustles and was letting me stay there in between our Texas shows. We wandered over to the apartment complex's pool area to soak in the atmosphere and get a feel for what was what. It was a beautiful night in Austin. The moon was out and it was quiet as the country with the wind blowing through the trees. We talked the night through at the edge of the lapping water and then headed out to Cisco's for breakfast as the dawn crept in. And we have been together ever since.

Iris was an artist and a true free spirit. She painted and she sketched and music filled her days. She really believed in what I was doing with Murphey—she felt the songs and supported the work. She had an eye for beauty in all its forms and always stopped to smell the roses—literally.

Iris and I got married near Lake Travis, 1973. Lots of famous faces here. (Photo by Scott Newton.)

I had some stage shirts, cool shirts, and would wear them when I took her out. She always remarked on that: "Cool shirt." I opened car doors for her and pulled out chairs and she liked that, too. On my off days, we went to restaurants, swam in Lake Travis, and ate enchiladas at Rosie's off Highway 71. I didn't quite realize it at the time, but I was wooing her. In any case, we fell in love and would marry within the year.

CHAPTER 21

The Brown Album

1972

On July 17, a couple of days after meeting Iris, we started recording sessions for Jerry Jeff's new MCA record, the one I will call the Brown Album because of all the shades of brown on the cover. Jerry Jeff had found a recording studio in Austin, the most primitive on the planet. It was in an old abandoned Rapps Dry Cleaners on West 6th Street right across from an eatery called Mad Dog and Bean's. The studio had been gutted to make one big room that had high ceilings and walls covered with burlap. There was a 16-track Ampex tape recorder in the center of the room, no mixing board, no central room, wires running everywhere, everyone flying by the seat of their pants. Primitive yet futuristic.

Michael Brovsky was Jerry Jeff's big bear of a New York manager-agent who had put together an MCA record deal. Brovsky had been in The Serendipity Singers, a folk group that had a hit with a song called "Don't Let the Rain Come Down." His was the voice that said "Ah ha" every time in the chorus. Brovsky came to Austin to produce the sessions. He was wearing platform shoes and he had a long beard and big hair and was a real New Yorkie type and was wearing what looked to me like British Carnaby Street clothes. He really stuck out in Austin and got a lot of attention. Brovsky showed up with some noise reduction equipment he had brought from a studio in New York. To Brovsky's credit he was unfazed at the recording layout before him. He took one look at this primitive studio setup and said, "Whatever . . . let's do it." And he let Jerry Jeff do it, whatever he wanted.

Jerry Jeff had a vision with the music and the sound. And he had a band that would roll with that vision. Jerry Jeff said this is the way it was going to be recorded and Brovsky was going to capture it, whatever it took. He originally wanted Jerry Jeff to record in New York, LA, or Nashville, but Jerry Jeff was having none of that. He didn't want session players. He wanted some Austin-funky and that's what he got. I wonder what that record would have been like if Jacky Jack had recorded it in Nashville? Or in the City of the Angels?

Jerry Jeff was going to record his new songs here and now, no doubt about it. So Brovsky and the engineer hustled around plugging stuff in, testing all the wires. There was no recording console and everything had to be plugged straight into the back of the Ampex. In a way that was unique, the sound and recording guys had their shit together and the mics and wires all worked and we got sounds and when we listened back, it sounded pretty damn good and it all went down on reels of 2-inch tape that began to stack up.

It was a painstaking job to listen to a playback because everything had to be switched over from record to playback, each individual track, and the VU meters that tell you if you are distorting or not have to be set again and maybe the mix changed slightly, so we just never listened to playbacks during recordings. We didn't listen until the end of the evening; that's when the party began.

Jerry Jeff was all feel, all vibe, all into the moment. That's why I think I fit in so well. I had a similar musical disposition. To set the mood just right, Jerry Jeff would show up to the studio about seven in the evening with a galvanized washtub and begin the process of making a tub-load of sangria. He mixed a cosmic concoction with apples and oranges and placed it outside in the doorway that opened onto the 6th Street sidewalk. Everybody would have a few glasses of sangria and then we'd go in and start playing. And we would cut everything once or twice and we couldn't listen to playbacks until the end of the night. People would come in off the street to see what was going on and they might end up on the record singing background or playing the backbeat on a rock. There was an Austin piano player, Roosevelt Williams, also known as the Grey Ghost. It just so happened Roosevelt was walking down 6th and looked in the doorway and saw some musicians jamming in there and he was drawn into our campfire of music. Jerry Jeff saw him and asked him in. The Grey Ghost sat down at the piano and played on "Moonchild," a great moody sensuous track that really typifies the vibe of the album. Spontaneous and fun.

We were recording live for the most part, Jerry Jeff singing and playing his guitar, the rest of us working it out and playing along. It was recorded like that, live. We'd work it up and cut it. It was very organic and grew by itself. There were no overdubs except for the occasional background vocals. Gary and I were greatly influenced by the Beatles and would sing Ohs and Ahas and Jerry Jeff loved it. He told the engineer to keep the tape rolling at all times, including catching all the talking and conversations.

We cut six or seven songs that night, all that Jerry Jeff had ready. And the next night we did the same songs again. We had two or three takes of everything, all recorded live. "Charlie Dunn," "Good Lovin' Grace," and "Hill Country Rain," all written up at the Lazy H in Red River the summer before. There were some pretty crazy songs, too: "Hairy Ass Hillbillies and the Continuing Saga of the Classic Bummer, or Is This My One Way Bus Ticket to Cleveland."

This was only the second album I'd ever played on and it was still hard to believe we were recording an album for sale on a major record label, an album with so many rough edges, unconventionality, humor, and rascal attitude to it. Jerry Jeff knew it was working. He did not necessarily know where he was going with it and relied on us to help shape it. He accepted suggestions on arrangements and maybe agreed to change a word or two, but other times he would tell me, "Bob, when you make your album, then you can do that."

But I think he relied on each of us to watch him and notice what he liked and what he didn't and to be able to latch onto his sometimes-quirky time signatures and U-turns and be there at the finish line with him. Jerry Jeff took to the nonconformity of the band. We were not country, not rock, not folk, but all these mixed together into a new hybrid. He loved playing and singing and he loved that we would go anywhere with him, as high as the Moonchild. He trusted us and the direction we were going. The same direction he was going. It wasn't planned and no corporate head designed a music career path for him. But I didn't know any better and had faith in his innate sense of knowing he was onto something. A New York cowboy come to town going for it and making something fresh.

In the studio, we would warm up by jamming together on something familiar. Blues and reggae, country, and jazzish numbers. Songs we all knew and wished we'd written. And Jerry Jeff was in the middle of it playing and encouraging me and Gary to sing songs like "Not Fade Away" or even "Daylight Come and Me Wanna Go Home." This was garage band. We were getting tighter and reading each mother's minds and playing with wild abandon.

Both *Geronimo's Cadillac* and *Jerry Jeff Walker* were recorded first or second takes at the most. On *Geronimo's Cadillac*, Murphey and I knew the songs so well we just sat down and recorded how we played them onstage, one pass through. With Jerry Jeff, we were winging it. New territory with every passing note. It was a country rock painting done by many hands. This wasn't Nashville or New York where Jerry Jeff said he couldn't be himself. This was Austin, Texas, the Oasis. Where the groundwork for a musical revolution was being planned without anyone knowing it was being planned. We all flourished and grew more confident with our gung-ho attitude and willingness to try anything.

Jerry Jeff was always working on a song in the studio and sometimes we'd record as he was still writing it in his head, changing verses midstride in real time. He wanted it as live as he could get it. Rawness and experimentation with a band that would follow him anywhere was the rule of the day. He had been a solo acoustic folkie. That's how I first saw him. Jerry Jeff moved to Austin looking for inspiration and musicians to help develop his new songs and create his new undefinable sound. He didn't care too much about mistakes or being a bit out of tune. Because it was all about *feel* with Jerry Jeff.

♪

One night Murphey came by the new studio to see what we were up to. He probably felt somewhat abandoned because his band was playing on a new Jerry Jeff album. What the . . . ? He watched and listened for a while then went for a sandwich at the shop next door. In about an hour he came back with a song. It was called "Alleys of Austin" and he played it for us. It was another Murphey masterpiece that captured his take on what was happening right then and there in Austin, Texas.

I brought Iris with me to the studio to impress her. She met Michael and the rest of the band and everybody was friendly and we were all getting along and this was a key part of the arrangement. She liked Gary and Craig and though McGeary was a bit different, she liked him too. We were all young and we were friends and we hung out together and had fun even when not playing music. We carried on this recording routine for a few days and then finished up for the time being. The record wasn't complete; there were more songs to be sung and stories told. Unbeknownst to us at the time, that would happen in the Big Apple.

We had some time off and Iris and I would swim at Lake Travis with Craig and his wife Dana. Dana's father was Dan Strait of Strait Music in Austin. He and his wife Janet had a big stone house on a high cliff overlooking the lake. We ate picnic lunches, went swimming with our friends, no big worries and . . . life was good.

In August we played a double concert with Murphey and Jerry Jeff at a club in Austin called Mother Earth. The band did double time and we were onstage for a full five hours if we were on a minute. On the second night the place was packed to the rafters and Eddie Wilson, the president of Armadillo World Headquarters, brought Willie Nelson to see what was going on. I had seen Willie on Ian Tyson's TV show *Nashville North*. All his great songs made my head whirl. "Crazy," "Hello Walls," "Night Life." The place was packed with wild, enthusiastic fans, clapping and dancing in time. The night had a big impact on Willie when he saw all the rednecks and hippies loving the same music, smoking joints, drinking beer, dancing, and singing together. Cogs were turning in the Willie brain, and I think the phrase "What would Willie do?" was born right then in the head of Willie himself. Willie didn't have long hair then but when he showed back up in Austin six months later, he was growing the hair that he's probably never cut.

The Murphey band was sounding great. We had played a few shows and had spent time recording together so we were getting tight as a drum.

We got ready for the eastern US tour. Murphey was a great player: he played a Martin, and could fingerpick as good as anyone

Double concert at Mother Earth in Austin. The band never left the stage. Then Willie walked in . . . (Poster by Bill Holloway.)

and he loved to rock. After all, he'd played in cover bands too and knew his way around many styles. The band was unique and people took to us everywhere we had played so far. But these were mostly hometown gigs with the exception of the Whisky shows. How would we go over in big cities like New York, Baltimore, Boston, and Washington, DC? We'd soon find out.

We drove to Memphis, stayed the night, then drove Roanoke, Virginia, and played a club called the Crazy Horse. Nobody had any idea who we were, it was a dance club, and they weren't used to singer-songwriters. It was a tough audience and someone yelled out, "Hey, play some Grand Funk!" And Murphey just yelled back, "This is the GRANDEST funk you'll ever hear!" and launched into "Harbor for My Soul," from *Geronimo's Cadillac*, rocking gospel. It appeased the drunks, and for us in the band it was fun and a paid rehearsal in a sense. There was a lot on the line.

In New York, we played the famous Bitter End for a four-day run and stayed at the Holiday Inn in Manhattan. On the third day, Murphey and I were up on the roof with guitars and singing country songs. He used to call me Cosmic Bob and he had actually made a hand-tooled leather belt for my birthday with "Cosmic Bob" tooled on it. That "cosmic" name was going around and everything was cosmic and I might have said something about a cosmic cowboy but I can't really take credit for it. All I know is that it was in the air. Murphey wrote "Cosmic Cowboy," the whole song, right then and there.

Just as Murph was wrapping up singing "Cosmic Cowboy" on the rooftop, the phone rang over by the pool. A hotel attendant picked it up and called out, "It's for you, Mr. Livingston."

On the line was Jerry Jeff, calling from a studio in New York right up the road. He said he was finishing the album we'd started back in Austin and had connected with some musicians from upstate who were already laying down tracks. He wanted Gary, Craig, and me to come over "right now" to help wrap it up.

One of the players he'd found was a young guy named Patterson Barrett—a talented kid who would later move to Austin and play with the Austin All Stars and Buddy Miller.

That night in New York we recorded "L.A. Freeway" and "Old Time Feeling." We'd never heard "L.A. Freeway" before, a song that Guy Clark had written and given to Jerry Jeff. Brovsky had hired a session drummer named Andy Newmark, an A-list player in New York who'd recorded with Cat Stevens, Sly Stone, and John Lennon and the Plastic Ono Band. I was only one degree of separation from a Beatle! I played bass with Andy on "L.A. Freeway" bashing the drums with an intensity I had never felt before. He was the driving wheel and he was going to take me with him. It was killer. Hillis rose to the occasion with an iconic rousing lead hook at the end driving off into the sunset, getting out of the city on that LA freeway! We were all singing to high heaven.

We had a few more Murphey gigs to do on this eastern tour and there were a couple with both Murphey and Jerry Jeff on the bill. One of the most memorable nights we had was at the Main Point in Philadelphia. I think Jerry Jeff was opening the show and we were deep into it when suddenly all the lights went out from a major power outage. Jerry Jeff took it in stride, not in the least nonplussed, and gathered as many candles as he could and had someone go across the street to buy more. We filled the stage with those candles and sat on the edge and played purely acoustic. It was like the old days, the *real* old days playing and singing in a dim candlelit room. I'll never forget it, and I wish it could be the same way again right now today.

Next night, the Murphey band made our way out to Long Island to play a club called My Father's Place. Jerry Jeff stayed in NYC to mix the new album. Larry Coryell, the great avant-garde jazz guitarist, opened the show, got drunk, stood on a chair, bent over backwards, and absolutely shredded it. After his show, I told him how much I loved it. "Don't patronize me, man!" he said.

On September 4, 1972, we opened for the Kinks in Baltimore. It was an unconditionally untamed evening. For our part, we played a good show and the Kinks crowd gave us a lot of love, although they were a bit rowdy and expectant as if something wicked this way comes. Between our show and the Kinks', there was a bomb scare and the concert was halted for an hour while authorities looked in vain for something nonexistent. All the while the Kinks were backstage drinking whisky and beer, shouting, arguing, and getting drunker and drunker.

They finally gave the show the all-clear and the lights went down and the Kinks ran onto the stage. It was a whiplash-slapdash show from the beginning to the end with the band pouring drinks down their throats and beer all over the stage. The keyboard player massacred the B-3 organ and poured beer over the keys and inside the works. Ray Davies slipped in a puddle of beer and literally did a backflip and knocked himself out. The rest of the Kinks stayed onstage with brother Dave stalking around the stage playing the chords to "You Really Got Me" with no vocals. They were openly pissed but playing for time for Ray to recover. After about thirty minutes, Ray Davies came back all apologies and they went back over the hits, this time with vocals. After their show, the Kinks got into a brawl in their own dressing room and beat the crap out of each other. We had a bird's-eye view and saw it all and were laughing so hard and looking at each other wild-eyed. I've never seen or heard anything like it before or since. And I thought *we* were rough and rowdy. Maybe this was the show and they went through it all perfectly every night. In any case, this is the way the Great Cosmic Cowboy East Coast Tour ended, not with a whimper but with a bang. It was gonzo and the sky was not the limit.

The next day, we began the long drive back to Austin and there was plenty of time to think and ruminate and roll everything around and try to process what we had done and where I was going with it. I was relatively happy on the road. We were making our bones and learning to play together as a band and sounding damn good, not some back-up musicians that didn't have the feel.

Murph was a great bandleader and he was rolling with it all. We played his music with our own personalities scattered around all the grooves on the record. People loved this new sound. It was folk-rock, because we had simply combined folkies with rockers. But Herb Steiner was now playing steel so they started calling it *country rock* or *progressive county*. We were going somewhere and it looked like up.

♪

Murphey didn't like it all that much that we were playing and recording with Jerry Jeff on our time off from him, and I can understand and might feel the same if I was in his shoes. But it seemed natural for us to be doing it, and we were very fortunate to be playing and recording. We were really Murphey's band, though, and tours were being planned and his Geronimo's Cadillac Texas Western persona was getting a lot of press and making a lot of fans. There was never an edict that we couldn't play with Jerry Jeff, but we knew how Murphey felt. We were all just putting one foot in front of the other. Jerry Jeff would later say "something's bound to come out," but for now, there were more good times to be had both on the road and off. It was a mystery and things were coming to a head and a showdown was on the horizon, even though none of us ever wanted that showdown.

Meanwhile, it was plain as day that I needed some downtime and a real place of my own. A permanent address.

CHAPTER 22

Things Get Real on Lake Travis

Still 1972

The couch I was sleeping on was hard and lumpy and I was sharing it with an old dog named Beauregard, after a Confederate general. I don't remember where I was, just the dog and the couch. *I'm done*, I thought as I rolled off of the uncomfortable piece of furniture. I didn't know what part of town it would be in, but my antennae were out. I was going to find my own place. Put down some roots.

One of the best music stores in Austin was Strait Music. Dan Strait and his wife Irene (Dana Hillis's parents) lived out on Lake Travis in a beautiful Texas limestone house on a cliff overlooking the lake and the world's greatest sunsets. One Sunday afternoon, Craig and Dana Hillis and I all found ourselves hanging out at the Straits' place swimming in the lagoon and relaxing on the deck. Shake Russell and Johnny Vandiver were there. They were in a band called the Ewing Street Times and we were all friends. I told everyone I was looking for a place to live and I pictured a little cabin in the woods on the lake. A friend of Dan's suddenly said, "I have the place for you."

She drove me to another part of the lake where there was a perfect little cabin on a tiny country road across from some more land and then the water. One big room and two small bedrooms, plenty of space. I took it. Earlier that morning all I'd had was a spot on a couch, a couple guitars and a bass, an amp, and some clothes. Now I had my cabin in the woods. It was unfurnished, so Salvation Army was my next stop. Bed, cooking stuff, couch, table, chairs. I'm good. I bought a Baldwin piano from Dan at Strait Music and put it front and center in the big room. My cabin would play an integral part in the making of Michael Murphey's next album, *Cosmic Cowboy Souvenir*, and would also be the setting for the knock-down drag-out to come.

Iris had a place in the city but she spent a lot of time with me out at the cabin. She would paint, I would play piano, and then we'd go eat in town. Murphey lived out on Lake Travis too, on Comanche Trail just around a curve a few miles away. I got a Bluetick hound dog and named him Jake after a song I'd played as a kid, "You Gotta Quit Kickin' My Dog Around." "Well I had an old hound and his name was Jake / I found him out in the old canebrake / I figger'd he'd make a real good hound / soon as he learned his way around . . ."

Willie Nelson had moved to Austin too and it wasn't long before we got a tour with him up to West Texas and back. Besides seeing Willie from a distance at Mother Earth, I had never met him. The first show was in Abilene at the Municipal Auditorium. We drove up to the loading dock and there was a small RV parked in front of the backstage doors. On the front of the RV was a sign that read "Remember Me." Willie and his drummer Paul English were in the RV playing chess. Paul was mysterious and looked like the devil. He was funny, had an odd way of talking, and acted like a character out of a Western novel. Willie had started to grow his hair long and was working on a beard like ours. With our red beards Murphey, Willie, Gary, and I looked like brothers from different mothers.

Willie and Paul were set to play the show, just the two of them. On the spur of the moment, Willie asked Gary to play bass with him that night. Gary didn't know the material all that well, but he got through it fine. Then we played in Lubbock, my hometown, and Tony Joe White was also on the bill. I felt a hollowness not knowing a single person I could call up. My parents had long since moved back to San Antonio and I was no longer close to anyone in the Hub City. During the show, I kept thinking that someone I knew would walk through the door. It turns out that some old friends did walk in but couldn't get near the backstage to say hello. Regardless, Tony Joe was great, first time I'd ever seen him live.

I can't quite remember our mode of transportation, but I am sure it was supremely funky. A van, maybe, or two cars. Murphey never had a bus when I was with him. We played in Arlington the next night, but the crowd was nothing to write home about. None of the crowds were good on that tour. Most of West Texas didn't even know who Murphey or Willie was. Willie at that time was trying to get his story out. There was a vast collection of his classic songs that others had recorded that the folks who didn't show up to these performances would have loved and then could have said, "I was there."

Back in Austin we played the Armadillo for two nights to enthusiastic audiences who were glad to be where the total buzz was. In October we played two shows at Castle Creek with Murphey. Castle Creek was one of the hottest clubs in Austin. It was owned by Tim O'Connor who had come to town with only a wooden sign that read "Castle Creek," which he nailed on the door. Jerry Jeff rambled in right before the show was to begin and surprised us in the little backstage area, telling us he had just received a package from the mastering plant at MCA with mixes of the new album. This was it! He wanted to have a listening party later that night . . . at my house. He had already invited a lot of people, so what could I do? Castle Creek was jammed with Austin fans and we tore it up. Everybody sang along with many of the songs, especially "Geronimo's Cadillac." Murphey had taken to wearing all white onstage and with his long blond hair and red beard, he looked like the Methodist picture of Jesus. Murphey sang, "Jesus told me and I believe it's true / the red man is in the sunset too." Jesus appears in several of Murphey's songs, so I guess he must think about Him a lot.

After the show, Jerry Jeff bought a couple of cases of beer and scrounged up a reel-to-reel tape recorder and some speakers so he had everything he needed, he thought. The whole band, and friends they invited to hear the new record, were at my place. Everybody was having a lot of fun playing guitars and listening to Pink Floyd's *Dark Side of the Moon* on the stereo. It was a beautiful Austin night. My earth mother Iris was in the kitchen cooking fried green tomatoes.

After a couple of hours, around 2 a.m., Jerry Jeff went out to his car and got the tape recorder and the speakers and handed everything, including the tapes, to a fellow who knew what was what and started putting it all together. The tape recorder man said, "Hey, where's the amplifier so I can plug the speakers in?"

Jerry Jeff said, "What are you talking about? Amplifier? Just plug the speakers into the tape recorder."

The guy said, "No, no, you have to have an amplifier, the speakers can't plug straight into the tape recorder!"

It suddenly dawned on Jerry Jeff that he hadn't gotten everything he needed after all. The beer, the food, the tape recorder, the speakers, yes—but he hadn't thought to bring an amplifier with him. That broke the chain. It was late and we couldn't go anywhere to rustle up an amplifier at that hour. The full impact of not being able to listen to the tapes *right now* hit him like a Muhammad Ali punch in the gut. To say that Jerry Jeff was disappointed in the extreme didn't cover it. He boiled over and in three seconds flat he went into a rage. Some of it was very comical and symbolic.

He grabbed the reels of tape and ran out to the winding country road in front of my house, holding on to one end of a tape and sailing the reel off into the distance, unwinding most of it. He did the same to the second tape, and we watched it unspool and disappear into the night. A long line of tape.

He abruptly turned and barged back into the house and soon the party guests started leaving in droves. He calmed down at some point and picked up his guitar. We were listening to some music on the stereo and he was tapping the base of his guitar in time to the music. The way Jerry Jeff would explain it later was that while he was keeping the beat with the guitar he heard a slight crack in the bottom and he decided to just "GO, GO, GO right through with it!" And he began pounding it harder and harder and finally the guitar splintered.

After the demise of said guitar, Jerry Jeff poured a can of beer on my head and squashed an avocado on the wall. Quite a statement. At one point, Iris chased him around the kitchen table with a cast iron skillet. He was begging for something to happen. And it did. He began swinging and all hell broke loose and we found ourselves in the brawl described in chapter 1. Go back and read it again to get the full effect......... I'm waiting . . .

We each took our lumps and were scratched and bleeding from the rocking and rolling on the sharp rocks poking up from the ground. I got to my feet breathing hard. Jerry stood up and in rare silence he headed for his car. It was a beautiful old restored '39 Plymouth, a convertible. He was parked in front of my mailbox and I said, "Jerry Jeff, don't go." His car began to roll. "Hey, Jerry Jeff! Don't run over my mailbox . . ." That was all he needed to hear: he gunned it and smashed into my painted country mailbox and sent it spinning. He raced off down the quiet lane, tires squealing, dogs barking everywhere. Back in the house, Iris and Jerry Jeff's girlfriend Murphy Stadler were in shock. We were all in shock. I don't remember how Murphy got home; maybe she slept on the couch. Nobody said much. We cleaned up everything in silence and went to bed and tried to sleep.

Early the next morning the phone began ringing and on the other end was a gravelly cracked voice. I knew whose it was.

"Hello?"

"Bob . . . this is Jerry Jeff. Hello? Hello??"

"Yeah, I can hear you."

"I need help. Can you come get me? Can you?"

"What are you talking about? Help for what?"

"After I left your house I couldn't drive. I ran off the road through a bob-wire fence. I've got some problems here. Can you come get me?"

I thought about it. "Yeah, I'll come get you."

He was calling from a house near the lake but in the woods. He gave me the address and I drove over there and it was indeed a pitiful sight. The beautiful car had gone through a fence and the bob-wire was wrapped around all four axles. There were three flat tires. Jerry Jeff was sitting on the back bumper. We looked at each other and broke into laughter. The whole mess had to be towed away and fixed up to live another day. Jerry Jeff couldn't remember most of the night before but was all apologies, and neither he nor I ever held it against each other. I don't think.

The new album was called *Jerry Jeff Walker*. His face was on a brown cover, rough-and-tumble ragged, with energy bursting out of the seams. There is an indefinable approach to the songs that was different than any other Texas record at the time. Nashville was king but Austin was era-defining with new music emerging every day. Jerry Jeff believed heart and soul in the songs and in this new sound. He wanted it to sound live, like we were performing at a party. And the recording sessions *were* a party. He was determined to go against convention and record at his own rather than at a record company's comfort level, which you couldn't fathom anyway.

He was singing genuine out-of-the-box tunes, some really good and considered great in certain quarters—late at night, out on a fishin' boat or at the tail end of a fraternity party. One rabid Jerry Jeff fan told me that when the drunken frat parties were over and the guys had taken their dates home and gone back to the fraternity house where there was beer . . . that's when they put on the Jerry Jeff.

Jerry Jeff never told us what to play but counted on us to make it gonzo. There was a lot of movement in those songs and the recording sessions were full of stories, both in the song and out. Jerry Jeff was there at every stage of the recording and production. Sometimes he'd drive the engineers crazy. He pored over photos and wanted the perfect visual. He insisted that everything be done his way and he made sure it sounded right and that he liked what he was hearing and if anybody doubted what was going on in this funky-ass studio they didn't need to be around there. Jerry Jeff wanted to capture the moment, of playing guitars late into the night, of our drinking sangria and telling stories and learning new chords. Eccentricities were encouraged at all times. We played on the record with youth and vigor. The band's approach was to follow Jerry Jeff "Mr. Bojangles" Walker wherever he went and to add some turns and twists of our own whenever possible. I feel we were successful in that endeavor.

All things considered, Brovsky did a pretty good job with Jerry Jeff, lacing up the patchwork of songs into a relatively cohesive and much-loved record. The best move Brovsky made was to flow with it and let Jerry Jeff and the band do it our way. Jerry Jeff undoubtedly knew he was onto something with this particular group of musicians. He had faith in the songs and in the down-home lo-tech recording process. It was different than anything he'd ever done. It was different than anything any of us had ever done, and there was a change in all of us and it was infectious.

The record that MCA was given caused quite a stir among the brass in Hollywood. They had never had an album like this to promote. It wasn't rock, it wasn't country. It was as raw as it gets. It was before Johnny Rotten. They didn't know what to make of it. But Mike Maitland, president of MCA, made the decision. He didn't understand this wild unvarnished project but there was something there. He must have had a hunch because he went with it.

Thank God Jerry Jeff's contract with MCA said they had to release whatever he gave them. I heard that when Willie Nelson recorded *Red Headed Stranger* he was rumored to have said that "the record company *has* to release whatever I give 'em, like in Jerry Jeff's contract." JJ's album was released mid-1972 to some fanfare. It sold well and people took notice. MCA was pleased, considering what could have happened. Nobody knew much about this demographic of album buyers or about the music they liked. But the audience for the music we were playing was growing. "L.A. Freeway," the first single, would peak just inside the top 100 at 98 on Billboard. It was a worldwide release on a major record label and it followed close behind Murphey's *Geronimo's Cadillac*. It looked good for all of us. Jerry Jeff, Murphey, and the city of Austin were getting a lot of attention in the press. The progressive country scare was unfolding. Only now can I see it.

CHAPTER 23

I Just Want to Be a Cosmic Cowboy

1972–73

In those days the major record labels required many of their artists to produce at least one album a year, and Murphey and Jerry Jeff were no exceptions. From 1972 onward into the '80s, it was a new album every year no matter what. In late October of'72 we began rehearsals for a new Murphey record that would be called *Cosmic Cowboy Souvenir*. We chose my bucolic cabin on Lake Travis as the perfect space for a band to rehearse and let the music spill out like wildfire.

Things had taken an ominous turn that stemmed from our East Coast tour. Michael was having a hard time singing; his voice became raspy and sounded like a tumbleweed blowing past. He was diagnosed with nodules on his vocal cords, right before rehearsals were to begin. We had been out touring hard and I think that Little Richard must have possessed Murphey just like he'd possessed Paul McCartney, and Murphey had pushed his voice to the limit singing songs like "Harbor for My Soul" and other rockers, with whoops and impossible screams. I think the keys for many of the songs were too high and he had to really push it night after night. We were a band full of color and individuality and we played loud with lead guitars and steel guitars and sang our heads off. Murphey was spurred on and he rode above all of this taking vocal chances he'd probably never taken before.

He had blown his voice out. It could be repaired if he would follow his doctor's orders. And those orders were not to sing, or even speak a word, for the next seven weeks after the surgery. But there was an album to be done, and the pressure was on to stay on schedule. That was a bad decision on everybody's part: the record company, Murphey's management, and Murphey himself. They should have let him get well, reschedule a month later. But maybe it was a case of keeping your record deal at any cost, no matter what it does to you. I myself have been down on my knees in a studio trying to sing past a badly torn voice and going to any measure to get there when I should have been home in bed. *Geronimo's Cadillac* had made a respectable debut, and A&M Records wanted a follow-up ready ASAP. They stuck with the schedule.

All the while Murphey had been writing songs. They were hot off the press, and he had never actually sung many of them. We had to come up with a way to rehearse everything without his singing. So I became Murphey's voice. Every day before the band got to my cabin, Michael would show up about 10 a.m. with song lyrics and instructions all written out on a yellow legal pad. I still have some of these pages. Here is a typical entry: "Wrote new song 'Blessing in Disguise.' Go to piano, I'll whistle the melody." He began playing the chords and whistled the melody and I followed along as best I could, learning as he was whistling, and I would sing it out and if that wasn't right he would shake his head vigorously, *No no no, that's not it.* The next time through he nodded his head even more vigorously as if to say, *You got it!*

Then the band would arrive and we would run down the new songs. I'd read notes about them that Murph had written out and then I'd sing them. This curious technique of learning and presenting the song became the template for working out all the arrangements for the album. Murphey also responded on the fly, writing comments for me to read: "McGeary, do a fill coming into last verse"; "Craig, you and Herb split leads."

We managed this way and since these were great songs we had a blast playing them. But there was a lot of frustration and tension building in Murph. I didn't know it at the time, but the doctor had told him he could never play in a smoky club or bar again, and smoky bars and clubs like the Saxon Pub and the Armadillo were all we played. Murphey was sweating bullets and thinking about how he would make a living, how it would all pan out. We were all wondering the same thing.

We were paid $75 a week for two weeks of rehearsals. Murphey told us, "Don't worry, boys, we'll all make good money when we make the record." Coincidentally, my electric bill came a few days after rehearsals ended. The total was almost $250, which is something like $1,600 today. Up to then, electricity had been around $25 a month—those electric guitar amps were sucking a lot of juice five to six hours a day. When we met at my house to discuss the Nashville recording trip—Murphey had found his voice again and was telling us about the motel where we'd stay—I asked if he could help me with the bill. He paused and then said, "We *all* have to give 100 percent and if *you* can't give it . . . then you're fired!" This was in front of the whole band. I may have told him I was going to kill him if he didn't get out of there immediately. After he left, we sat around in silence. Gary said, "He'll forget all about it. He won't fire you." Sure enough, early the next morning Murphey called me to say, "Forget everything I said yesterday. We are all going to Nashville to record as soon as they can find studio time." We left for Nashville a week or so later. The electric bill was never mentioned again.

We recorded some of the rehearsals. John Inmon, who would later go on to play with Gary and me in the Lost Gonzo Band, was the engineer. John was gifted, a lead guitarist who could

Bob Livingston, Jerry Jeff Walker, and Michael Murphey at the Kerrville Folk Festival, 1973. (Photo courtesy of JLS Hall.)

shred it. He had played in a band with Gary called Lavender Hill Express. John had a 4-track reel-to-reel TEAC tape recorder co-owned with his brother Jim, a talented mixer and sound guy who would go on to work with Frank Zappa—if that isn't gonzo, I don't know what is. Gary asked John to bring the tape machine and record all the songs. We set the gear up in my spare bedroom with wires running everywhere. Overnight my place had become a recording studio. I loved everything about it.

These rehearsals were held during the daylight hours so the band was free to play some shows with Jerry Jeff at night. We played the Armadillo and more shows throughout November and December. An eventful year was winding down. And we were still *Murphey's* band. But that was about to change.

In January 1973 we headed for Nashville for the *Cosmic Cowboy* sessions. We recorded at Ray Stevens's studio on Music Row. Remember Ray Stevens? "Ahab the Arab"? He'd made a lot of money as a songwriter and had built a world-class studio that was booked 24/7 and had produced major hits.

Bob Johnston was once again driving the boat, but the tone

and vibe with Murphey was different this time around. Michael got his voice back but not fully and he was uptight. He'd been under a lot of pressure and was about ready to bust. A&M wasn't cutting him any slack and I think his New York managers were pushing him to record before he was ready.

It was late morning on January 16, 1973. We were in the studio, sitting in our places with our instruments, tuning up. We hadn't even warmed up yet. No 12-bar blues to shake out the cobwebs and loosen up. Then Murphey said into the open mic, "Okay, we're going to cut "Cosmic Cowboy" and if we don't get it on the first take, it won't be on the album. Count it off, McGeary!" "Cosmic Cowboy," the great song that the record would be based on, would not be on the album if we didn't get it on the "first take." It was a startling statement and was hard to absorb.

After hearing the playback, Bob Johnston calmed Murphey down and loosened him up. We all loosened up. In the end, we made a magical record away from all the drama and tension. I sang all the background vocals and Murphey gave me credit on the album as "The Robert Livingston Uncivil Opera Appears by Permissiveness."

The songs were brilliant and funky. Funky good. Listen to "Temperature Train." The studio had a lot of different instruments scattered around and Bob Johnston was forever egging us on to try new things and go for it. Gary made a Moog synthesizer sound like a Viking horn on "South Canadian River Song." We were already doing "Harbor for My Soul" in our live shows and we got a great live cut. "Cosmic Cowboy," "Prometheus Busted," "Blessing in Disguise," "Drunken Lady of the Morning," and "Rolling Hills" were all remarkable and soulful. Murphey had written most of them for this record in a fairly depressed and fearful state. Is that not amazing?

We recorded *Cosmic Cowboy Souvenir* in three 10-hour days. The album would do nothing less than launch the Cosmic

Cowboy progressive country music era. We didn't know that then, of course, but we knew that we had hit a sweet spot and had done something special.

The next morning we went to the studio to listen to all we had done. Bob Johnson and the engineer had a reasonable mix up and everything sounded terrific and wondrous. Our part of the recording was done and we were going back to Austin the next day. Envelopes with paychecks for our work were handed out and we were flabbergasted and disappointed with the paltry amount we received. Murphey's hard-assed New York managers were running the show now and they must have taken us for rubes who would play for anything so they paid us far less than what the Nashville Musicians Union said we were owed. Same as it ever was. We lit a fuse when we called the musicians' union whose president was as hard-assed as any of Murphey's New York managers. Murphey would have to pay us what we were owed. Needless to say, it did not go down well with him or his managers. So . . . we were fired. It was as if a line had been drawn in the sand and we were put in an unacceptable position. Everyone in the band but Gary stepped over the line and fired themselves.

We walked out of the studio into the bright sunshine of a crisp January day. We had just recorded what some would say was a masterpiece and now we were walking away from it. Walking down Music Row past the record companies, RCA, Warner Brothers, and Columbia. Past the publishing houses of Acuff Rose, Tree Music, and Universal. Past the kid with a guitar about to knock on Atlantic Records' door. We were passing it all by as we made our way to the band van for the long drive back to Austin with our brooding thoughts.

Bob Johnston caught up with me and said, "Don't worry, man. I'm going to get you back. It'll all come out all right. Murphey needs you. Just be cool." This was the second time Bob had intervened to get me back in the fold. But this time, it was not to be.

Things were moving too fast and the die was cast. Or as we used to say in the Gonzo Band, "the cast is dead." We were on our way back to Austin eventually to join up with Jerry Jeff for good. Everybody was going back . . . everybody but Gary Nunn. He stayed on in Nashville with Murphey and told me at the time that Michael needed somebody to stand by him. And that was probably true.

It wasn't until a few years ago that I finally learned what Gary was really thinking when he didn't return with the rest of us to Austin. Gary and I were being interviewed for a documentary in Luckenbach, and we were reliving that incomprehensible day in the Nashville studio. We had decided to go to the musicians' union and fight for our rights. Eventually we would get paid what we were owed, but I had never been sure why Gary stayed on with Murphey and I had felt a little betrayed at the time. He and I were best friends and roommates but there was some distance between us for a while.

During the interview Gary said, "I had a song on *Cosmic Cowboy*. It was the first song I had ever recorded on a major record label." The song in question was "Song of the South Canadian River." Gary had composed the music and Murphey had written the lyrics. It was a brilliant, orchestrated piece, one of a kind. Gary said he thought that if he had left with the rest of us Murphey just might have taken his song off the album. "This was a big chance for me and I just couldn't let that happen over a few hundred dollars." At last I understood what Gary had been thinking and I could see and appreciate his reasoning. It turned out to be an auspicious decision because for his loyalty, Michael took Gary with him off to London to mix *Cosmic Cowboy Souvenir* at Abbey Road Studios. On that fateful trip Gary wrote "London Homesick Blues" and changed Texas country music forever.

As for me, when all that went down in the studio, the ball—already rolling fast—picked up speed and turned into a blur. I didn't have to leave with the others. I could've stayed on with Murph, maybe even gone to London. But we'd taken a vote, and I had to stick by mine. That door had closed. It was time to see what lay beyond behind the next one.

CHAPTER 24

¡Viva Terlingua!

1972–73

Bumping along in the back seat of our gonzo van from Nashville to Austin, I tried to process the events that had unfolded. We had just thrown our hearts and souls into recording a new album with Michael Murphey and now our connection with *Cosmic Cowboy* had been tossed out the back door. In the most basic of terms, we were all in need of an immediate infusion of cash no matter how small and I was mulling over my options, which weren't many. A couple of days after I got home I called Jerry Jeff and told him what had happened in Nashville. He was happy as a clam because that meant we were free to be a part of the new record he was planning and beyond that to the tours that would follow.

Jerry Jeff wasted no time in getting us over to his house out on Camp Ben McCulloch Road for a meeting. He told us about Luckenbach, the little town outside of Fredericksburg, and how he wanted to record his next album live there in the town dance hall. He said he was still working it out but had found someone in New York who owned a mobile recording studio in a bus and had secured his services to come down at the end of the summer and set up in Luckenbach to record. That sounded good to us and suddenly before the sun had set we were out of Murphey's frying pan and into Jerry Jeff's raging fire.

Meanwhile, we had a lot of work with Jacky Jack before the recording was scheduled to kick off. Gary was in England with Murphey, and who knows what was going on? We played at Castle Creek to try it all out. Jerry Jeff, Michael McGeary, Craig Hillis, Herb Steiner, and me. At that time, Herb was just sitting in. Jerry Jeff didn't know him very well even though Herb had played on that first MCA record, the Brown Album. After the first set at Castle Creek Jerry Jeff confided that he thought Herb was playing too much and too loud. He wasn't used to the steel. McGeary told Herb to "tone it down a bit. Don't be so busy." Herb followed McGeary's advice and after a more nuanced second set Jerry Jeff was sold and confident enough in Herb's skills to ask him to join the band full-time and to come to Luckenbach to record with us. We played a few more shows in August, winding up at Liberty Hall in Houston, a great venue full of our growing audience tapestry. Colorful long-haired men and earth mothers were swaying and dancing dreamlike, sometimes with kids in tow. There were many short-hairs there too, crewcuts and nicely parted heads against the cowlicks. Everyone was having a great time drinking beer and singing along as Jerry Jeff showed off his powerful new folk country band.

At the end of March, Murphey and Gary came back from England. Gary was depressed about the trip because he was homesick and not really making any money. But we roped him into coming with us to play a five-night stand at Kenny's Castaways in New York City. Jerry Jeff always played in New York. It was his home turf and a lot of folk singers and fans there were wondering what had happened to him. He'd gone off the map. This new album had caught a lot of people by surprise. It was far and away different from the Jerry Jeff they knew. It was funky and raw and loud and it resonated with what was going on elsewhere in the country as '70s musicians looked outside the box for something new. Our ragtag Texas band packed Kenny's every night, two shows a night, and *three* shows on Friday and Saturday night. The last show on Saturday started at 2:30 a.m.

After the first show, a reporter for *The New York Times* wrote a review that was very favorable and said Jerry Jeff "was backed up by an adept five-piece cowboy band." The next night during the late show Jerry Jeff pulled out that review and read it to the audience from the stage. It just so happened that there was another reporter from the *Times* in that night's audience who would write yet another review of the show. He misunderstood Jerry Jeff when he was reading the previous review and wrote that "Jerry Jeff Walker was backed up by a four-piece deaf cowboy band." We laughed so hard at that one. When we got back home Jerry Jeff got Michael Priest, one of the great Armadillo artists, to paint a drumhead with an old geezer in a cowboy hat holding an ear horn and the words painted overhead, "The Deaf Cowboy Band." Our first band name.

Stars like Kris Kristofferson, Rita Coolidge, Delaney & Bonnie, Harry Belafonte, and Phoebe Snow came out to the shows. There was a buzz going 'round. They were coming to see what Jerry Jeff was doing next and judging by the crowd's reaction, everyone found the answer. A lot of folkie singer-songwriters and coffeehouse pickers came out. The shows were a radical departure from the folk singer Jerry Jeff they were used to. This was a new and edgy high wire balancing act. The audience was literally dancing and singing in the aisles and Patrick Kenny himself said he'd never seen anything like it in his club.

After the Kenny gigs, Gary went back to Austin to decide what he was going to do with the remainder of his life. Craig Hillis, Michael McGeary, and I did some northwest shows with Jerry Jeff while Gary stayed behind deliberating. We were playing in Seattle and the club was packed, hanging from the rafters. If you died in the crowd you would still remain standing up. During the set, Jerry Jeff broke a string and turned to me and told me to sing something while he changed the string. I remembered the song that Ray Hubbard had written in Red River about the redneck mother. I barely knew it myself, but it only had three chords and a cloud of dust so it wasn't hard to follow. The crowd's reaction was immediate and they roared and sang along.

The next night, we played in Portland at the Roseland Theater, a whale of a building with a dance floor. About halfway through the set, Jerry Jeff turned to me and said, "Play that song about the redneck!" So I sang "Redneck Mother" again and this time we all sorta knew the chords and the band played it great and the place went buggy and people started pouring beer on their heads and singing, "Up against the wall, redneck mother!" Jerry Jeff noted the reaction.

On the third night of the tour we played the Palomino in North Hollywood where movie stars would come for their fix of country music. That night our background singers were Robert Duvall and Will Sampson, the Indian in *One Flew Over the Cuckoo's Nest*. They were doing the "ohs" and "ahs" and Jerry Jeff said, "Let's do 'Redneck Mother' but this time . . . I'm gonna sing it." So it became his song and we played it a few more times on our way back to Texas and the Luckenbach album.

Gary was disillusioned and disgusted with the music business and was threatening once again to leave it and go back to pharmacy school at UT. Jerry Jeff happened to walk into a club in Austin called the Squeeze Inn and found Gary at the bar. He told Gary about his recording plans in Luckenbach, which got Gary's attention. We all talked it over and it seemed like a totally original idea. There was no album concept like it out there. Once again Jerry Jeff's vision, even though he didn't know how to articulate it right then, drew us in.

On Saturday, August 11, 1973, we headed to Luckenbach to start rehearsals. When we arrived we saw the grand shiny bus that was the world-class mobile recording studio parked right next to the dance hall. This was my first trip to Luckenbach, and I didn't know what to think about any of it. It was a wooden town all weathered and worn with one street, a general store and post office on one side and a dance hall on the other. Coming out to greet us was the Prime Minister of Luckenbach, a wizard of a man named Hondo Crouch. He had a business card that read:

> Hondo Crouch
> Imagineer

Hondo was a legendary Texas Hill Country character. He had been an All-American swimmer and became a storyteller bullshitter entertainer, poet, writer, bigger-than-life figure. He owned the whole town of Luckenbach with his partners Guich Koock and a woman named Kathy Morgan who had an airline pilot husband who would buzz the little town in his own plane from time to time. Jerry Jeff had met Hondo a few years earlier and had become pals, hung out with him a lot, and saw him as a father figure. Hondo dispensed sage-like homespun wisdom, cracked jokes, and basically kept everything lively at all times. Hondo's daughter, Becky, a sassy whip smart Texas artist writer if there ever was one, would write about Luckenbach and Hondo in a book called *Hondo, My Father*. Everything you need to know about Hondo and Luckenbach and how it came to be is there.

Michael Brovsky, still Jerry Jeff's manager-producer, had a penchant for bullshit. Brovsky was the man Jerry Jeff turned to when he decided to do something off the beaten path, which was most of the time. The mobile recording studio could record in almost any situation inside or out. They had miles of mic cords. There were only a few of these state-of-the-art mobile studios around at that time, and this one—owned and operated by an outfit called Dale Ashby and Father—was the best. The engineer of the

Playing washers in Luckenbach with Texas legend and "Imagineer," Hondo Crouch. (Photo by Gary P. Nunn.)

album would be Marty Leonard, who called himself Sundance and would later help us record the Lost Gonzo Band's first album. The team was in place.

It was hot in Texas in August 1973 or, as Woody Guthrie said, "It wasn't hot, it was damn hot!" The Ashby outfit had arrived a few days before and had commenced to set everything up, running mic cables and wires into the dance hall and in the trees across the street at the back of the general store. It wasn't long before they realized there wasn't nearly enough electricity in the town to accommodate all those tubes, compressors, power amps, noise reduction units, and guitar and bass amps. But with Hondo's help, the county came out, inspected the scene, and ended up rewiring the whole town for electricity to provide plenty of juice for what was to come.

At the time, I didn't think much about whether we were recording in a studio environment or otherwise. I'd only played on three records up to then. With Murphey we had recorded *Geronimo's Cadillac* and *Cosmic Cowboy Souvenir* in pristine Nashville studios.

With Jerry Jeff, it was pure spur-of-the-moment recording wherever we were. If a track went by that had a mistake—or "clam" in studio parlance—it could either be fixed or disguised or left as it was because Jerry Jeff liked it. Out-of-the-blue harmonies, talking and joking around during the song, were left in the mix. The *Jerry Jeff Walker* album was made in the primitive conditions of Rapps Cleaners and now we were in Luckenbach recording in a wide-open dance hall and outside under the massive oak trees with scorpions crawling up the walls and bandy roosters clucking. It wasn't really any different when we went into Nashville studios later on down the road. Records recorded lickety-split, making it up as we went along, engineers always being caught without the tape moving—it drove them crazy and became a game with Jerry Jeff to try to catch them off guard.

There were no motels or accommodations of any kind in Luckenbach, so the band checked into a cluster of rustic little motel cabins called the Peachtree Inn tucked back a-ways on a side street in nearby Fredericksburg. Out at the site we set our amps up first outside and then inside on the dance floor in front of the stage, picking our spots and settling in around Jerry Jeff who was urgently trying to finish six songs at once. McGeary set up his drums on the stage behind us. We baffled everything with bales of hay and Sundance set up mics on it all. We needed a piano, so we brought mine from Austin, a Baldwin spinet. The leg got busted during the move and the crack is still there.

Michael McGeary had a friend from California named Kelly Dunn who played a Hammond B-3 organ. McGeary told Kelly there was a lot of music being made with these galoots from Texas and if he came to Austin he would blow everyone away with his playing. And he was right about that. Kelly had showed up a few months before and we had all jammed together a few times at Gary's house. Jerry Jeff liked what he heard and asked Kelly to come along to Luckenbach *with* his B-3. After we set everything up, a couple of gals showed up. "Sweet Mary" Egan was a fiddler from Austin, a virtuoso with soul who played with a band called Greezy Wheels. Joanne Vent, who sang with a gospel voice, fit right in on some of the background vocals.

This was the general daily order of things: We would wake up at the cabins late, eat breakfast in town, and get out to Luckenbach around 2 p.m. When we pulled up, Jerry Jeff would be mixing up a batch of sangria wine in a big galvanized tub. We would hang out for a while, watch the sky and the clouds drift by, drink some sangria, start to fool around with our instruments, and jam, getting loose.

The band was Jerry Jeff on guitar, Herb Steiner on steel, Gary Nunn on piano, Michael McGeary on drums, Kelly Dunn on Hammond B-3, Craig Hillis on lead guitar, Sweet Mary on fiddle; Joanne Vent joined in whenever things needed a feisty edge. I played bass and sang the harmonies to the high heavens. Willie's harmonica player, Mickey Raphael, showed up just in the nick of time to play on a few songs. Don't ask me why, but I thought Mickey looked like an Egyptian pharaoh.

Jerry Jeff had three or four songs he knew he wanted to do: "Little Bird," a song he had recorded before; "I Like to Sleep Late in the Morning," by a folksinger friend, David Blue; and Guy Clark's "Desperados Waiting for a Train." The rest of the album was up for grabs and would be recorded on the fly.

The first song we cut was "I Like to Sleep Late in the Morning." Then came Murphey's great barroom ballad from *Geronimo's Cadillac*, "Backslider's Wine." Herb Steiner added a weepy country steel.

Jerry Jeff made up a song, seemingly on the spot, a two-beat called "Gettin' By." The verses were different every time he sang it. "Hi, buckaroos, Scamp Walker time again . . . think it's time to slide one by you once more . . ." Forever after, Jerry Jeff opened his shows with "Gettin' By." He also wanted to get his recipe for sangria wine down in a song, so he wrote "Sangria Wine" with his ingredients of "lemons and limes . . . and tacos, nachos, and burritos, who knows . . ." We tried it a few different ways: country, rock, bluegrass. Somebody said we should play it reggae, even though most of us didn't really know what reggae was, much less how to play it. But Michael McGeary, who had dabbled around the smoky rasta edges of reggae music back in LA, gave us some ideas. He had Craig Hillis play what would turn out to be the signature guitar lick that begins the song—"deda-dedel-le, deda dedel-le." He told me to play something on the bass that was an answer to Craig—"dum-dum, da-dum." There were plucking steel and fiddle parts and B-3 in there, too. It sounded funky, it was country reggae, and it worked. "In Austin on a Saturday night, man, it's time to make up some Sangria wine . . ." Even the crickets were singing in time! Hondo was always hanging around with us, and when we sang the chorus, he sang along, "Oh, oh oh oooh-oooh oh, I LOVE . . . San-gri-a wine!"

Next was Jerry Jeff's own song, "Get It Out," an off-kilter rocker. Guy Clark's "Desperados Waiting for a Train" was somber and floaty with the train screaming off into the distance at the end and Craig playing a Les Paul full of steam and smoke.

We recorded everything mostly dead-on and only overdubbed some background vocals, "oohs" and "ahhs" and "fight for your rights!" on "Backslider's Wine." Locals and tourists would wander into the dance hall to listen and sometimes sing along. Everything was wide open and had a live feel to it and Brovsky and Sundance captured everything. We were making progress, but we needed something else to kick things into higher gear. Jerry Jeff decided to do a live concert on Saturday night and record it all. Somebody made up some flyers advertising the show with $1 admission.

It was August and the flyers worked wonders. Several hundred people from all over the Texas Hill Country turned out and crowded into Luckenbach and the dance hall. It was

Someone passed along a few rare photos taken during the recording of *¡Viva Terlingua!* inside the Luckenbach Dancehall. Far as I can tell, they're the only known shots from *inside* the hall during the recording. (Photographer unknown; photo courtesy of Bob Livingston.)

triple-standing-room-only: redneck farmers, cowboys and hippies, frat boys and sorority girls, bankers, carpenters, hucksters, preachers and teachers. All literally hanging from the rafters and standing on tiptoe looking over shoulders into the windows and doorways, trying to see and hear and be a part of it, spilling out into the street and over to the general store where long-neck Lone Star beer was the order of the day. The mystery, excitement, and anticipation of the event were palpable. We were used to playing for packed houses with hell-raising crowds, but this night was something special and magical. It was only later that I understood how historical it was.

We climbed in over the crowd, took our positions, picked up our guitars, and kicked it off. At first, we did songs from the Brown Album: "Hill Country Rain," "Charlie Dunn," and a screaming version of "L.A. Freeway." We played some of the songs we had recorded earlier in the week, but none of these Saturday night takes ended up making the cut for the album, though we did catch a couple of spontaneous spur-of-the-moment keepers that night.

Jerry Jeff wanted to record "Redneck Mother" but said it needed a third verse: "All it is is two verses and the choruses and you do that weird spelling thing." I called Ray Hubbard up to see if he had left anything out. Hubbard couldn't believe we were recording his song and mumbled a crazy third verse that never made the final cut. When we did it that night in Luckenbach, it was the first time most of the crowd had ever heard it but they got the words fast and sang louder than the band on the choruses.

In the intro to "Redneck" I said something like, "Here's a song by Ray Wylie Hubbard!" Later, during the mix-down, Jerry Jeff decided to leave this little shout-out on the record, and after a few months of the new record's release, a few hundred thousand people knew Ray Wylie's name and that he had written "Redneck Mother." It was also the first time Ray's middle name "Wylie" was heard publicly, and it stuck. He has been known as Ray Wylie ever since.

Earlier in the week, sitting under the massive Luckenbach oak trees, Gary sang the song he'd written in England, "London Homesick Blues." It was mostly a true story, an autobiographical account. Gary had been depressed and homesick and it was all in the song. It had been the worst winter in London in twenty years and it was cold as a witch in a flat that Murphey had arranged for him. To save energy, during the day the landlord would turn off the heat in all the flats. He probably thought, concerning his tenants, "You need to be at a job or in school. I'm not going to heat you during the day." Gary was cold and lonely when he reached for the guitar in the corner, and the first thing out of his mouth was, "It's cold over here and I swear I wish they'd turn the heat on."

So he brought "London Homesick Blues" to Luckenbach and played it for us one afternoon under the oaks. It begins with "It's cold over here," and I had an idea that he should kick it off with his second verse, "When you're down on your luck and you ain't got a buck in London you're a goner." I felt he should get to the London part right away.

We all knew "London Homesick" was special, but what happened that Saturday night with the song was pure magic. We had just played "L.A. Freeway" and Jerry Jeff suddenly turned to Gary and said, "Play that song about London you sang yesterday!" We had never had a chance to rehearse it and didn't really know it. We had only heard it once. Gary went with it and started singing it slow and uncertain while we struggled with the edges. After a couple of verses and choruses, however, we knew the changes and the words, and as the song progressed and the choruses came drifting by, the crowd took to it as their own. When we got to the last choruses of "London Homesick Blues" that night, we just kept singing it over and over: "I wanna go home with the Armadillo . . ." Everyone was singing along maybe ten choruses, maybe a hundred: ". . . good country music from Amarillo to Abilene." The crowd wouldn't let us stop. The crescendo and the end, the roar and urgency from the crowd, otherworldly. I at least had never experienced anything like it. And then I wanted everyone, including whoever might be listening to the record later on, to know that Gary Nunn had sung it and not Jerry Jeff. So I yelled, "That was Gary P. Nunn!" The dance hall had turned into bedlam, with people screaming and cheering. What a reaction!

Mr. Producer Brovsky came running out of the mobile unit and shouted to us, "That was great, but the tape broke. You have to do it again." We were wild-eyed and breathing hard from the thrill of the crowd and getting through the song. And now we had to gather ourselves up and do it again. That was when Gary says on the recording, "I have to put myself back in that place." So, we played it a second time and this time the audience knew what was coming and sang on all the choruses. "London Homesick Blues" would go on to be one of the great Texas anthems and the theme song to *Austin City Limits*. I can't imagine Texas music without it.

After that Saturday night's mythmaking, we slept in Sunday morning to early afternoon, but we all wanted to get back out to Luckenbach to listen to what we had done that week. Jerry Jeff, who was probably staying at Hondo's house through all of this, had gone on ahead. The night before, someone in the crowd had given the band some organic something or other, and that morning everybody decided, *what the heck, we're off work*, so we all took a bit of that. Ready or not, here we come. Now, I'm not saying it was a good thing to do or a bad thing to do, or that I'm proud of it, or not proud of it. I wouldn't do it now, but the point is we *did* it then and that's all there was to it.

As we drove back into the rapidly changing Luckenbach landscape, my consciousness was altered in a definitive way. The dance hall swayed back and forth from the heavy rhythms of the night before and soon it changed into a beautiful shade of lavender blue and it scooped us up and took off and flew to Paris, with us in it. Down below, we saw Jerry Jeff waving. I guess he got our attention because we swooped back down closer to the ground. Jerry Jeff ran up to us and snagged our boot heels, dragging us back down to earth, announcing "Hey, I just remembered, we have *one* more song to do!" Holy moly! How are we going to manage *this*?

We pulled ourselves together and went to work. It was called "Wheel," an old song Jerry Jeff had around for a while but had never recorded. It was packed with great imagery, and each chorus ended with "the wheel kept spinning 'round." If you listen to that cut, you can hear the ebb and flow of the broken wheel and some pretty psychedelic musical sketches painted right in there. As for myself, I was holding on to my bass and to reality for dear life, trying to play something coherent. It's a wonder I ever made it out alive and without horns.

All week long a photographer and good friend of Jerry Jeff's, Jim McGuire, had been snapping photos for cover ideas. He'd taken a shot of Hondo's hand pointing to a bumper sticker by Rusty Cox advertising the Terlingua Chili Cookoff that was pasted on the door of the dance hall. Jerry Jeff saw that photo and decided it was the cover shot, and the record became *¡Viva Terlingua!* It made no sense to call the album that because we were in Luckenbach, but that was what was so good about it. As the Gonzos used to say, *What it is, what it is . . .*

With that, we stuck a fork in the recording and called it done. It was being mixed and the cover was taking shape, but the band still didn't have a name. Then, a couple of weeks later, we were on our way to a gig at Castle Creek, a funky club in Austin. We were riding in Gary's Checker cab he had bought in New York and spray-painted black like a cosmic limo. The Checker was perfect for a band. The back seat was way back there and there was plenty of floor space for amps and drums. I know exactly what kind of car it was and how it rode and how much space there was because the year after I borrowed that black Checker limo from Gary to bring Iris and our brand-new baby son, Tucker Boots, home from the hospital.

On the day of Jerry Jeff's wedding, Iris (holding baby Tucker) and I walked into the frame and Scott snapped the shutter. (Photo by Scott Newton.)

Gary was driving. Hillis was trying out an Eric Clapton riff. Cowboy Herb was holding court on stocks and bonds, and

McGeary was going on about something or other. We were a band without a name, no identity. I used to introduce the band at shows. I'd always come up with a different name: "Jerry Jeff Walker and the Unborn Calves" or "The Rodeo-dee Riff Raff" or "The Bluebonnet Plague."

I was in the back seat reading Hunter Thompson's *Fear and Loathing in Las Vegas*. It was gonzo this and gonzo that. There were gonzo states of being, and one of the characters was called Dr. Gonzo. I said, "Hey, boys, let's be the gonzo band tonight. The Lost Gonzo Band." Now *that* stuck! Gonzo described us to a tee and especially it described ol' Jerry Jeff. After I introduced us he said, "Now, I like *that* one." Nobody knew exactly what gonzo meant but it sounded like us and it sounded especially like Jerry Jeff. After all he was as gonzo as you could get, just south of Hunter Thompson. So the Lost Gonzo Band, in name and in spirit, first appeared on the inside cover of *¡Viva Terlingua!* with a double-spread sepia photo of all the musicians. You can see it hanging on the wall of the Luckenbach bar.

¡Viva Terlingua! was released in November 1973. After all these years the album still holds water, rough-hewn and real. It's so loose I've had musicians remark to me, "What's the big deal? I could play that. It's so loose and funky. That's why I love it."

Jerry Jeff and the Lost Gonzo Band packed them in wherever we went and everybody in the room knew the words to the songs and sang them louder than us. And everyone who's still alive today who played on that record is still in the game. Viva *¡Viva Terlingua!*

CHAPTER 25

Hard Traveling on the Far World's Roads

1987

Back home Jerry Jeff wasn't touring, so I stayed on in India with Iris and the boys and forgot about Texas for a while. I called my State Department friend, Tim Moore, in Madras and told him John was going home to Texas, but I was sticking around and would be available for shows. This time I wanted to play with some local musicians. Tim said it was an interesting idea, and he knew of available musicians in the different areas and started planning a solo tour for me that would start in a month. While the tour was being planned in far-off New Delhi I was with my sweet family jumping in the river, eating vegetarian, working up my solo set, practicing on my Gibson J-45, and only occasionally going into town for supplies, dodging traffic and flies.

The tours took intense planning from both the State Department and myself. E-mail wasn't yet widely used, so we sent telegrams back and forth with questions and answers. The State Department people are very, very good at what they do. But I had to come to understand that and see it for myself and not be freaked out when they told me about the places I was going, like Pakistan. But they also sent the names of the musicians I was going to meet, rehearse, and play with, so the tour looked promising and exciting.

I played shows in major cities and their surrounding areas. Public and private concerts, schools and community organizations—wherever we could spread the American way. Many of the shows were held in consulates and the corresponding American centers with local tabla and sitar players who were dubious that it would work. But it always did.

Tim asked if, instead of staying in hotels, would I be open to what they called "home hospitality" for accommodations? It was always good to have a nice hotel on the hard road, but occasionally I would stay with a family for the two or three days I was in the area. The State Department would put me in these situations that could have turned out weird I guess but I'd go with it and it was always interesting and enlightening to meet and stay with local families. When I was in Mysore I stayed in the modest home of a wealthy man who owned incense factories. He had an American wife and three children, and the interaction was a good experience for all of us. I'm sure the State Department had an eye on this family for just this type of thing—the cultural aspect. They didn't live in a palace and the wife cooked great authentic local food and we talked endlessly late into the night about our lives. "What's it like to run an incense factory?" "What is your kitchen like in Austin?" The kids called me "Uncle."

It was hard traveling: planes, boats and trains, taxis, and once even on a camel. Okay, it was only a couple of miles, but I lost my harmonica holder on a red sand dune in Rajasthan off the back of a camel. I loved the trains, depending on how long the ride was. I'm sure on many occasions they put me in out-of-reach places they had always wanted to get into but never had such a willing fool to make the hard trek. In my show I told stories the audience could grasp. As I noted before, most people in India

After a State Department performance in a village in Rajasthan, India. The villagers paid me with a goat. (Photo courtesy of Bob Livingston.)

understood some English even in those hard-to-get-to places and it helped if I slowed down my talking and enunciated clearly. I did my best to make sure they could understand me and I knew I was reaching them.

I was traveling with my cowboy hat and my Martin guitar in a gig bag slung over my shoulder. I stuck out in any crowd. I couldn't do anything with that hat but wear it all the time in these railway stations and the un-air-conditioned airports. My boots were stuffed away in my bag to be worn only in the shows. I'd be standing there, as Jimmie Rodgers said, "waiting for a train" and since I was redheaded and freckle-faced, I would have a crowd of people gazing at me in silence. Many of my fellow travelers had never seen anything like me before and they were unabashed gawkers. I had to get used to it and find some kind of comfort level with the mouths hanging open, eyes wide and staring.

A lot of the time I was accompanied by a State Department public affairs officer or an Indian liaison officer. They would go out into the field, travel with me, and conclude all the arrangements that hadn't already been made. These diplomats were all smart and seemed to have it wired. At first, they felt they had to be with me all the time for fear of a repetition of a situation like that of an itinerant blues player from North Carolina named Billy Stevens who went rogue on them. Billy bought a motorcycle and sped off with a young woman on the back—they were never sure whether he was going to turn up at the next gig or not. He never checked in to any of the hotels they had provided but rather would stay with whomever. Then, at the last minute, Billy would walk into the auditorium, set up quickly, and deliver the goods.

Sometimes it was like a spy novel, and I would go with the flow and imagine I was an agent on a big adventure. One night I was on my way to Lucknow for some shows and I was waiting on a lonely railway platform for someone the Department said would show up. As I stood there in the darkness with my guitar and bags, no one else in sight but a few sleepers in the shadows, an Indian man in a threadbare suit appeared out of nowhere asking my name and handing me a package: "Here, Mr. Robert, this is for you." The parcel was bursting with the odor of wonderful South Indian vegetarian food and the aroma made me drastically hungry. The man waited with me without another word until the train came and I was securely packed away on board in my berth and ready for the long haul to Lucknow. His last act was to hand me a folder and have me sign my name that it was all received. Inside were my papers, train tickets, itinerary, correspondence, and even a few press reviews. After my dinner, I crawled into my bunk, this time with blankets and a pillow, and slept the whole night through rocking and rolling across the Indian countryside.

I learned to get around very well in India and later in the other foreign countries, and the key was always English. The King's

First US State Department tour in India, 1987. (L–R): Bob Livingston, bass and guitar; Pinson on drums; John Inmon on guitar; and PAO Tim Moore on banjo. (Photo courtesy of Bob Livingston.)

English, they called it. Our audiences were usually middle-class and upper-echelon folks, businessmen, artists, and media types. I played in Gujarat in the city of Surat, where Mahatma Gandhi had defied the dreaded British salt tax and marched to the sea to make his own salt. At the university, the English professor who introduced me said, "Mr. Bob has come to India to play American country music and to learn the country music of India."

I also played several gigs under the table, and if the government of India knew about it they would get mad for sure. I played a hotel in Bangalore and met the Russian Bolshoi Ballet troupe who were also performing in town. We lounged around the hotel pool during the day and ate papaya with lime. I played for the Nehru Centenary Celebration and brought Iris, Tucker, and Trevor along to be the Livingston Family Singers. There was a big bazaar and festival and a lot of different musics being played so I thought it would work out to have the whole family sing with me. Iris

The Livingston family singing at the Nehru Centenary Celebration, India. (L–R): Tucker, Trevor, Iris, and Bob. (Photo courtesy of Bob Livingston.)

has a pretty voice and we worked up some songs. Thirteen-year-old Tucker was playing pretty good guitar by then and Trevor was learning the mandolin. We all had costumes made by the local tailor with the same hand-loomed fabric and we went over like gangbusters.

We opened with "Country Roads," because it was the most famous song in the world at that time. Everybody in the audience knew at least the chorus and I quickly realized that the way to reach folks who had no idea about American country music was to play "Country Roads." "I'm going to take you walking down some country roads and tell you stories about the beautiful women and ugly men of the Wild West," I'd say, and they would laugh. "Almost heaven, West Virginia . . ." They would think, "Oh, so *this* is country music, okay, I know that song." They're in the pocket on the first song; they're already singing along and clapping.

I know some very rudimentary scales but for the most part Indian music is beyond me. A clerk in a vitamin store once told me he studied Hindustani music, practicing the scales and learning the ragas. Then he woke up one day and realized he had no musical talent whatsoever and his life was wasted. In Pakistan, I did a show at the Islamic Heritage Folk Life Center, and we did a workshop and I played with a world-class sarangi player who was a master of the archaic forty-stringed, bowed instrument. His name was Allah Rakkar. He was one of a kind and among the last sarangi players. He was gruff and reminded me a little of Jerry Jeff. He said that his great-grandfather, grandfather, and father had all played the sarangi and that he only had daughters and "they won't play." The Center was videotaping and recording him play this instrument, capturing it to be archived there forever. That afternoon, we did a workshop together and he could not speak a word of English and of course I could not speak a word of Urdu except for As-Salaam-Alaikum and Khodahafez. Those are my only two Urdu expressions, one a greeting ("Peace be unto you") and the other a response ("God be with you"). Through a translator, Allah Rakkar said it was "an honor" to play with me and I said, "Yes, and I'm just really glad that you can play my songs with me, because there's no way I could do what you do." And he told the translator to tell me, "Tell this man that he speaks the truth."

CHAPTER 26

Collectibles

1973–75ish

With a new Jerry Jeff record to support, we hit the road. Hard. We felt obliged to live up to our new name, the Lost Gonzo Band, and took no prisoners. We were a lot more confident now and played high-energy balls-to-the-wall country rock 'n' roll led by Jerry Jeff's indefatigable spirit. The last song played for the evening was always the encore "Hill Country Rain." Jerry Jeff would come back onstage, with the crowd at a fever pitch, and have his guitar to his ear and get that Strat into an open-C tuning before I'd kick it off on piano. There was a sort of preamble where I sang the chorus slow and dramatic: "I've got a feeling / something that I can't explain / it's like dancing naked / in the high Hill Country rain . . ." Then Jerry Jeff would join in with droning licks while McGeary kept time on the hi-hat. "Sometimes I just wake up hummin' / feelin' that the world is right . . ." On the last choruses the song would crescendo into a wild loop with choruses one after another, Craig ripping hair-raising leads all over the changes. I would stand up from the piano and begin to jump up and down, and we sang "ohos ohos" like the Rolling Stones in "Sympathy for the Devil." Jerry Jeff and Gary would begin to jump up and down too and we would all be bouncing up and down and really rock it and try to blow the roof off and the back wall down and the crowd would go crazy and jump up and down too. The whole place singing and jumping. "Hill County Rain" was the go-to encore song and no matter how much they screamed and cheered Jerry Jeff wouldn't come back out for another one because it was in that open tuning and he didn't want to go to the trouble of getting it back in standard tuning. Well . . . sometimes the crowd would be so insistent we might come back, and if we hadn't played it before, we'd do Willie Nelson's ace in the hole, "Pick Up the Tempo." It was all very exciting and wild and we'd head back to the hotel usually with a slew of hangers-on who wanted to keep it going and party.

News of Jerry Jeff and the Lost Gonzo Band was spreading far and wide and more die-hard fans were signing up for life and the shows were always sold out no matter how big the venue. I watched it all like a movie, the crowd's faces singing between quaffs of beer, people dancing and jumping, dust rising and stage lights flashing.

Many times after shows we went to local FM radio stations and would play live on the air with acoustic guitars and cardboard pizza boxes for drums. There was one station in Gilroy, California, KFAT (the name later changed to KPIG), that broadcast all over the San Francisco area. We'd be there all night playing and spinning our favorite records. It was so much fun.

We had roadies who worked like Trojans on the marathon. We traveled mainly by bus, big Prevost buses with bathrooms and kitchens and bunks, but it was always hard for me to sleep. We would leave after the show and drive 500 miles through the night, guitars out all the time. Jerry Jeff never wanted to go to bed and always wanted to play into the night. He encouraged us all to play our songs too. And Jerry Jeff cut a few of my songs because of this practice. I'd go at it for a while, but I just didn't have the stamina and would always feel like crap the next morning if I pulled an all-nighter.

After a while we started flying and living in and out of major airports. The security was not as tight as it is today, so we traveled with little acoustic instruments to fritter away the hours. I had a Gibson mandolin that never left my side. Gary brought a fiddle he was trying to learn, and Jerry Jeff had a little Gibson that he carried around strapped to his back when he wasn't playing it. We would sit in the lounges and play and Gary and I learned Irish jigs and all of this was done endlessly and the time flew by until we were ready to board. Meanwhile the roadies drove all night with the equipment truck so who knows what kind of shape they were in by the time they arrived to set up.

On one tour we played the Whisky in LA and were staying at the Holiday Inn, a big fifteen-story structure in North Hollywood. Craig was having a hard time on the road and was homesick. He remarked to Jerry Jeff that he was thinking about just jumping off the roof. Breaking the silence, Jerry Jeff said in an up-all-night voice, "Craig if you jumped, knowing your luck you'd see someone in the window you'd like to meet on the way down!" That broke the tension, and we all laughed as it was such an outrageous thing to say. But it wasn't long before Craig left the band and the road. Gary wanted John Inmon to be the next guitar player and everyone readily agreed. And so it would happen that John became a Gonzo.

After the runaway success of *¡Viva Terlingua!*, we began working on an album that would be called *Collectibles*. The old Rapps Cleaners studio where we recorded Jacky Jack's Brown Album had turned into Odyssey Sound, a proper studio with a control room and a massive Neve console separate from the big cutting room. They had a room off to the side with a pool table and vending machines and we spent a lot of time in there too. I asked our manager Brovsky whether, since we had good recording budgets, "Why don't we take some of this money and buy some equipment and record either on the road or even go out to my house

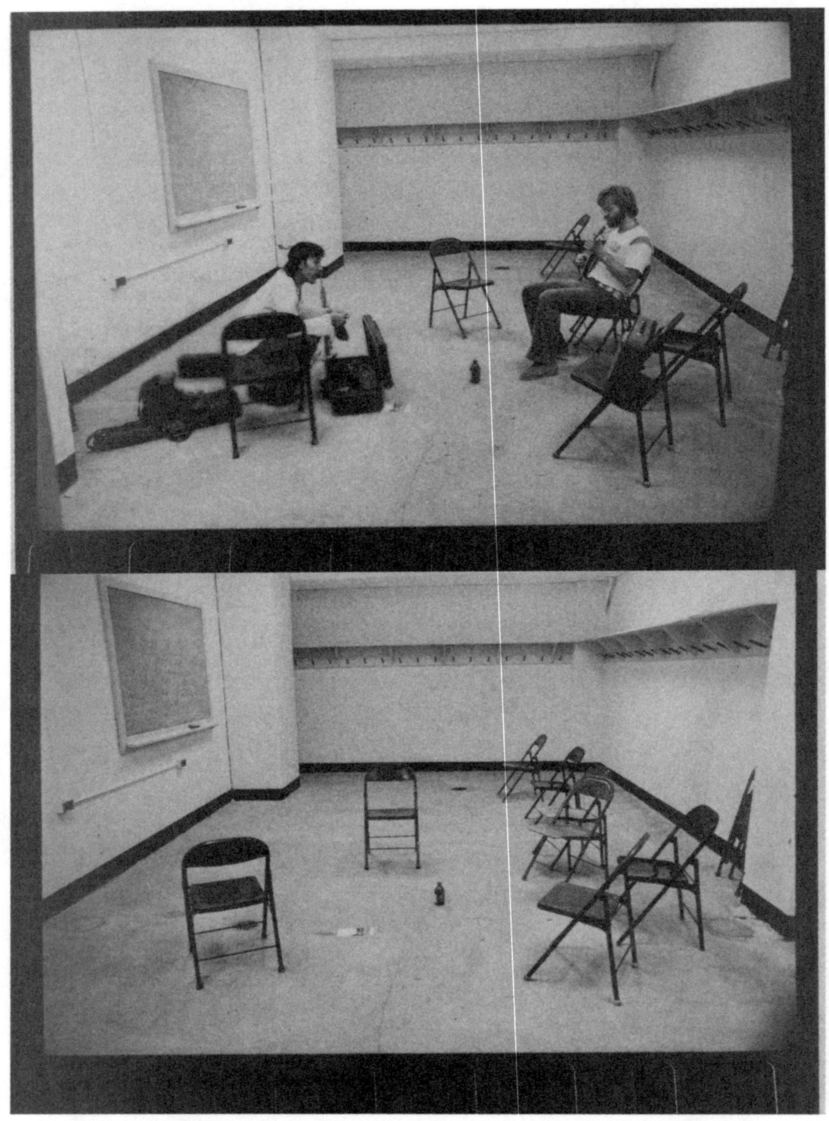

Backstage in Nashville with Tomás Ramirez, 1978. (Photo by Jim McGuire.)

in the country and make records like The Band's *Big Pink*?" But because Brovsky now had a stake in the studio he was making money hand over fist with it and there was no way he was going to let us do that.

Jerry Jeff decided he wanted to have horns on the new album. Mike Mordecai is a local trombone player, arranger, booking agent, and fixer-upper with anything jazz. He sent out a call to all horn players he knew. We assembled at about 7 p.m. and there were eight cats there wetting their reeds and playing runs. A couple of trumpets, three or four saxophones, and a couple of trombones. We started jamming and by 10 p.m. two of the players disappeared. By midnight a couple more had drifted away. At 4:30 in the morning there was only one horn player standing, Tomás Ramirez. The Jazzmanian Devil. One of the hottest sax players alive. He got the gig. Tomás called a couple of his friends, Bill Joor on trumpet and Jim "Squank" Baker on valve trombone, and suddenly we had a three-piece horn section in the Gonzo Band.

The next night we started laying down tracks. It was a drunken wild session with Jerry Jeff making up lyrics on the fly. There was a song called "Will There Be Any (Up in Heaven)." Something about, "Will there be any beer, pool tables, girls up there in Heaven? . . . On our way home tonight there'll be itty-bitty rabbits shining itty-bitty flashlights on the road to make it safe." Something like that. Really out there. It was a crazy song and we did as much laughing as singing. My brother Donald happened to be in Austin on one of the nights of the recordings. He and a Methodist minister friend came down while we were in the middle of recording "Will There Be Any." On the chorus, Gary, John, and I were on our knees with our arms outstretched singing the chorus, "Will there be any up in Heaven? / Lord before I go I've got to know. . . . I've got to know!" The minister friend looked at Donald with amazement and asked, "Are they *really* recording a record?"

When you listen to *Collectibles*, you can tell the mood and the shape everybody was in, loose and ragged. Jerry Jeff didn't really have the songs prepared and we couldn't believe we were making a record either. We cut a new song Jerry Jeff had written about our

Jerry Jeff and the Gonzos sing "Will There Be Any Up in Heaven?" (L–R): John Inmon, Gary Nunn, Donny Dolan, Bob Livingston, and Jerry Jeff. (Photo by Ron McKowin.)

exploits in airports, especially DFW. "Wingin' it home to Texas / homin' on the morning plane / I'm wingin' it home to Texas and I lost my bags again / And that Dallas airport sucks." Somewhere in the middle of the recording the band fell totally apart, no one was sure where it was going next, we were still working it out. Miraculously, on the fly, it resolved and everyone came roaring back into the right place. It was exhilarating and funny and gonzo and we laughed hysterically. But we didn't know that would be the take that ended up on the record. Jerry Jeff was laughing and said, "It's great! It's perfect." We could have cut it again, but that rascal left it like that, fallen apart and loose and thundering back together, same as it ever was. We *were* winging it! And it was perfectly gonzo.

It was the loosest, most rambunctious record we ever made. And the amazing thing was that the fans just loved it. They bought a lot of records and Jerry Jeff's popularity only grew from it. No one abandoned us. We toured to support *Collectibles* with a big band: Kelly Dunn on B-3, Gary on bass and piano, me on bass and piano, John on guitar, and a new guy on drums named Donny Dolan. Tomás, Bill, and Squank were the Gonzo Horns. A nine-piece band on the road. Plus our fearless road manager Jack Borders and Bobby Lemons, our sound man, who would dial us in just right every night. One of our roadies was Slappy, better known as Farmer Dave Gilstrap, who was also a songwriter, responsible for "Ro-deo-deo Cowboy" and a few other songs Jerry Jeff recorded. The tour required bigger equipment trucks, more vehicles, and more hotel rooms.

Kelly Dunn was a wild man! Kelly and Tomás. They were wild and lived the rock 'n' roll lifestyle and trashed rooms like Black Sabbath did. Kelly painted his room phone orange once and they threw a few chairs and tables out windows into the swimming pool. Stuff that they had heard that other rock bands had done. I don›t know why they acted like that, though I'm sure they were under the influence and were just trying to have fun and blowing off steam. Boys will be boys, I guess? We were having great fun and played a lot of places, but it *was* hard traveling, and we lived in a state of exhaustion most of the time.

¡Viva Terlingua! sold a lot of records and went gold. It was really a high point in Texas music and in 2014 *Texas Monthly* placed it as one of the top five all-time Texas albums. *Collectibles* was drunken and sloppy and the songs were not as strong, and MCA came down on Jerry Jeff and Brovsky, or maybe just Brovsky. Many of the fans loved *Collectibles*, but MCA couldn't understand it at all. It just sounded like a big party, which is why a lot of people loved it. I'm not saying it didn't sell a lot of records, but it didn't sell as many as *¡Viva Terlingua!* and MCA wanted more sales. They wanted something sort of mainstream like other country acts were recording. Jerry Jeff was never going to be pigeonholed like that, but he agreed to play it straighter for the next album.

So Brovsky and Jerry Jeff decided the next album would be recorded in a studio in Nashville and we would use some key Nashville session players mixed in with the Gonzo Band. Kenny "Heart of Gold" Buttrey was the drummer, Norbert Putnam on bass, David Briggs on piano, Weldon Myrick on steel guitar, and Johnny Gimble, the Texas grandmaster, on fiddle. All A-list players, the best of the best. The rest of us—Gary, Jerry Jeff, and I—sat around in a circle with acoustic guitars and sang. John played electric lead like always and Kelly was on the B-3. It was a big group crammed into the studio. And we played everything live, as always.

Ridin' High was different, and Jacky Jack had to be organized or face David Briggs's scowl. Jerry Jeff only had two originals on this record, so eight of the ten songs were by his friends and were already written and arranged. We got in our song circle and kicked it off. *Ridin' High* opens up with a song that Gary and I wrote called "Public Domain." We wrote it in Santa Fe, New Mexico, and at Gary's house in Austin and we imagined Jerry Jeff singing it when we wrote it. Next is Willie's "Pick Up the Tempo." Willie does it as a waltz, but we rocked it up in 4/4 and played it as a closer or encore for years afterward. Guy Clark's beautiful "Like a Coat from the Cold" follows and then "I Love You," a Jerry Jeff song about his wife Susan that he wrote to get him out of trouble, he said. After that is "Night Rider's Lament," a song by Michael Burton, who had been raised by Native Americans in Alaska. John Inmon's "Goodbye Easy Street" came next. Bill Callery's "Pot Can't Call the Kettle Black" follows and then we got a good version of Jesse Winchester's "Mississippi You're on My Mind." Chuck Pyle's "Jaded Lover" follows, and the album closes out with one of Jerry Jeff's most famous and wild concert songs, "Pissin' in the Wind."

I was a little intimidated by all these hot-shit Nashville studio players. I had played with Buttrey one time before but we never

Bob singing his song "Public Domain" at a Jerry Jeff/Gonzo show, 1977. Rare performance with a Telecaster. (Image by Scott Newton.)

actually met. It was when I'd played the bass on the *Geronimo's Cadillac* album and Buttrey came in and overdubbed drums on it. The first time I met Norbert Putnam he was literally dragging his bass behind him down Music Row. Norbert had played on more hits than you could count and was probably one of the top, if not *the* top, bass players in all of Nashville and the world. He's also been part of the Muscle Shoals Rhythm Section. And he was dragging his bass, an old beat-up Fender Precision, kind of like mine but even older and more beat up. He said he hadn't changed the strings in six years. It was probably all bullshit but there was some rust on them and he said he was afraid to change them because the guitar had such a good tone. And he was right about its having a good tone, an incredible tone.

All these guys made a living by being able to hear a song once and get it down right in one or two takes. Three at the most. They would cut three or four songs in three hours. It was amazing. I had a great time sitting in a circle playing guitar and singing with John, Gary, and Jerry Jeff, and besides, Jerry Jeff recorded Gary's and my song, "Public Domain!"

CHAPTER 27

It's a Good Night for Singin'

1976

The bus was a self-contained traveling hotel, rehearsal space, and green room. A fortress refuge in which to keep the rabble at bay. Willie used to live on his bus whether he was on the road or parked in his driveway. There were twelve bunks stacked in threes. We didn't use the top bunks for sleeping but rather stored our bags and guitars up there. We were lucky that we didn't have twelve to fourteen people on board like some bands did. That would have been a nightmare. I always tried to get the second bunk from the bottom at the rear right. It was the quietest bunk, I figured. Everybody else tried to get that bunk too. I know John Inmon did. One of us would try to outmaneuver the other to get that little oasis. I used Mack's earplugs to sleep. They were the most massive, but even with them in I could still hear the party going on and it was hard to get any real rest.

We were coming off a major tour and Jerry Jeff was anxious to get back in the studio and throw down some songs he loved to sing. Michael Brovsky would work the recording sessions into the middle of the tour and there wasn't a lot of downtime for deep reflection. Jerry Jeff always had his ear tuned to new songs,

Singing harmonies with Gary P. Nunn, 1976. We were Gonzo brothers. (Photo by Ron McKowin.)

especially ones he heard at late-night picking sessions out on the road. He watched how the other musicians and the audience took a shine to them and sang along, the true test. So as we closed in on Nashville, he started making a list. We rolled into Nashville

More singing with ol' Gary P. Nunn. (Photo by Scott Newton.)

late at night, rode hard and put up wet, but dove right into the session the next morning. We followed the same formula as we had with *Ridin' High* and recorded *It's a Good Night for Singin'* surrounded by a slew of great Nashville session players, with us in the middle.

To get things kicked off, we got a rocking cut of "The Heart of Saturday Night" by Tom Waits, followed by "Standin' at the Big Hotel" by Butch Hancock, "Old Five and Dimers Like Me" by Billy Joe Shaver, "Couldn't Do Nothin' Right" by Gary P. Nunn and Karen Brooks, and Jerry Jeff's own classic story song "Stoney." I had co-written "Head Full of Nothin'" with Rick Fowler a few years before in Red River, and that made the cut too along with Rick Cardwell's "Dear John Letter Lounge," Bill Callery's "Leroy," then "Won't You Give Me One More Chance" by Lee Clayton, and two songs by longtime Jerry Jeff running buddy, Keith Sykes, "Very Short Time" and "Someday I'll Get Out of These Bars."

Gonzos unhinged at Public Domain, 1976. (L–R): John Inmon, Kelly Dunn, Bobby Smith, Mike Holloman, Gary P. Nunn, and Bob Livingston. (Photo by Scott Newton.)

Gary and I wrote "Roll on Down the Road" about the times when Jerry Jeff couldn't remember the lyrics and he would grasp for something and it was "roll on down the road" or "let it roll" or something like that. So one day at Public Domain Gary and I were sitting around and we said, "Let's write a song for Jerry Jeff." And we took those two lines, "roll on down the road" and "let it roll," and that became our chorus. In the song, we followed a guy who starts out betting on racehorses in Santa Fe then goes to New Orleans and takes a gambling boat called the *Delta Queen* and loses everything and ends up in New York or LA trying to make it as a songwriter. To our surprise, Jerry Jeff liked the song and ended up choosing that to be on the record as well.

"Up against the wall!" Me leading the charge with (L–R) unidentified reveler, Susanna Clark, Jimmy Buffett, Rusty Wier, me, and Jerry Jeff. (Photo by Ron McKowin.)

I wrote "It's a Good Night for Singin'" in Austin out at my little cabin in the woods at a campfire under a slip of a moon. Jerry Jeff liked the good-time feel of it, so that's how we closed the record, all of us singing together:

It's a good night for singin'
I got too drunk and my ears are still ringin'
but it's so good to see you
It's a brand new day!

After the recordings we invited a lot of Nashville friends over to a bar to take photos for the cover. Jerry Jeff and the band were in a circle playing and singing with Guy Clark, Teddy Wilburn of the Wilburn Brothers, Jim Stafford, Susanna Clark, John "Toad" Andrews, and a further cast of ruffians all howling at the moon. Nashville photographer Jim McGuire snapped the cover photo.

The album *It's a Good Night for Singin'* was released by MCA in 1976.

CHAPTER 28

Two Worlds

1989

What began as a dusty bus ride west with Jerry Jeff and the boys bound for California turned, a month later, into a flight across the world—back to India on another State Department tour. One minute I was trading songs in L.A., the next I was rattling through the Indian countryside on a herky-jerky train with a thousand people riding on the roof, lurching toward Bombay. Then—bam—back to the States, barely time to catch my breath, launching into another Jerry Jeff tour starting at Jonathan Swift's in Cambridge, Massachusetts.

I flew straight into Boston, arriving massively jet-lagged, and went to the hotel to crash and then get ready for the show that night. Johnathan Swift's, the big rambling folk club on Harvard Square, was packed tighter than a redneck's fist. I mustered up some cosmic gonzo strength and dove into the sea of energy that was electrifying the room. There was an aisle down the center of the room with Harvard Law and Medical Schools on either side outdrinking each other at a pace never seen before. There were insults, occasional fistfights and outright brawls, with backs slapping on slippery floors, and through it all they were laughing and hollering and singing at the top of their lungs, "It's up against the wall, Redneck Mother!" It was the Gonzo Compadres band with

Jerry Jeff, John Inmon, drummer Freddie Krc, and me. Freddie walked backstage with a piece of graffiti he'd copied down from the restroom wall: "The world is flat. – Harvard class of 1491."

I had come into this free-for-all of my own free will. But still, I felt like I was in a Fellini movie watching it all happen. My role in the movie was that of the jet-lagged bass player, Cosmic Bob, who entered the scene with a crowd shouting his name. I was to play bass guitar with a group of rag-tag musicians while singing along to a song about a redneck mother, whatever that was. In the scene, we are supposed to play loud while the audience is pressing the stage, singing and yelling. It's hotter than hell and sweat and beer are pouring from everyone. We went off script and the band turned up and some production people arrived to secure the area and try to calm things down. The band kept turning it up. I turned up to 11 and the intensity in the room mounted 'til the rider fell off his horse and a riot broke out at our feet. Still the band played on and the rioters sang along with us. It was high drama. The Secret Service was called to get a president's daughter to a secure location.

I was watching this Fellini film from a distance and taking notes. Between the weight of the jet lag and the nuclear bomb of culture shock I was still hyper-aware of how unique it all was. Two worlds. From sitting quiet on a riverbank down in South India thinking lofty esoteric thoughts to singing "Redneck Mother" out loud with hundreds of others as the teeming uninhibited room shifted and came closer.

Our hotel was just off Harvard Square, and I woke from the nightmare with a gasp, determined to get out into the sunshine. I walked on the red brick streets and sidewalks and bought a high-tech Panasonic cassette player/recorder that I kept for years after. Plugging in my earphones, I strolled through Harvard Yard listening to *Bach's Greatest Hits* by Eugene Ormandy and the Philadelphia Orchestra. It was a revelation and the most beautiful music I had ever heard and it was all in the movie. Cosmic Bob walked amidst the dark bronze statues of great men's ghosts scattered around the immense Harvard Yard, the center of the university. On the periphery of the Yard in a weathered dark-redbrick student dormitory/library there was a promising young law student in his garret trying to keep his wits about him after the previous night's Jerry Jeff show. He would later become a federal judge, but right then he was cramming for an oral argument scheduled for later that night with the hangover of a lifetime . . . and no voice left.

Ray Wylie's song "Redneck Mother" got a lot of mileage. Once upon a time after an outdoor show in New Delhi an older woman in a beautiful sari came up and said, "I enjoyed your program, Mr. Bob, but tell me one thing. Can you play that song, 'Redneck Mother'? I very much enjoy that one."

"What? How did you ever hear *that* song?" I was flabbergasted!

"Oh, I listen to the bluegrass show every Sunday on Voice of America. You can hear it there."

I myself have listened to Voice of America while out on the far world's roads. I actually heard "Navajo Rug" and "Public Domain," among other Jerry Jeff and Lost Gonzo Band songs, amazed to catch them through the static of sound and time.

CHAPTER 29

Lone Star High Drama in New York City

1975

The day started when Gary Nunn's phone rang. A familiar voice: "Hey, is Rick Beresford there?"

"Rick Beresford? No, he doesn't live here. Who is this?"

"This is Eddie Wilson. Who is *this*?" So Eddie Wilson, the bigger-than-life president of Armadillo World Headquarters, makes another entrance into the story.

"Well, Eddie, this is Gary P. Nunn."

"Hey, Gary, I was just trying to find Rick. Somebody gave me your number by mistake, I guess. I'm looking for a song 'cause we're working on an advertising campaign for Lone Star Beer and we need someone to write a commercial. I need a commercial. I need a song."

Gary didn't miss a beat. "Hey, Eddie, you don't want Rick Beresford to do this, you want the Lost Gonzo Band. We'll come up with a song."

Eddie said he needed it quick.

Gary called me straight away and told me to get over there. Something big was happening. They need a commercial. But they want it to be a song, too. They'll play it on the radio. They want

Jerry Jeff Walker and the Lost Gonzo Band on a TV show, 1974. (L–R): Gary P. Nunn (on piano), Bob Livingston, Donny Dolan, Jerry Jeff, John Inmon, Jim "Squank" Baker, and Tomás Ramirez. (Photo courtesy of Bob Livingston.)

to mention Lone Star in the song in some way. I got a guitar and it came right out:

> Dancing in the moonlight under Lone Star skies
> In a Lone Star state with a Lone Star high,
> And the nights, they never get lonely.

A lot of "lones" in there. Just lonely and lone all the way.

Gary loved it and I wrote the whole thing down that day. Two days later we played it live on acoustic guitars for Eddie, lawyer Mike Tolleson, and the rest of the sagebrush suits at the Armadillo and at Lone Star. They loved it and we booked studio time at Odyssey Sound and cut the song almost overnight. We did a one-minute version and a thirty-second spot. And we recorded an extended version for the radio. Gary wrote a spirited bit for the end, "Bean taco and harina tortilla all night long."

During that summer of 1975, they played our Lone Star commercial over and over on most country radio stations in Texas and the region. They made television commercials that were aired nationally especially during the live broadcast of several baseball games leading up to the University of Texas winning the National Championship. In the commercial, a guy in a bar in Austin walks over to a jukebox and puts a quarter in. We hear "Dancin' in the moonlight" and "The Nights Never Get Lonely . . ."

Armadillo artist Jim Franklin hand-painted brilliant posters depicting armadillos crawling out of Lone Star longneck bottles and other surreal Texas images. The advertising campaign was successful for Lone Star, and the Lost Gonzo Band was a big part of it. Other artists recorded the song. The Pointer Sisters and Freddie King both recorded "The Nights Never Get Lonely" and they made commercials out of them. Freddie King did it pure blues rock and later told me he loved the song and he was going to release it as a single. But he died the next day or so. Damn! A hot Tejano group called Sunny & the Sunliners recorded it in Spanish. Lone Star Beer sales went through the roof. It was all good and I was itching to have more opportunities like this.

After the release of *Ridin' High* and the intense touring that followed, the Gonzo Band wanted a record of our own. We had meetings with Brovsky, who said he was sure he could get us a record deal.

There was some concern on Jerry Jeff's part about our doing our own thing and I think he wanted to be part of it, to control it. But the plan was to record our songs and eventually leave Jerry Jeff and go out on our own. Brovsky seemed to think this was doable and, true to his word, landed us a record contract with MCA. We found some time between the Jerry Jeff tours, and in 1975 we went to Nashville and recorded our debut record *Lost Gonzo Band* at Starday Studios. Our lineup was Gary, Inmon, Dolan, Tomás, Kelly, and me. Marty "Sundance" Leonard, who

First Lost Gonzo Band promo photo for MCA Records, 1974. (Photo courtesy of Bob Livingston.)

had been the engineer on *¡Viva Terlingua!*, was now pushing faders and turning knobs for us. Michael Brovsky was the producer.

We were nervous but ready to go. For the most part, we played live on all the basic tracks, only overdubbing some lead instruments and background vocals. We kicked off the record with Gary's "Loose and On My Way," about breaking free—which we were definitely trying to do. We would open Gonzo shows with it. "Desperados" was a song Murphey and Gary wrote, a real rocker, and John shredded the lead. Gary's "Give Me Some Money" found a place. John's "Love Drops" was a cool blue-eyed soul song. "Reality" was written by Gary and Bud Shrake (under the pseudonym M. D. Shafter). We would write more songs with Bud over the years. John had a truly great song I still love, "Railroad Man." I had a couple of songs on the album, "Take Advantage of Your Chances" and "Those Were the Days." I recorded "Take

Bud Shrake writing our Gonzo bio. He said about me, "Bob Livingston is the most worldly of the group and hopes to visit Houston someday." (Photo by Scott Newton.)

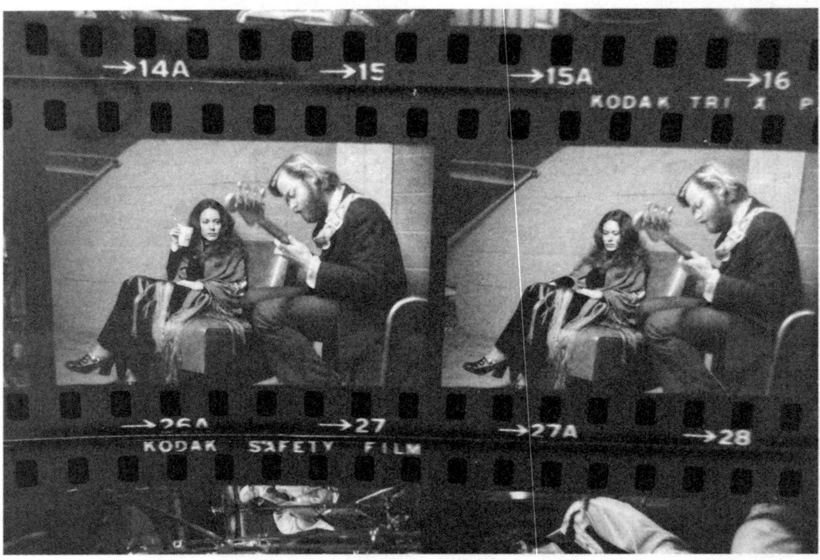

Practicing backstage as Iris looks on at the Texas Opera House, 1975. (Photo by Scott Newton.)

Advantage of Your Chances" on my album *Original Spirit* and I still play it. Rip-roaring bluegrass cosmic. "People Will Dance" was a Gary Nunn disco song, and MCA would later put out a dance compilation album and include that alongside Elton John and The Who. They even called that special album *People Will Dance!* The record closed with Gary's "Fool for a Tender Touch." Gonzo reggae into the sunrise on the drag.

We cut the record in three days so we could get back on the road. I overdubbed my vocal for "Those Were the Days" at 3 a.m. on the last night, down on one knee with the microphone low, on and off a piano bench, the pressure on, trying to get the words out with a blown voice. The album was released later that year and we got a lot of press and there was a buzz about it, and we were off to a good start. We opened all the Jerry Jeff shows and from then on it was billed as "Jerry Jeff Walker and the Lost Gonzo Band." We played in front of a lot of people and the record sold reasonably well, enough to warrant a second album, *Thrills*, that was released the next year.

The band was to be given an advance against royalties. Besides the recording budget, we were each to get a lump sum of $5,000, which was a lot of money back in 1975. I remember walking out of the lawyer's office after we signed the contract and in the elevator Gary and I starting to sing "Give Me Some Money," which later he turned into a song for *Thrills*. We waited for the money. And waited. And waited.

Meanwhile, I thought I'd do something good with my share so when the deal finally went down, I bought an old farmhouse on five acres outside of Oak Hill up a dirt road. It was perfect, and Iris and I said we'd take it on the spot. It didn't hurt that we saw one of the most beautiful sunsets of all time. That was the deal clincher. We watched this magnificence every day, and Tucker and Trevor would later run wild and free through the woods and trails.

The wheels on the bus kept going round and round and the rhythm of the road took us to more towns and venues than I can remember. The Gonzos would open the show for an hour. There was a fifteen-minute break, and then we went right back up there with Jerry Jeff, "Hi, buckaroos, Scamp Walker time again . . ." He would invariably play one of his marathon sets just to keep us on our toes so we were onstage three to four hours some nights. It was exhausting, but we didn't know any better. It all seemed normal to us, and we had a lot of stamina and we were living it. This was our job!

We played Carnegie Hall—twice. The first time was with Doug Sahm. I took Iris (who was eight months pregnant) with me, and she looked ravishing in a lavender dress that she had bought for the occasion. Backstage, Tomás played some quiet clarinet to our still-in-the-womb son, Tucker Boots. The Carnegie Hall show was a sellout, and they wanted us back.

CHAPTER 30

The Only Civilized Answer Was a Fist

1975

For the second Carnegie Hall show, we flew into New York and stayed at the Plaza Hotel. As we walked into the stately old school and hotel, Tomás, our Lost Gonzo brother and sax player, was wearing a T-shirt that read simply, "Eat More Shit!" The fellow at the desk didn't flinch. He had probably seen it all. I rolled with it too. Tomás was also wearing a long dangling earring and some sort of cosmic cap that draped to his shoulder. He was a wondrous sight.

John Carradine, the venerable actor, walked into the lobby and then into the plush elevator with us. Carradine had been in *Grapes of Wrath* and done a lot of Westerns and horror flicks like *Billy the Kid versus Dracula*. He was a Shakespearian character, standing there with us, wearing a dark blue three-piece suit with a gold watch fob and a cocky black beaver hat. His hands were gnarled from arthritis, and he walked with a cane. He looked like he'd just stepped out of a movie. He gave Tomás a glance, then a complete once-over, and noticed his T-shirt. He rolled his eyes and stared at the ceiling. As if everything was normal, I said to Mr. Carradine, "I believe I know who you are, sir." He looked at me with a nonchalance betraying his obvious disgust and said, "Yes, I do believe you do, sir." Then he suddenly punched a button for the next floor—no matter that it wasn't his destination—and exited the scene with a flourish, never looking back. When the door closed, Tomás and I broke out laughing!

The night before the show we were up in Jerry Jeff's and Susan's suite. Gary Nunn, folk singer Rosalie Sorrels, and I were drinking some celebratory champagne and watching the Dallas Cowboys get soundly beaten by the New York Giants. Tom Landry was coaching Dallas. Jerry Jeff was getting more agitated and pissed as the game went on, cursing Landry, screaming at the television, laughing and drinking champagne. He was really taking this seriously. After a blown play by Roger Staubach, Jerry Jeff suddenly picked up a brass lamp from an end table and hurled it at the television. The heavy lamp missed the TV but bounced off the back wall, flew back across the room, and hit him in the head. That quick. "Bam, bam!" Jerry Jeff looked dazed and put his hand up to his forehead, saw blood, and said, "I'm bleeding, I'm bleeding." Then quick as a whip he turned at me and said, "You're not so tough" and immediately started to clumsily strangle me and chase me around the room for a while, with me yelling, "Jerry Jeff, what's the matter with you?"

We were all having a great time up to this point and still everyone was rolling with it like they might have at the Roman Colosseum. Champagne can do crazy things to you, I guess. Susan was telling Jerry Jeff to calm down. We were all saying to "calm down." Jerry Jeff ended up on top of me on a bed and he had that look in his eyes again of no surrender. I threw him off and he came at me again, so I hit him. In those days with Jerry Jeff the only civilized answer was a fist. I've thought long and hard about it and there was no other alternative that would have worked. I'll spare you the gory details.

It got out of hand for a minute and there was wrestling around and then a few punches thrown. I looked up at Susan and Gary and they were staring at us in with their mouths wide open like in the cartoons. I was breathing heavy, I'd just hit a fellow human being, my compadre, my band mate, *my boss*!

Jerry Jeff got up growling. He rubbed his jaw and shouted, "Okay, all right, ALL RIGHT" and went for the little Martin guitar that he carried on planes. He started whirling that Martin around over his head like a bullwhip and he said, "All right, let's go party! We're in New York City!" I said, "I'm not going anywhere with you," and Susan said, "Yeah, no, we're not going anywhere and neither are you." But he headed for the door, strumming the Martin, to where we did not know. "Come back, Jerry Jeff, come back!" But he went storming down the hall past people poking their heads out of their doors and then slamming them on sight.

Down on the street, Jerry Jeff hailed a taxi and went to The Bottom Line, a famous listening room. Steve Goodman, who wrote "City of New Orleans," was playing that night and he was in mid-line when Jerry Jeff walked through a sea of people and onto the stage. Goodman said, "Jerry Jeff, what the hell . . ." Jerry was still holding the little Martin and he said, "Here! You take it. I'll break it," and he gave that Martin to Mr. Steve Goodman on the spot and walked off the stage and out into the night and back to the Plaza Hotel and slept until right before the show. Whenever these knockdown drag-outs would occur, Jerry Jeff never really held it against you. There's an old blues song that says "champagne don't drive me crazy," but maybe it does . . .

At the show that night, a young woman streaked the stage just as we kicked it off with, "Hi, buckaroos, Scamp Walker time again . . ." Boom. It was electric. Here she comes! The crowd went wild and stood on their seats, whooping it up and singing along. After a few songs, the manager of the hall walked onstage and shouted out to the rowdy audience, "This is highly inappropriate, sit down in your seats. This does not happen at Carnegie Hall!"

John Inmon, Kelly Dunn, and me (on clarinet) backstage, Carnegie Hall. (Photo by Iris Livingston.)

And the fans rushed the stage all the more and threw empty beer cans onto it. *Pick up the tempo and take it on home!*

They didn't pull the plug, but for a while after that Carnegie Hall placed a moratorium on Texas bands like us. The guy was so pissed. He couldn't understand any of it. The music, the fans, the beer. They were used to Pavarotti and here is Jerry Jeff turning it into a roadhouse bar. Well, it was hard to imagine that, with all the red velvet and chandeliers in the room. The night was a sellout and that made the manager even madder and that was the last time we darkened that hallowed door.

It was always Jerry Jeff's crowd. I never played a gig with him when they weren't hanging from the rafters and thronging out in the street peering in. Guy Clark, and most of his contemporaries, couldn't pack them in like that. All things being equal, we were a damn exciting band and would push Jerry Jeff, and push him and push him. We were pure dynamos and gave him a lot of energy. Even when he was too wobbly to play, the Gonzos would push him. I would push him. He depended on me for that. It was hard to fathom. If I had even one all-nighter, I felt so miserable and exhausted the next day I would swear at myself. Like Jerry Jeff sang, "I was so damn bad last night / I'll be good for the rest of my life!"

CHAPTER 31

The Lost Gonzo Air Force

1976

Jerry Jeff wanted an easier way to tour without spending time roaring through the night on a bus followed by the equipment van. We started flying to gigs a lot. There were two Pipers—Navajo Chieftain models—and we had pilots who were businesslike and competent flying us from show to show. Then the pilots started getting into the music and road scene and would always come to the shows and help out. Steve Keith, a fiddle player from Ohio, joined the band, played ripping country leads, and flew high and low with us.

Meanwhile, our road crew would drive a truck with all the equipment on the ground; they left after the show and drove through the night. Among the crew were our road manager, Jack Borders, who flew with us a lot; our sound man, Bobby Lemons; and our roadie, a fellow named David Gilstrap who went by the name Slappy or Farmer Dave. Besides being smart as a whip, he was also a good songwriter. Jerry Jeff recorded Slappy's "Ro-deo-deo Cowboy" and I would later record a song of his called "Country Western Swing" on my *Gypsy Alibi* album. These days, Slappy is a PhD up in Michigan.

When we got back to the hotel someone would usually say, "Let's meet in my room." I never would volunteer mine if I could help it. Sometimes I couldn't help it. When we got back to the hotel much of the time I'd go put my stuff up in my room and I may even have a bottle of wine with me but I would walk in the room and the door would close behind me and suddenly I was in a pristine, cool, quiet space; it was like a switch had been flipped and all the loudness and craziness was left in the hall and I'd put the bottle of wine on the table and I would never take another look at it much less take a sip. And I hardly ever went back to the party. It was all camaraderie and the Russians at the gate.

We went through several of the Upper Midwest states: Illinois, Wisconsin, and Minnesota. Once we played in St. Paul. We had a good night, packed as usual and hot as a sauna, but when we came outside it was freezing cold. Someone said there was a party, and we got there before Jerry Jeff. It was a houseful of people filled with food and guitars. The owner of the house and the host of the party had a big aquarium on one end of the room. A gigantic aquarium. It took up the whole wall and was full of fish and starfish and all kinds of sea creatures to include maybe even an eel or two. The guy was real proud of the aquarium and really it was interesting to watch the fish. Calming. Suddenly the door burst open and there was Jerry Jeff. He came in the room and one of the people at the party said, "Hey, hey, it's Jerry Jeff ! Hey, Jerry Jeff, do something! Come on, DO something!" JJ just stopped and looked at the crowd. He was coming to hang out, but NOOOO. Most times on the road, he couldn't be just a normal guy. They wouldn't let him. His reputation preceded him wherever he went. Everybody expected him to do some outrageous act, so when the guy yelled "do something!" Jerry Jeff walked over to the aquarium, took off his hat, plunged it in the water, and stirred it up like a big vat of stew, around and around and around, and fish and sand and little buildings and eels were all swirling around in a whirlpool tornado! Then he turned in his boots, left his hat floating in there, and just stormed out and slammed the door behind him. *That* sure brought the party to a standstill. The guy was so pissed off he just took Jerry's hat and threw it out the front door after him. There was snow on the ground and more coming down.

The cops showed up. "You folks keep it down, you hear? Somebody's been yelling out in your front yard disturbing the neighbors!" Actually, that's what brought the party to a standstill, at least for us, and we took off pronto. On the way out we found Jerry Jeff's hat on the front lawn, frozen solid, a block-of-ice hat. I grabbed it and took it back to the hotel and left it by the door of his room. When he got up in the morning, Jerry Jeff found the ice hat waiting for him.

To look like a top-notch, professional outfit, our amplifiers and road cases had the Jerry Jeff Lone Star logo on the side. We played really loud, trying to outdo each other. I had a Fender Showman brain for my amp with two 15-inch JBL speakers. It had a lot of power and bottom end. It was a tube amp, analog, and it sounded great. I played a Fender Precision through it. That was my sound. And we were really trying to play over the crowd because they were screaming and singing the songs so loud you could barely hear yourself even though you were playing balls out.

Later on in the heyday of the Gonzo Compadres—"four guys in two cars," John Inmon, Freddie Krc, Jerry Jeff, and I—we were playing at a rock club in New York City called Tramps. It was completely packed, 1,800 people, sold out. We are doing all our usual songs, "Hi, Buckaroos," "Navajo Rug," "L.A. Freeway," "Redneck Mother," "London Homesick Blues," "Trashy Women," "Pissin' in the Wind"; on and on and on and everybody in the crowd knew every word to every song and sang with gusto. We did "Man with a Big Hat" to a sea of Lone Star and Shiner bottles. Tramps had flown in cases of Texas beer for the occasion and all the New York fans were singing "drink up while the drinking is free, drink to my compadres and me!" and they'd raise their bottles high. After the show I went back to the sound man and asked how it was. The guy's name was Rocky, I think, and he was from New York City—the Bronx or somewhere. Rocky said, in his New York accent, "The crowd was screaming and singing so fucking loud that I had to turn the PA up louder and louder, louder than any heavy metal band I've ever had in here. My head is spinning, I have a fucking headache! You guys bring out the craziest crowd I've ever seen. They know every word to every fucking song. Let's do it again!"

And we would play long sets, at least two hours but more like two and a half to three hours a night. Jerry Jeff would play everything he knew. Sometimes we played so long that people would start leaving. It wasn't that they wanted to go, it was just they were so exhausted and drunk they couldn't take it anymore. They had to get to work the next day. But we kept on playing. We would play and play, louder and louder, jumping around; it was really a workout. Judging by the power of the songs and the crowd's reaction I felt like we were playing nothing but hits. And in a way, we were.

Gary and I would trade off on piano and bass. When we got to "Hill Country Rain" I'd play the piano and do a voice intro: "I've got a feeling, something that I can't explain, it's like dancing naked in high hill country rain." Gary would play the bass and he could really rock it and I would play the piano so hard I thought I was gonna break it. Especially on the end where there was this gigantic crescendo and I would be playing octaves, hitting the piano with both hands, marching up with an arpeggio from F to G, A, B, C, D, E, F and up and up to the next octave and over and over to the top of the keyboard and back down and over again, root notes with both hands as thick as I could make it, pounding it, bashing it.

Jerry Jeff called a good set. He would always start the show with "Gettin' By." That was our sound check song. It had everything in there, started out with the guitar and the bass and the kick drum and by the time we're playing that song halfway through the mix was in place. It had vocals and harmonies, leads and his motto, "Gettin' by on gettin' by is my stock and trade, livin' it day to day." Everybody in the audience knew it and everybody was singing on the first song, then all the way to the end of the night. We would usually do "Navajo Rug" or something like that next and with the first four or five songs we would be in our groove and the energy just went up and up.

Whether traveling by bus, plane, or train, it was a whirlwind of activity. We had to be up early to get on or in whatever conveyance there was to take us and throw our stuff in. We had some gigs in Canada, we had just played at Massey Hall in Toronto, and we were late getting to the train station next morning so we just left the rental cars out on the street and made a mad dash for the train. The train to Montréal was just starting to pull out but we threw our bags on and jumped. The CBC was filming the train ride for a documentary and they filmed us abandoning our rental cars on the street still running with the trunks open. The camera guys barely made it on themselves.

The train was full of French Canadians, almost all French-speaking. I had a little concertina with me. We were in the club car singing along with my concertina when I started doing the French song "Alouette." All the French Canadians started singing along and they were drinking and laughing. Later the CBC crew filmed Jerry Jeff singing "Mr. Bojangles" from the back of the train with the tracks disappearing. We got to Montréal that night. It was cold, snowy, and beautiful like in an old black-and-white movie.

It was a big band, eight people on the road. Things were getting a little crazy. Everybody we met wanted to hang out with Jerry Jeff. He would end up coming back to the hotel late at night or early in the morning and it was harder and harder to get him awake when we had to leave.

Me, Gary Nunn, and John Inmon on a Jerry Jeff show, c. 1974. (Photo by Ron McKowin.)

We called our road manager, Jack Borders, "Pud." The Miserable Pud. Not sure how he got that name, but it fit as he was a bit miserable and grumpy. Jack would tell us the next day's flight was at 8 a.m. so we would get up at 6 and get to the airport at 7 and find out the flight really wasn't until 1 or 2 in the afternoon. We called that being "Pudisized" and we never knew whether it was happening or not. He was like the boy who cried wolf: To be on the safe side, we always had to believe he was telling the truth and show up when he said. And we never missed a flight.

CHAPTER 32

Joe Ely's Magic Demo

1975

We were playing in Lubbock with Jerry Jeff one windy night with dust storms making everything snuff-colored. The show was at the Municipal Auditorium, a cavernous armadillo shell, horrible acoustics, wild and rowdy rednecks, frat boys and sorority girls and some long-haired hippies right up front. It was a typical JJ audience. After the show, a fellow named Johnny Hughes walks up to me backstage and says, "Here, Bob," and he hands me a cassette. Then he says, "This is really great. You gotta listen to it." It turned out to be an album's worth of songs that Joey Ely had recorded at Don Caldwell's studio with Lloyd Maines and Jesse Taylor along with other Lubbock hotshots. And it *was* great, full of new raw country rock songs about the flatlands done with retro sweetness.

I loved what was there and thought there was magic to it. I took the tape back to Austin and kept it in my glove compartment and would listen to it driving around town. One day I played it for Gary and he was similarly impressed. About a month later we were at a music industry powwow for songwriters at the Hilton Hotel and Jack Parker, the newly appointed head of country music at MCA, walks up and engages me in a conversation. We had met him because he had been a promo guy out in the field in

Boston setting up radio interviews and in-stores and that kind of promo thing when we were touring both with Jerry Jeff and as the Gonzo Band. We were always friends with Jack. Jerry Jeff didn't have much use for promo people because, for some reason, they made you be places and do things *they* wanted you to do to help promote *your* record. Jacky Jack didn't get it, or refused to get it—he wanted to do what *he* wanted to do. A smart promo person would have said, "Okay, Jerry Jeff, what do *you* want to do?" Everybody would have come off a lot better.

Jack Parker told us that as the new head of country music he could sign three acts immediately and wanted one of them to be from Texas. "Do you have any ideas?" he asked. And Gary looked at me and said, "Bob, are you thinking what I'm thinking?" And I said, "Yeah!" And both of us told Jack that he had to hear Ely's tape. Gary had to leave, but I got the tape out of my car and headed up to the penthouse suite where all these MCA suits were drinking and eating and talking about record sales and recording budgets. Jack Parker said, "Let's hear it."

I had a cool little Radio Shack cassette player, a little portable that everyone could hear. The first song I played them was "West Texas Wind": "Do you know why the trees bend at the West Texas border?" And when it came to Lloyd's steel lead there was nothing but magic on the tape and in the room. He was painting a Rembrandt with his steel. In a way, it's a *perfect* recording and when these guys were listening to it and Lloyd played that steel part I started grabbing my heart strings and pulling at them for dramatic effect. Pulling on my chest. And these MCA boys bent into the tape recorder for a closer experience. Put their ears close. These jaded suits from LA who had the biggest acts in the world on their label couldn't believe what they were hearing. Their jaws dropped. I'm not kidding. "That's really great! Who is this guy?" And then we listened to the whole tape and Jack asked, "Where can we see him?" And in a couple of days they had it all figured out and had flown to Lubbock to see Joey play at the Cotton Club.

A few days after, one of the vice presidents at MCA called me to thank me for turning them on to Ely. He said they really wanted to sign him but they couldn't make a deal with his manager. "Do you think you can get Michael Brovsky interested in managing Ely? We can talk to him." And in the end, they signed Joe and he was on MCA for years. The heartbreaker of the whole thing was that they didn't put out those original demos for the first album. They re-cut everything in Nashville and it just wasn't the same. To me, the MCA record didn't have the same feel and magic jumping out of it like those original demos.

CHAPTER 33

Turn Me Loose, I'll Never Be the Same!

1974–75

Bobby Bridger walked through the backstage crowd to introduce himself at the third Kerrville Folk Festival, in 1974. I was there to play with Jerry Jeff and the brand new Lost Gonzo Band. Bobby had just played a great set and we were up next. I would come to find that Bobby was a great songwriter and had albums out and had written a beautiful piece of music, a musical, called *Seekers of the Fleece*. It was an amazing epic ballad weaving song into song with musical interludes and narration written in Shakespearean couplets.

Bobby's a Louisiana boy—soulful to the core. He can channel Elvis with his voice, but he's got his own thing going. He plays Martin guitars in alternate tunings, all fingerpicking, never with a flat pick—his style is all about touch and tone, drawing out the music with bare fingers. We were all living in or around Austin at the time, that wild, never-a-dull-moment town. Life was a blur of guitars, good food, and great company. Bobby loved the Gonzo Band, and the feeling was mutual. We were kindred spirits, spending time together out at Lake Travis, laughing, jamming, and soaking it all in.

Me and Bobby Bridger at Yellowstone National Park, 1975. (Photo by Melissa Tatum.)

Then Bobby invited us to be part of the recording of *Seekers of the Fleece.* He didn't want to record in Austin. Instead, he talked us into heading up to Colorado to cut the album at a studio called Denver Sound. He had everything lined up: players, engineers, the whole setup. But Bobby had something even better—he had Slim Pickens. Yes, *that* Slim Pickens: cowboy actor, rodeo clown, and legendary character. A big fan of Bobby's, Slim showed up and agreed to do the narration for the record. He kicked it off with that unforgettable voice: "The year is 1822. Jim Bridger lives in old St. Lou. He's learning 'bout the blacksmith trade . . ." In the studio, I could never get out of my mind the image of Slim riding that atom bomb down whooping it up and fanning his mount with his hat at the end of *Dr. Strangelove.*

We recorded all the music with Bobby on lead vocals, while Gary, John, and I handled the harmonies. John's brother, Jim Inmon, ran the board as our engineer. The towering redheaded singer, Mike Williams, dropped by to lay down some deep bass

I played Hugh Glass in Bobby Bridger's musical *Seekers of the Fleece*. Here Hugh is drawing a bead on Jim Bridger. Hugh said, "Fer your youth, I forgive ye." (Photo courtesy of Bob Livingston.)

harmonies. I played bass on some tracks and added a bit of mandolin here and there. But John was the real standout in the tracks—his guitar work was nothing short of stunning. Bobby has always gone to John to whip things into shape and play whatever instrument is needed.

The morning of the first sessions, the door burst open and in walked a wild-looking fellow in buckskins and moccasins and a skunk-skin hat and with a long gray beard. He shouted, "Turn me loose, I'll never be the same! I'm Timber Jack Joe, the last of the mountain men!" Timber Jack had retired from being some sort of bulldozer operator who to hear Bobby tell it could operate with surgical skill around the ground he was shaping up. Timber Jack had quite a lot of acreage somewhere up there in Utah or Wyoming, but he actually lived like a mountain man on the road. He would shoot an elk, tan the hide with the brains of the beast, and make it into a beautiful, pure white, gorgeous, fringed, full-on outfit. He had beads, and mojo and bear claws hanging around his neck. He wore red long underwear under the whole thing and you could see it peeking out. He carried a .45 pistol in full view much of the time. He was a character in all dimensions. Timber Jack had a hand-painted sign on his Winnebago outside with the colorful proclamation that read *Timber Jack Joe and Tuffy! The Last of the Mountain Men!* Tuffy was Timber Jack's dog. His RV was full of Indian blankets and costumes, authentic Native American and mountain men clothes. And he pulled a horse trailer behind carrying the most beautiful Appaloosa pony you'd ever want to see.

One time, we walked into the packed Night Hawk restaurant on 19th street in Austin for breakfast and once inside the door Timber Jack yelled out to the high heavens, "Woo-hoo! Turn me loose! I'll never be the same!" Of course this startled everyone sitting there and got us all a lot of attention, what with all our beards and the guitars we were dragging in. A server came up to welcome us and see what on earth? Timber Jack said, "Honey, you're as pretty as a picture and I'll give you six beaver pelts to come back to the mountains with me." He would charm women, and they would go out and see his rig and horse trailer. Timber Jack had the horse and even a fox that would curl up with him. He'd pose the girls in authentic Native American dresses and put them atop his appaloosa. Pretty as a picture. Around Utah and Wyoming, his dog Tuffy was just as famous as he was.

Timber Jack had a cameo in the movie *Jeremiah Johnson*, and he provided a lot of the costumes for the film—that's how Slim Pickens knew him. Bobby told us that Slim was one of the largest holders of Western costumes for all these movies. He had Hudson Bay cloth, and piles of Indian blankets and costumes. Authentic. You may not know the story of Slim Pickens. He was a rodeo rider who became a rodeo clown but wanted to get in the movies. He moved to New York, got a gig at Carnegie Hall operating the elevator backstage, and one night the manager of Carnegie Hall tells Slim the only person who can use the elevator that night is Leonard Bernstein: "Don't let anyone else on it but Mr. Bernstein." Slim says, "You got it."

The renowned Jascha Heifetz was making a guest performance that night. He's probably the greatest violin player in the world and was carrying a Stradivarius, the greatest violin in the world. Jascha is downstairs in the green room and it's time for him to go up and he's trying to get on the elevator, and Slim, who is manning the elevator, says, "You can't get on here now."

Heifetz says, "What do you mean I can't get on?"

"Only Mr. Bernstein is allowed on this elevator tonight," Slim says.

"Don't you know who I am? I'm Jascha Heifetz."

And Slim Pickens says, "I don't care if you're Bob Wills hisself. You ain't getting on this elevator!"

After we finished recording *Seekers of the Fleece* we all went up to the mountains to have a *rendezvous*. A meeting and a ceremony. Bobby had written a beautiful song of the same name that paints a colorful picture of the Native Americans and white men meeting for the first time in a peaceful party that lasts for days. There were several teepees already set up with more coming. We painted one for Timber Jack. Other mountain men showed with their teepees. There were many ragged hunters, all dressed in mountain man wear. Authentic elk, dear, and bear hide. They had flintlock guns in the crooks of their arms and huge knives in their belts. We had a colossal bonfire going, and we all got ready to sit in a big circle of songs and stories. Jim Inmon was there to record the whole thing.

At the ceremony around the big fire we were solemnly presented with beaver pelts with words and whoops. But you can't cash in a beaver pelt except in that neck of the woods You just have to put it on your wall or make something with it. I made a deal with one of the mountain men to make something with it. I can't remember what I gave him in return, but he made me a beautiful beaver hat out of my pelt. It had a leather bill and an abalone button. It was funky and gorgeous.

Meanwhile, it was story time and they formed a circle of storytellers around the big roaring bonfire. Someone brought out some real moonshine. I'm not exactly sure what was in it, but it was clear, and it was clear that it was white lightning. The jug was passed around the circle and you *had* to take a drink. And you can hear it in those old recordings as the jug gets passed around, the gulping of moonshine, the hiccups and burps. And everybody had to tell a story. Many of them were hunting stories, unbelievable tales of killing grizzlies and fighting off a wolf pack. One cowboy named Bob Eggers told a harrowing story of a grizzly wandering into his camp that he had to shoot with his pistol at close range. We were wide-eyed.

Michael Burton—the writer of "Night Rider's Lament"—was in the circle. He told us he was an orphan raised by Native Americans. He also told us of an incredible experience with his hunting-guide uncle. Michael laid it out. "The grizzly was at 150 yards and he's already smelled us by this time, and so he's bearing down on us, and my uncle says, 'Okay, Mike, here's this double-barrel. If he gets through me put it in its mask and let both barrels go. That's the only thing you can pray for.'" All this time the grizzly is roaring and running at them full steam ahead, and Michael says "I'll get him" and he gets down low and his uncle starts shooting his big bear rifle at the grizzly, bam, bam, bam! And the grizzly is already dead in his tracks but is still running and runs over them and into the forest behind another 50 feet and collapses in a dead heap.

At that point Slim Pickens says, "You know, I own a little piece of property right near where you were talking, and you know the Indians had some burial mounds up there with a lot of artifacts and last year we discovered some . . ."

"Turn me loose, I'll never be the same!" Timber Jack brings his mojo to a Lost Gonzo Band show. (L–R): Timber Jack Joe, Gary P. Nunn, Bob Livingston, Bobby Bridger, and Bobby Smith, c. 1976. (Photo by Scott Newton.)

Then the jug would go around the circle again and another character would tell something about killing a bear in Taos, and Slim would say, "You know, I own a little piece of property over there near Taos, and there's a buffalo jump on it . . ." and he would tell his story, and it turned out that Slim owned land everywhere across the country.

Bobby is a true genius and continues to write and paint and record and make movies. He recently re-released *Seekers of the Fleece* with a new mix, and it sounds great. It's part of a trilogy called *A Ballad of the West* with two other musicals, *Pahaska* and *Lakota*. Bobby also wrote a science fiction whirlwind musical called *Aldebaran* about a dolphin caught in a whirlpool in the ocean who's then spit out into a black hole in space. They are all brilliant.

Bobby's rendezvous was a great experience for all of us, a sepia-toned snapshot from another time. We rushed back home carrying tales of Indians and mountain men, Slim and the story circle, and the moonshine and Timber Jack Joe. Thank you, Bobby, for giving us all that. Turn me loose, I'll never be the same!

CHAPTER 34

I Survive a Revolution in Bangladesh

1989–91

The US State Department asked me if I wanted to go to Pakistan, to Islamabad, Karachi, and Lahore. Pakistan was in the news and there were a lot of killings, including some foreign diplomats. They put the tour together in a few weeks while I was in India. In this peaceful setting it was hard to imagine the strife all around the region. The Russians were still fighting in Afghanistan and there were thousands of Afghan refugees in the country. There was a lot of fighting but most of it was tribal, or Muslim against Muslim, or Sikh against Muslim. I was not too far away from all this. And what's more, the Gulf War was still in full swing around the corner in Iraq!

They said I'd be safe. I maybe foolishly felt protected in some way. So I went for it and I played the shows, took part in the official events, and met an array of fascinating Pakistani musicians, students, and audience members. One night after a concert in Islamabad, I went out for an evening stroll with my State Department man. We walked into the neighborhoods and through the very public square where militants had gunned down a dozen people the week before. I asked him if we were safe. "We are safe," he said. "Nobody knows who we are." It is a fine thread that the State Department must weave to do what they do, whatever it is that they *really* do. That thread was never more evident than when I was finding my place in such a volatile neighborhood. As long as the State Department felt I could spread some good news about America they challenged me to do just that. A tour of India was next and there must have been some decent relations going on with both countries, even at this level, to make something like this happen. India talking to Pakistan on a funky country music level.

The next night, we played a show in Chandigarh, in a university auditorium filled with Sikh students—young men in turbans, full of energy and curiosity. After the show, they swarmed around us, laughing and talking excitedly. They said they loved the music, tossing out compliments and questions in rapid fire. "Do you ride a horse at home?"

Trying to keep up, I smiled and said, "I've heard Sikhs are the best cooks, the best lawyers, and the fiercest warriors."

One student grinned and shouted, "And the best terrorists!"

The whole crowd erupted in laughter and cheers. I gave a tight smile, caught off guard and unsure how to respond. That's when my State Department guy leaned in and said calmly but firmly, "Time to go."

Seconds later, we were hustled out and into a waiting bullet-proof Chevy Suburban, engine running, doors slamming shut behind us like a scene from a movie.

I loved traveling in the embassy cars. They felt safer than any of the rest of the cars on the road. Our drivers were usually gruff, burly men with the pedal to the metal. We would always take a different route each time we left the hotel or the venue. We would turn right one day and left the next, down a different street, sometimes going far out of our way before getting back on track. But truth be known, I never felt threatened in any of the countries they sent me to. Most folks were glad to meet and greet Americans,

All Pakistan Radio Live! 1994. (Photo courtesy of Bob Livingston.)

especially the artists, musicians, poets, and painters that my State Department friends were bringing to them.

The good response I got in Pakistan paved the way for me to go to Nepal and Bangladesh. State Department public affairs officers (PAOs) in one country would book me again when they were posted somewhere else. That was the case with Diana Prochel. She loved that part of the world and would only accept posts in that region. Every two years, the State Department played fruit-basket turnover, and everyone went to other posts. Some transferred out but others like Diana were hardcore and would say anchored in South Central Asia for the duration of their careers if they could. Some of these posts like Pakistan and the Middle East and even India are considered hardship posts. The Foreign Service folks get paid a lot more money to be posted in these exotic and beautiful though not altogether secure cities. I first met Diana in Bombay where she lived with her mother who had been a disciple of Mahatma Gandhi. She lived in an American compound in a spacious, authentically colorful wide-open apartment with several rooms full of treasures. There were guards at the gate and a contingency plan. Later on, Diana was posted to Karachi and then Bangladesh and arranged shows for me there. And that brings us to Dhaka, Bangladesh, in 1991 where I got to play an extraordinary show with some amazing musicians and, unbeknownst to me or anyone else in my State Department retinue, it would turn out that a revolution was about to begin.

The first Gulf War was still going on and there was a lot of tension in the air. I played in Dhaka at the Shilpakala Academy. After that there was a series of shows and workshops and meetings and press conferences in other cities. These tours were always hard work but I considered it high adventure and a different awesome experience every day. I played the Shilpakala Academy with Chandan Dutta, the greatest tabla player I'd ever heard. The tabla is a set of two hand drums considered to be from India but in reality used throughout the Indian subcontinent. Chandan can make that tabla speak. He still lives in Dhaka and he plays all over the world as a music ambassador. Someone recorded the performance that night straight off the mixing board onto a cassette tape. It was given to me after the show. It's lo-fi but cool as it distorts in all the right places. We did a spirited version of Buddy Holly's "Not Fade Away" with Chandan shredding it. Later my producer Mr. Lloyd Maines and I added it as a bonus track to my record, *Gypsy Alibi.*

The show was exhilarating but that night and the next day things were going on in the background that we had no power over. I was in the care of the US State Department so who really knows what was happening in Bangladesh that hot humid day. We had heard there was going to be a citizen strike the day after the concert—the opposition party was striking against the government. It might be hard to drive around the city, they said, "but we have to get you to a press conference right now." They

East meets West! The great tabla player, Chandan Dutta, played with me in Dhaka, Bangladesh. (Photo courtesy of Bob Livingston.)

picked me up in a nondescript embassy van and drove me to the American Center in downtown Dhaka. The Center is not in the US Embassy but on the fourth floor of an office building the United States owns. It houses the library where locals come for a dose of US news and to watch American movies. There are also offices for the Public Affairs and Cultural Affairs officers and their large staff where diplomacy is being born and planned using these cultural outreach nuts and bolts.

We arrived in the parking lot behind a gate and after we parked I was looking at my guitar. The driver said, "Do you need your instrument, sir? You can leave it in the car. I will watch over it. It is very secure here, sir." I had a fleeting moment of laziness and thought I'd just leave it there because I had no scheduled programs until the next day when we would fly up country. But who knows, I might play a song or two up there for the reporters. So I told my driver I'd take my guitar up.

That turned out to be a good move. They took me up to the fourth floor to an immense office complex where I was directed to sit behind a gray metal table in front of twelve or so reporters and another number of photographers. I put my guitar case next to me on the floor ready for anything. I thought. The State Department is all about publicity for things they are doing and bringing to these countries. There would be write-ups in local papers for the whole country after our kickoff in Dhaka. The show generated a lot of interest because I was from Texas, wearing a cowboy hat, and had played with one of Bangladesh's favorite-son musicians, Chandan Dutta. A lot of press was in the room, writing in every language you can think of: Urdu, Bangladeshi, Hindi, English.

The press conference began. "What is it like for you, Mr. Bob, to be in Bangladesh? Do you like it here?" As I was answering, one or two of the local State Department tribe wandered over to the large windows that ran the length of the building. Someone said, "Oh my god!" and the reporters and government folks rushed over to the window and I rushed over there with them. We all looked out at the city to smoke rising above the buildings. Across the intersection was an office building where over 500 people were standing on the flat roof staring down as smoke rose from below. It was eerie and incomprehensible and there was nothing to compare it to. More gray-black smoke billowed from the streets below, then someone in the room said, "It's starting!" just as a large mob came roaring around the building into the square.

The streets were full of angry-looking people who were attacking everything, smashing the windows of every car they saw, trashing motorcycles and hauling them out into the middle of the square and setting them afire. There were a couple of suspicious men in expensive shirts open at the neck with walkie-talkies in their hands, their ears to the receiver, directing the mob giving orders and pointing. The mob broke into the American Center parking lot. The van that brought me there was getting trashed.

The brigands hauled cars, vans, and motorcycles out from the lot into the wide street square and burned them to the ground, tires exploding. Most of these motorcycles and cars belonged to the Bangladeshi reporters and local State Department personnel standing next to me, who were looking down and sobbing, "Oh my god, oh my god."

The folks in charge seemed not to know what to do though I was hoping a plan was being devised to turn off the spigot outside and things would go back to normal. We were physically cut off from the US Embassy across town and I'm sure they didn't want to send in the Marines for a Texas folk singer. We didn't know how serious this was and whether our lives were in danger but so far no one had tried to enter the building. We needed to get out of there as soon as possible, and meanwhile all our transportation was up in smoke. But my guitar was with me!

An ingenious plan was hatched. The CAO called some mucky muck across town and said, "Our visiting dignitary, Mr. Robert Livingston, is having heart palpitations and needs to be removed as soon as possible and we are requesting an ambulance." They were using me as a plausible excuse to get us the hell out of there.

At the time, there was no telling what was going to happen. How did they get an ambulance there so fast with mayhem rampant in the city? The only answer, I thought, was that there were powerful forces at work that didn't want to use a hammer when a dinner knife would do. They sent an orange ambulance with lights on and sirens blasting. We walked down the four flights of stairs out into the mob that was still rampaging on the periphery. Suddenly it all stopped when we stepped out of the building. There were only six of us, all Americans. We began to walk through this crowd towards our rescue ship past the sea of faces and many were smiling at us and for some reason I didn't feel threatened. They looked at us then out to the cars burning then back at us. It was like, "Heh heh, look what happened. Wonder what you're going to do now?" They were staring at me like they stared at me in India at the railway stations. They didn't have anything against me or any of these other Americans. This revolution wasn't against the USA but against what may have been a corrupt government about to be replaced by another corrupt government.

What happened there was indeed the start of a major revolution and the Bangladesh government fell. And the generals were watching.

At the same time this was happening I was just a hop, skip, and a jump away from the Gulf War blowing up Iraq. Under these bizarre circumstances they had to cancel my shows and get me out of the country and back to America. One result of Saddam Hussein's attacking Kuwait was that the thousands of Indian citizens who were working in Kuwait poured out onto the Jordanian desert and were stranded, waiting out the war. All the commercial aircraft in India had been sent to that area to rescue these unfortunate people, so there were no planes available. Everybody was trying to get out of there, and now I was stuck with this pesky revolution problem. All the remaining programs I had scheduled, the shows, the workshops, the train rides to who knows where, all of it was cancelled. The ambulance took me to Diana Prochel's house where I was staying and I quickly packed my bags for a red-eye flight to Calcutta. It happened *that* fast.

Stranded in Calcutta for four days while waiting for a flight out, I found a way to spend my time. Calcutta is almost more than you can handle. Energy and movement of people everywhere. Humid, hot, loud, and beautiful. They stashed me into a State Department apartment somewhere within the maze of Calcutta streets. They sent a car every day if I needed it, but I did a lot of walking and looking around the jam-packed colorful streets.

They told me I had to get to Bombay to catch a Lufthansa flight back to the US, but there were no flights out of Calcutta. So they put me on a train—a magnificent train—rolling west across India in Maharaja Class. It took three days.

I shared a compartment with an Indian professor and a Sikh gentleman with a long beard that he stroked thoughtfully as he peppered me with questions about everything under the sun. Eventually, he coaxed me into opening my guitar case. I played a song of mine that seemed right for the occasion called "Everybody Knows That This Ain't Art," and his eyes lit up, wide with surprise and curiosity.

We rolled into the colossal railway station in Bombay, and I grabbed a taxi to the international airport. The flight was delayed—just another act in this ongoing drama. I dozed in the lounge with one eye open, watching Hindi news on TV, its garish Gulf War footage flashing by, while my own little revolution in Bangladesh barely rated a mention.

CHAPTER 35

Exit Stage Left

1976

We were working with Jerry Jeff on a new project, a 24-song double album that would be called *A Man Must Cary On*. It was a collection of mostly live tracks recorded in Luckenbach and on the road and it was a tribute to Jerry Jeff's old friend and mentor, the late Hondo Crouch who had passed away some months before. We recorded a lot of fun stuff, from Dave Gilstrap's "Ro-deo-deo Cowboy" to a strong version of Rusty Wier's "Don't It Make You Want to Dance." Jerry Jeff wrote a song called "Derby Day" for Susan and he recut "Mr. Bojangles" . . . again. He kept trying to get it right and would do it different every time, different chord progressions in the "He jumped so high . . ." part.

Gary and I had written "Roll on Down the Road" for Jerry Jeff. In a rowdy show, if JJ was ever at a loss for a word or a lyric, he might say "roll on down the road!" or "let it roll!" to fill in the missing lyrics. We said that's the chorus and wrote the song about a rambler gambler scamp kind of a guy and we were thinking about Jerry Jeff the whole time. We played it in a song circle one night when Jerry Jeff was there and we sang the chorus and he kind of perked up and everybody was singing "roll on down the road, let it roll" and he thought it sounded good, never once thinking that we wrote it actually for him. It was one of those songs that just fell into place and sure enough, he recorded it on *A Man Must Carry On*.

It was Luckenbach again with the great mobile recording studio with mics everywhere, even hanging down from the oak trees under which songwriters picked in the afternoon. Towards evening the hens and roosters would perch in the trees and the mics picked up a lot of their clucking and singing. We started singing that song out of Music Man—"Pick-a-Little, Talk-a-Little (Cheep, Cheep, Cheep, Talk a Little More)"—and then "Goodnight, Ladies," and mixed it all together and called it "Stereo Chickens." That's the opening song of the album.

As *A Man Must Cary On* was being mixed and readied for release, Brovsky said he could get the Gonzo Band a record contract and we would go out on our own by the end of the year. We gave our notice to Jerry Jeff a year in advance. We didn't know how it would turn out but we were hopeful we could tour for a while and do some shows and record with Jerry Jeff too from time to time. So, all throughout 1976 we toured with Jerry Jeff with his knowing we were leaving him at the end of that year, which took its toll and JJ took to hanging out on the road with rowdy cowboys and their entourage and would bring them back to the hotel after the show.

By this time we were screaming across the skies at 275 mph with the Gonzo Air Force. We had the top-notch pilots, and they loved to hang out and be a part of show business. There were two planes, and we would moon each other at 10,000 feet. We played a lot of rodeos, and sometimes Larry Mahan, who was a six-time all-around world champion rodeo cowboy, would fly his plane alongside us. Meanwhile our roadies were in a big white truck down below on a lonely highway to Calgary. They would drive all night sometimes, ten hours to the next gig.

The year 1976 was winding down, Jerry Jeff was winding up, and the party was always on. We played several rodeos and

Willie's Fourth of July picnic—Jerry Jeff and the Lost Gonzo Band, with Leon Russell and Steven Fromholz chiming in. Gonzales, Texas, 1976. (Photo by Scott Newton.)

then went to Arizona to play Tucson and Phoenix. Jerry Jeff had asked Austin's rock 'n' roll doctor, Don Counts, to come along with us on some of these tours. We would be flying high, and Dr.

Flying the friendly skies . . . (Jerry Jeff asleep in the back). (Photo by Gary P. Nunn.)

Counts would be giving us acupuncture and foot massages and vitamin B12 shots.

We had a few days off between gigs. We were desperate for a little R&R and rented some cabins at a resort in Tucson out in the desert. We just hung out and swam in the pool and slept and ate good food. Salad.

Our road manager Jack Borders was suffering from a wart on the top of his head. Dr. Counts said he could take that wart off if Jack wanted and Jack said sure why not. So the day came and we all crowded around in a circle and watched Dr. Counts surgically remove Jack's wart. He stitched it up and put a big bandage on it. Perfect.

The next day, we flew over to Phoenix to play at an outdoor night rodeo. It was a good show and I changed into Cowboy Bob and wore my hat and boots. It was the tail end of the tour, only a few shows left. Jerry Jeff was hanging out with some crazy rodeo cowboys, real rounders, not stars, all beat up and creaky. After the show, he brought this new cowboy crew back to the hotel.

He brought cases of beer and found an old galvanized trashcan and filled it full of ice and beer and it was right outside his room, which meant it was right outside my room. All night long Jerry Jeff and the cowboys were banging the gong and that galvanized tub was getting banged and the cowboys were whooping it up with Jerry Jeff laughing and howling at the moon, telling war stories. I'm hearing all of this through a thin motel room wall. A fistfight or two broke out next door and I could hear them cussing. There were no prospects of sleep for me in this room, so I went down the way to Gary's room and slept on his floor.

Next morning the band woke up bright and early because we had a show that night at the Santa Monica Civic Auditorium opening for the Byrds. This was the country version of the Byrds with Gram Parsons, Chris Hillman, Clarence White, and Roger McGuinn. *Sweetheart of the Rodeo* was my favorite record. We were excited to hear them and do a good show. Remember we were traveling at our own pace in private planes, but we had a noon call at the airport and we were out in the parking lot loading our gear into the rental cars.

I was carrying my bags out and passed in front of Jerry Jeff's door, calling out to the guys in the parking lot, when suddenly Jerry Jeff poked his head out of his door and screamed, "Shut the hell up! I'm trying to sleep!" His face was red, almost purple, and he had been up all night and probably had only had an hour of sleep at best. I had only had a bit more than that and I was not in the best mood either. So I screamed back, "Now the shoe's on the other foot, right? Now you can't take it, *now* you want to sleep!" Suddenly the door flew open and Jerry Jeff came charging out into the parking lot. All he was wearing was a T-shirt. This was Sunday morning and church had just let out and the folks from the churches were coming to the Holiday Inn for brunch and they were spilling out into the parking lot chatting and milling around outside when Jerry Jeff entered the scene. They began running to save the wives and children. All the tension of the past year with its misfit mysteries finally got to Gary P. Nunn, who took some umbrage at the events that were being played out in public. There was an altercation between Jerry Jeff and him, with savage swearing and fists flashing.

Jack "The Miserable Pud" road manager, quick as lightning and taking it in stride, calmed things down and told Bobby Lemons to get Jerry Jeff back to bed and then wake him up and take him to the airport. "We play at 8:30." We piled into the van and flew to Los Angeles. We got to the Santa Monica Civic Auditorium with its perfect acoustics and high-end backstage accommodations and did a sound check.

Jerry Jeff walked through the door of the green room twenty minutes before he was to go on. Jerry Jeff and Gary both apologized and nothing more was said. We tuned up and charged the stage and played the show like we knew what we were doing and although Jerry Jeff was a little subdued he rose to the occasion and actually held up quite well. He had an amazing constitution, and it was all a blip in the review mirror to him. We stuck around to hear the Byrds from the wings and saw them sing "(I Like) the Christian Life." That was the last show on that tour, and it was all winding down. Down to No Man's Land.

So for better or worse, the Lost Gonzo Band was leaving Jerry Jeff to seek our own fortunes. Our last show with him was December 30, 1976, at the Summit in Houston. We opened for Linda Ronstadt and her band of California pretty boys. I remember Linda backstage in her short-shorts and knee-high socks and twin ponytails wearing a striped T-shirt with "Texas" on it. She was friendly and joking with us and, well, she *was* Linda Ronstadt after all, and she was incredibly cute and bright, so . . . it was cool in the extreme. In her autobiography she recalls a story about riding in a cab with Jerry Jeff in New York City and Jerry Jeff singing "Heart Like a Wheel" by Kate and Anna McGarrigle to her. She wrote that she sought out this song and recording it changed her whole direction and music. Jerry Jeff also introduced her to Gary White, who played for her "Long, Long Time," another gigantic hit for her. It's no wonder she had a lot of affection for Jerry Jeff.

This was our band's last night together with Jerry Jeff Walker, and the impact was not lost on any of us. We ran onstage and ripped it up, but the vibes were such that it was only an okay show. We left the building and in the end that's how we parted ways—the Lost Gonzo Band leaving Jerry Jeff not with a bang but with a question mark. Things would come back around with him and me in a fashion. The Gonzo Compadres would ride and rip and hoot through the '80s and '90s. But for now, the Lost Gonzo Band, armed with a new record deal from Capitol, was embarking on our own adventure, left to our own devices. And once again I was in a band in a van.

For the new album project we got some new blood in the band. Bobby Smith, who had played with Gary's old band the Sparkles, became the bass player and Mike Holloman from College Station was our new drummer. We recorded in Austin at Odyssey Sound again. The record opens with a song by Michael Burton, "Beacon in the Night." And then comes a song John and I had written called "Santa Cruz (After the Nick of Time)." We did a Walter Hyatt song and we recorded "London Homesick Blues" and Iris and I wrote the title track of the album that would be called *Signs of Life*.

The album was released in 1976. We'd been playing gigs on and off before that, but nothing really organized. There was already a disconnect with what we were told would happen and what *did* happen. Capitol Records, with the urging of Brovsky, agreed to give us some tour support money; each of us got $125 a week. We had to pay for our own food, but there was a separate expense account for gas and hotels. Jack had the credit card and charged everything on it. Brovsky had this idea that we should play all the showcase clubs on both coasts. I think this was the way record companies and managers worked things out. We had some local clubs we could play and make some fairly decent money, but Brovsky didn't want us to have any part of that. I had found a gig in Temple, Texas, called Bub's Tub and they were willing to pay us a thousand dollars to play for one night. I told Brovsky about it, thinking he would follow up, but he just said, "Not only have I never heard of Bub's Tub, but I never want to hear of it again!" So he sent us out to Los Angeles where we played the Whisky a Go Go for five days, and then up the coast. We opened for Randy Newman at the Celebrity Theatre in Phoenix. It's a great place, the stage is in the round and revolves so you end up playing to everyone, but I was a little dizzy at the end.

We played the Bitter End in New York City and My Father's Place out on Long Island. Some nights buzzards circled overhead and other nights it was packed and there were long jams with guest sit-ins.

Then Michael Holloman quit as our drummer. He had gotten a call from New York asking him to play in *The Best Little Whorehouse in Texas*, which was running on Broadway. It was a big deal and they offered him a lot of money. I tried to talk him out of it, but it was no use and, deep down, I didn't blame him. We needed a drummer fast. We'd heard about Paul Pearcy, another young guy who had played in a couple of Austin jazz bands, Forty Times Its Own Weight and Beto y Los Fairlanes. He was supposed to be hot shit, and we auditioned Paul and he *was* hot shit. Kick-ass! So we dodged a bullet on that one, and Paul picked up where Holloman left off.

In the middle of these changes, we still had another record to do for Capitol. It meant I'd be off the road for a while to record and hang out at Barton Springs with Iris and Tucker. A new baby was on the way! In those days, we never knew ahead of time if it was going to be a boy or a girl. I don't remember if ultrasound was

Our cute cosmic family backstage at a Ray Wylie Hubbard Band show at Memorial Stadium in Austin. (L–R): Tucker, Iris, me, and Trevor. (Photo by Scott Newton.)

even invented yet. All summer Iris would float around Barton's to be cool. The healing waters of Barton Springs felt wonderful for anybody, especially a young mother nine months pregnant with her second child. On August 24, 1978, the Gonzos were playing the Soap Creek Saloon and I knew Iris's due date was very, very close. Something spoke to me, I had a feeling not to go to the gig. I stayed home, thank God, and Trevor was born that night. He came out smiling, quiet, and calm. And that's been his modus operandi ever since.

For the new album, Brovsky told us that we "could be the Moody Blues of country music." That sounded good so we tried . . . a little bit of everything. We cut fifty songs: rockers, ballads, country, folk, jazz, and even psychedelic ravers. It was a plethora of sound, a tapestry of layers. We'd spend days in the studio going over parts we should have been rehearsing in someone's garage but instead were being charged studio time. After a few months of on-and-off recording and touring, Capitol sent a guy down to listen to everything. Instead of playing him just a few songs that were more or less finished, Brovsky played him everything in one sitting. Brovsky had completely misread Capitol's interest. The Capitol man turned to Brovsky and said, "Where's the country band we signed?"

Turns out we had no idea what Capitol wanted, or expected. If only Brovsky had pointed us in the right direction from the start. We weren't "country" enough for them, and in the end, it all unraveled. Capitol dropped us, and we figured we could at least take the tapes and release the record ourselves. But no—Brovsky erased the 2-inch masters to reuse on his other projects. Bulk-erased, gone forever. Believe it or don't . . .

CHAPTER 36

On the Road with Tucker Boots

1998

By the time the late '90s rolled around, my son Tucker had developed into quite a guitar player, singer, and songwriter. I taught him a few chords when he was a child and he ran with it. But he was mostly self-taught. Tucker is sharp and prolific. He's kept journals for years. He put out an album in 2004 that was hailed as a masterpiece and was a major download on iTunes. But in 1998 another tour of India, Pakistan, and Nepal was coming up and this time I offered Tuck the job to come with me to play guitar and sing harmonies. Tucker, no stranger to foreign travels, was in.

Tucker was into Eric Johnson and Monte Montgomery but didn't know a thing about country music. Even though he'd been to Willie's picnics with me a time or two he needed to get a better handle on some country licks. We went to see Champ Hood, who played brilliant acoustic guitar with Uncle Walt's Band, the Bluegrass Beatles. Champ knew a lot of basic country licks and he showed Tucker a couple of runs that he said he based all his country leads around. Universal licks Tucker uses to this day.

The PAO in Lahore was Donna Winton, a young gal married to a Syrian man named Said. She was all about mixing cultures up. She helped set up the 1998 tour, with shows in Karachi, Islamabad, Lahore, Peshawar, and several others in Nepal. Lahore is a magnificent old-world city, with palaces and temples and cobblestone streets, rich in history. It was called the Jewel in the Crown of India before the partition in 1948 and still had India all over it. Rudyard Kipling's *Kim* opens up with the title character sitting atop a giant cannon in front of the Red Fort in Lahore. It's still called Kim's Gun. We played a Set Department show in a packed hotel ballroom that night—wall-to-wall people and buzzing energy. At one point, I joked to the crowd, "If you've got a request, just write it on the back of a hundred-dollar bill and send it up front." After the next song, a Pakistani dude strolled up to the stage and handed me a single rupee note. On the back, he'd scribbled one word: *Elvis*. Without missing a beat, I launched into "All Shook Up."

Tucker and I played mostly public shows, but we also played a lot of schools. There were guards surrounding whatever venue we played, and I was glad there were as there was always what the PAOs called "an unspecified threat" that had to be weighed. As usual we took a different route each time to get to the gigs, sometimes circling in roundabout ways.

We played a lot and conducted workshops and made many new friends. At the University of Lahore we held songwriting and guitar workshops. Tucker was great in the guitar workshop, though invariably some kid would go all Eddie Van Halen on us and the students would roar. We gradually became a father-and-son act. Everyone loved Tucker—he was fresh, funny, and fearless, the kind of kid who never met a stranger. His youthful energy and charm balanced my cowboy-hat-wearing troubadour persona, and together we created something unique and heartwarming onstage. These shows often drew a lot of families, and we struck a chord—they laughed readily and they cried right along with

Rehearsal with Tucker in Lahore, Pakistan, 2003. (Photo courtesy of Bob Livingston.)

our sad cowboy songs. The State Department especially loved the father-and-son dynamic. It was a good story, and they knew how to sell it.

Most of the days were scripted, but sometimes we went off the map on the spur of the moment. The State Department was big on our meeting local people and visiting with them, eating with the mayor, going to his house, and being exposed to the culture. Sometimes we'd meet politicians, musicians, and movie stars. Lots of musicians. It was an exchange of ideas, it was part of the gig. When they figured out that I liked to do that kind of stuff they always had these events set up. We often stayed with local people, what was called "home hospitality." But they put us up in a lot of fine hotels, too. They literally made us stay inside the hotel and not wander off and they watched us and wanted to know where we were at all times. They wanted us to be safe. And the hotels were five-star with nice beds and bathtubs. But don't drink the water!

We played Calcutta at the American Center. A nice theater, libraries, a slew of offices, Fortress America. The tour had taken a toll on me. I'd developed a severe pain in my left leg. Something was bad wrong, but I didn't know what it was. In those days you could walk into a pharmacy in India and get whatever you wanted: "I'll take a gallon of codeine please." I was taking painkillers and muscle relaxers and all kinds of anti-inflammatory drugs trying to dampen the pain, trying to get some relief. But nothing would touch it. I was pretty spaced out, yet I still had to do the tours, and when I was playing in front of an audience I didn't think about the pain so much and could always transport myself to the show-must-go-on world. After I got back to Austin I had an MRI and discovered I had a ruptured disk—so that explained a lot.

Because I was so out of it at the Fortress America show I struggled and would go into La La Land and just stare into space while Tucker was playing his lead. When we'd get back to the verse where I was supposed to be singing something, or telling a story or a joke, I had already spaced out and couldn't do it. Tucker cued me, "Dad, you're supposed to tell a story. Start talking. Say something," and it was like, oh yeah, so then I'd tell the story. Strangely enough we had a pretty good show in spite of all of this. Muscle memory and auto-pilot.

After the Calcutta show, this cool cat comes up to me and he says, "My name is Sammit Roy and I am the world's foremost exponent of Bengali music. I loved your program and I have to beg you to come to my house for a visit tonight, please."

"Ah, I don't think we can do it. We're going up to Assam on the train early tomorrow morning for some shows up there. We have to get to bed early."

"Only thirty minutes. I just want you to come. Please, honor me and come to my humble house." He *was* a Bengali folk singer, with a pencil-thin mustache, urbane and charismatic. Tall and thin. Well-dressed. I asked our PAO about him and what I should do and he said, "If you can do it, it would be good. This man is famous and a big deal around here." I had to bribe Tucker to go.

Sammit Roy's place was a good 35-minute taxi ride away and up six flights of stairs. It was an enormous apartment, and the place was full of Bengali musicians and artists and media types. Sammit's parents lived there, and his wife's parents also lived there, and all their kids. Various faces peered out of the mists of this dwelling. There was a piano in the middle of the room and I don't know how they got that piano up there. Sammit's son was holding court. He was a Bombay session man visiting his big family and he was ripping some jazz on the piano to shreds. He began playing Nat King Cole's "Unforgettable" and Sammit began to sing exactly like Nat and then he sang one standard after another while the son was playing, and I was taking notes and watching like it was movie.

Tucker was nowhere to be seen, so I went looking. I found him in the kitchen talking with a young servant girl. She was about seventeen or eighteen, and he's in there talking to her, and she can't speak a word of English, and he's doing sign language, he's helping her chop vegetables, and talking to her and they are both laughing, her with her hand over her mouth. I'm thinking, *Okay, I get it.* Soon it gets to be about 10:30 at night. We'd already been there an hour and a half and I'm ready to go, and suddenly Sammit says, "You've got to eat with us. You have to stay for dinner."

"Oh, no. It's way too late, you know, we have to get up early."

"Please, you *must* have dinner with us!"

And Tucker suddenly appears from out of the kitchen and says, "Dad! We have to stay for dinner!"

"Whaat?"

"We've got to stay here, it would be an insult to leave."

And I am thinking, *What's got into Tucker*? I had never seen him so eager to stay anywhere after a show. He was usually the first one out of there.

So we stayed for dinner, and while we were waiting to eat, I found myself at the table with a bunch of Bengali guys swapping stories about the road and playing gigs. Sammit turns to me and says, "You know, Bob, I just love Tucker. What a wonderful boy—and such a *homeboy*—always wanting to be in the kitchen helping prepare the food." I just nodded and thought, *Yeah, right.*

Early the next morning we went straight to the train to go up to Assam, a northern state on the border with China on the Brahmaputra River. We were boarding at 4 a.m.; this was brutal. I glanced at the manifest, the passenger list that was taped to the outside of the compartment. I noticed immediately that a Mr. George Jones was among the train travelers that night. I searched for him through the night, but alas, never found him. But it got me to thinking and I imagined bumping along these wild Indian tracks with Ol' Possum, singing a train song together, imagining that Tucker would laugh at meeting him and then show him the Champ licks. I decided to put "He Stopped Loving Her Today" into the set and I still sing it whenever I need the saddest song ever written.

That night we played a music festival, videotaping the whole thing ourselves. There were a lot of ceremonial gifts and pronouncements. A State Department woman spoke and then the mayor spoke after her. All of it in English. When we got onstage they gave us these funny local hats and presented us with flowers and doodads. Then a musical group started with an exotic mix of instruments. They wanted us to sit in and who knows what we played but the people loved it whatever it was. All the while we were passing the video camera from one to the other onstage, Tucker and I, handing it off to strangers in the wings to get just a few minutes of us playing a song. It's a jerky-jerky high-energy piece of tape.

After the India shows, we played several venues in Kathmandu. The whole city is ancient and we stayed in the middle of town in

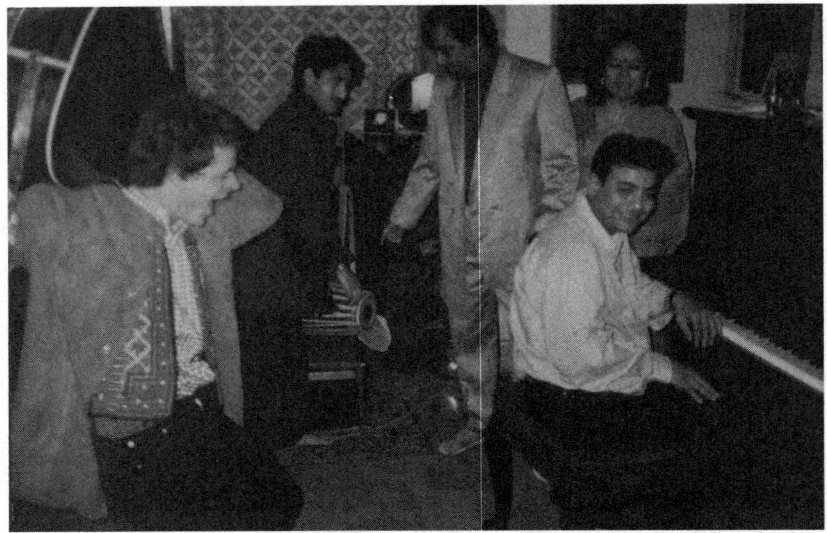

Tucker throws down a Stevie Ray move for Bengali musician Samit Roy (standing, center) and his family in Calcutta, India. (Photo by Bob Livingston.)

an old British guesthouse. We'd walk the streets and buy everything we saw. We were there about a week and every day Tucker would have a different plan for taking a trek in the Himalayas. It was going to be three days, then a week, not, "I'll just be gone the weekend."

We were scheduled to leave the next morning. Tucker walked up to me with the video camera. "Dad, I am videotaping you so you can't freak out, but I'm leaving for Everest Base Camp tomorrow for a month." This was in January and it was cold as a witch, but he did it. He was lost out on the ice sheets a few times and began to leave things behind. He sold the Swiss Army knife I'd given him for the trip to buy food and lodging at the many small guesthouse yurts along the way. He sawed his toothbrush handle off to save weight. At one point he and another trekker bashed down the door to an abandoned high mountain cabin and burned it for warmth. Tucker was gone for a month and we finally heard he was all right and had indeed made it to Everest Base Camp from a note he had written passed down the mountain through many different hands and into those of our State Department friend in Kathmandu.

CHAPTER 37

I Quit the Gonzos and Ray Wylie Calls

1979

The writing was on the wall. We'd lost our Gonzo record deal but we were still committed to a Midwest tour. We had no choice. Where was Michael Brovsky when all this was unravelling? There was talk of another record deal, but as far as I could tell, we were nowhere in the conversation. And now, we were out in the cold—literally—as the breaking point crept in with the dead of winter. We had journeyed into the badlands of the Midwest and the weather was turning against us. We were still on a pathetic retainer and it was becoming a financial disaster, and the longer we were out on the road the worse it became. I wanted to quit right then and there but knew I had to stick it out. I can't say what the other guys were thinking, though there was a lot of grumbling in the close quarters of the Buick band wagon. There were five of us packed there while our road manager, Jack Borders, and John T. Davis, our roadie and staff writer, were in the big white Chevy equipment truck that usually took a separate route and got there before us.

We had one more show to end this leg of the tour, a double bill with Ray Wylie Hubbard and the Cowboy Twinkies at the

Cotillion Ballroom in Wichita. That night was cold and snowy, a blizzard. We were all broke and edgy. There was way too much at stake and it didn't seem like we were making any headway. I had my family to take care of. Our tour support money had dried up. Ray and the Cowboy Twinkies were also broke and fighting with each other. Terry "Buffalo" Ware was the guitar player for the Twinkies, Dennis Meehan (AKA Clovis Roblaine) on bass, and Jimmy Herbst on drums. They were all great guys and were an eclectic band that served Ray's mad design well. But like it was with us in that bleak winter: there was enough desperation to go around for everybody. We were not as desperate as the hostages being held in Tehran we saw on TV, but still . . .

After the Cotillion Ballroom show there was a forlorn sadness hanging over us. We knew something was coming and we were all eager to get home. The next morning the truck wouldn't start. John T. Davis, who would later go on to write for newspapers and edit books, was our roadie at the time and drove the truck, among other jobs. The tour was over, we were miserable, and the truck with all our equipment was stuck in a snowbank with a blown head. Jack gave John T. a credit card and told him to have the truck fixed and drive it back down to Texas. The rest of us left for Austin, either in the Buick or on a plane. It took a week to repair the truck, and poor John T. was stranded in a cheap motel in Wichita, watching *The Beverly Hillbillies* and *Star Trek* in his underwear.

I got back to a freezing house. Our place wasn't well insulated and there was ice on the inside of the doors. Iris and the boys were cold but they rolled with the punches and were okay. We had two fireplaces and a big Dearborn heater and we had everything roaring all the time. I was glad to be back home, but things were precarious. I had a hard time compartmentalizing in those days. I couldn't leave the weariness of the road and the financial troubles at the door. And it all whirled around in my head.

CHAPTER 37

I called Gary and told him I couldn't do it anymore. I said I was going to have to go out and get a job. I was desperate. Gary told me to hang on and something would come up, but I just said it wasn't really working for me and I was quitting. I couldn't support my family. I guess I told John and Paul, but they were probably as shaken as I was. I didn't know what I was going to do but I had to try something else. I never thought about calling Jerry Jeff or Murphey, not even for a second. For some reason, those guys never entered my mind, even in such desperate times. Things were going to play out.

About a week after I quit, the phone rang with that old familiar jangle of fate I was starting to recognize—and sure enough, it was Ray Wylie. He asked what I was up to and I just said, "Nothing. I quit the Gonzos." He said the Cowboy Twinkies had broken up after that Wichita gig and he needed a bass player fast for a couple of gigs he had in Dallas that weekend and could I come play? All I said was, "Where do you want me to meet you?"

Playing with Ray that weekend was a lot of fun. A breath of fresh air. He was sardonic and funny and he was always on, always funny and punchy. There were some new songs and I went up a day early to go over them. He had an agent who was promising a lot of gigs coming up, but Ray had no band. Bobby Rambo was playing guitar on those two shows. After that weekend I was able to pay the electric bill, which took some of the pressure off.

Ray called again a few days later and asked me if I could put together a band—a guitar player, a drummer, and me. He said he had shows that week and the next and more to come.

I suggested John Inmon and Paul Pearcy, who were both looking for new gigs too.

"Yeah, that'd be great, call them and see what they think."

John and Paul said to count them in. Ray Wylie jumped at the chance to get John Inmon in the new band. Next weekend, John,

Making a video of Bill Oliver's anthem, "Barton Springs Eternal." I'm filming Aunt Pearl, AKA Joe Sears. (Photo courtesy of Bill Oliver.)

Paul, and I went up to Dallas and played a couple of shows with Ray Wylie and it was badass.

Recently I had a chance to talk to Paul Pearcy about the Ray Wylie days. He said, "I remember the first gig we played was in Norman, Oklahoma. You and John and me with Ray Wylie. We had no rehearsal and we played the show. Ray just started playing and you and John seem to know all the songs and all the harmonies." Ray did some eclectic covers. We did "Driving Wheel" ("I feel like some old engine, done lost its drivin' wheel . . ."), "Lost Highway," rock 'n' roll and "The Lonesome Fugitive" like Bruce Springsteen would do it. Ray would start strumming his guitar and we somehow knew where to come in and it sounded like we had played together for years." None of us could believe how easy it was.

The three of us—John, Paul, and I—had played a lot a lot of shows together with other incarnations of the Gonzos and we were tight as a drum. Paul and I were attacking the rhythm section and John just sailed over the top with leads and rhythms.

With this trio we recorded with Bill Oliver on his *Texas Oasis* album as members of his Otter Space Band. Bill is a lot of fun but dead serious about saving the planet. He's an environmental troubadour and he writes songs such as the Austin anthem "Barton Springs Eternal" and "If You Can't Break a Six-pack Ring, How Do You Think a Duck Will?" Paul especially hit it off with Bill—they've floated countless rivers together and shared more than a few campfire jams along the way.

So we throw in with Ray Wylie and he was the darling of Dallas. He was scruffy, wore black leather pants, and his hair was all messy. His wife at the time, D'Ann, looked like a model and her parents were Dallas lawyers who lived in a penthouse on Turtle Creek. Johnny and Jerry Crawford, D'Ann's folks, immediately loved us and would take us out to dinner and fight over who got to sit next to whom. Soon they would put us up in an apartment right under their penthouse that became our home away from home.

We might play four shows in a weekend. Once we drove up north to Dallas on a Thursday night, got up early Friday morning and played at NorthPark Center for a grand opening of some shop, then dashed across town to play for the Guy Laroche studio with fashion models everywhere, and then we played Whisky River that night. Then we played at NorthPark again Saturday morning and for a ritzy party for the American Cancer Society that night. To this day, Ray Hubbard has been the fairest band leader I have ever played for. He really valued us and didn't want us going anywhere else.

We were a four-piece band that sounded bigger. John could play anything, from rock 'n' roll to country, and had the ability to sound just like a steel guitar when called for. Paul really got around on the drums like always and I just powered through on bass with a lot of 8th and 16th notes. We all sang harmonies, so it was pretty powerful. We were a tight band from the git-go. Hand in glove.

Jimmy Buffett, me, and Jerry Jeff, posing backstage for an unknown fan. (Polaroid courtesy of Bob Livingston.)

Ray bought a Dodge van we nicknamed the "Butter Dish" because it was a soft yellow with a white top extension you could stand up in. There were captain's chairs and a bed in back with a cargo hold for amps and drums in back of everything. We needed a roadie-soundman and John suggested his brother, Jim. So it became the five of us driving everywhere, taking turns at the wheel, traveling many a mile in the Butter Dish. Later on, Ray's father-in-law, Johnny Crawford, bought us a bus, a 1967 GM 4106. It had been a tour bus back east and still had the various cities it had serviced up on the scrolling marquee: "Boston, New York City, Fenway Park . . ." The seats were still in it but we ripped them out and built two bunk beds and bolted tables and benches to the floor. It was a ramshackle creaky vehicle, a far cry from the Prevost buses of other bands. We all took turns driving; Ray especially loved to drive. But we needed a professional driver and Ray found Gary Mack, a Vietnam vet with a million stories who was a great guy and could drive through the night. We also had a man at some point, Dan Cook, we called "D-Boy." Dan would go on to be a guitar tech for the Moody Blues, Bonnie Raitt, and Jimmy Buffett. It was a good crew and we all got along and had a lot of fun whether making music or eating at Denny's.

During this Ray Wylie period, Gary Nunn went off on his own and started his own career. He'd written "London Homesick Blues" which so many people loved, but it was still hard for him. He was upset that I'd quit the band and thought we'd keep things going no matter what. Gary was tired of playing in a back-up capacity. He told me, "I can't believe you're going to be playing bass again behind anybody. You should be doing your own stuff. We could play the honky-tonks and bars." But it was not to be. The long and short of it was that playing with Ray and the guys was a lot more fun and lucrative than the Gonzos. And this was a damn good band.

Yes, we were firmly on the bus with Ray Wylie, but we still had a Lost Gonzo debt, a credit card balance, and payments on a truck and the Buick wagon. We were broke, but we had to square everything up. We wanted to retire the debt, had to. I started thinking outside the box. If you are a musician in Austin, you end up playing a lot of benefits for one thing or another. Well, let's have a benefit for ourselves. We'll call it the Benefit of the Doubt: "It's

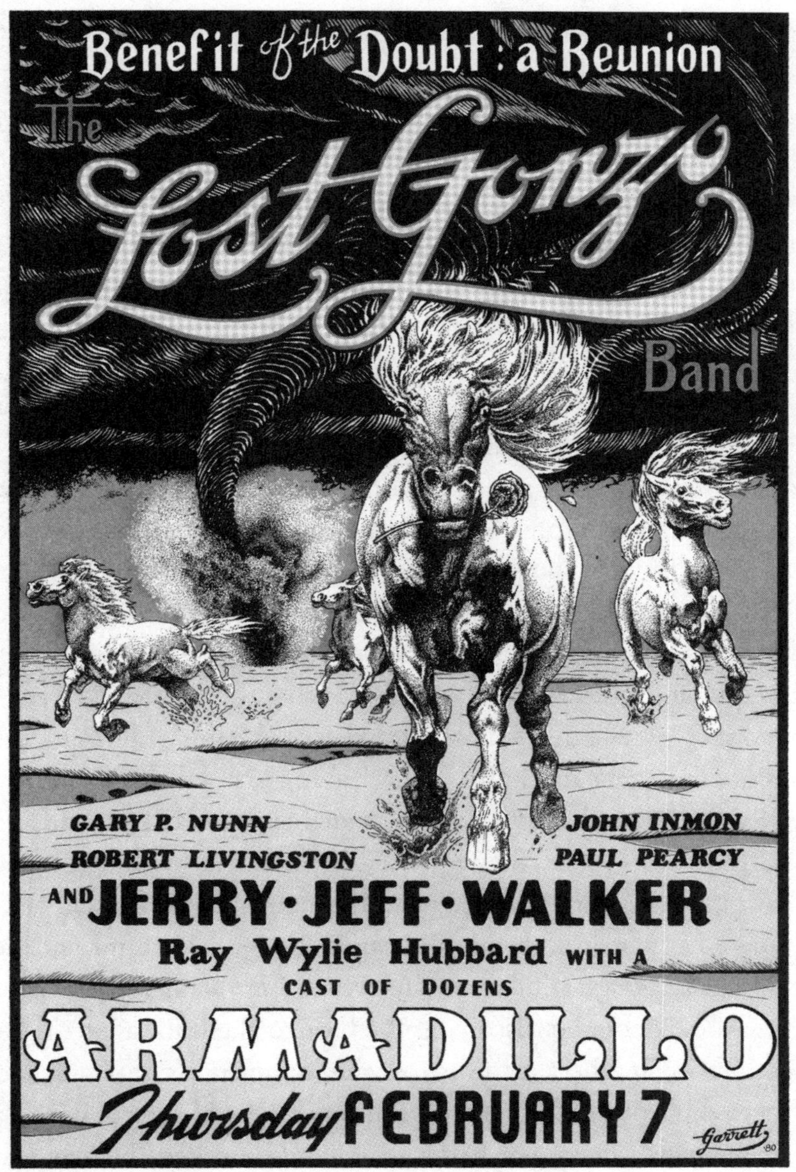

Poster by Danny Garrett, 1980.

doubtful who it benefits, but we're the beneficiaries of the doubt." There was really no better option, so the other guys agreed and it became a consuming project for me. We needed a venue so I asked Eddie Wilson of the Armadillo if we could play one last big bash—for ourselves. He agreed. We enlisted Danny Garrett, one of the Armadillo artists. Danny and Michael Priest and Jim Franklin had a complex where they created their poster art. Danny did an incredible poster for us. Jerry Jeff said he'd help us out, which was awfully nice of him, and Ray Wylie threw in too. We had the big show on February 7, 1980. It was a great lineup: Jerry Jeff, Ray Wylie, Gary P., John, Paul, and me. The Gonzos opened the show and then played with everyone else.

We also had the Nuclear Energy Dragon there. It was a cause we were involved in. Austin was part of the South Texas Nuclear Project—but it turned out to have major cost overruns and there were safety concerns and it became a big financial drain on the city. People were protesting, Austin was trying to get out of it, so we threw in with the protesters: "No nukes is good nukes!" An activist named Todd Samuelson had an extra-large mechanical dragon in his garage that he brought out of storage for the event. The dragon would emerge, with five or so guys in it, smoke blasting out of its mouth and burning red eyes. All the while Paul was bashing cymbals and lights were flashing and John was playing end-of-the-world chords and we made hissing dragon sounds on the mic and we stuffed fake money into its mouth and then he shat out an A-bomb. It was wild and fantastic. So we had theater, we had music and tears and camaraderie, everything, and we made just enough money to pay everything off, absolving us of the Gonzo debt and dissolving the Gonzo Band for a later date. So that was it. The Lost Gonzos were done and John, Paul, and I started playing full time with the Ray Wylie Hubbard Band.

Meanwhile, Jerry Jeff had a new band he called the Bandito Band: Freddie Krc, Bobby Rambo, Tomás Ramirez, and Ron Cobb. Our paths would cross every once in a while, but for the next couple of years I played with Ray. We made a record called *Something About the Night*, when albums were still being made. It

Ray Wylie Hubbard Band in 1980. (L–R): John Inmon, Ray Wylie Hubbard, Bob Livingston, and Paul Pearcy. (Photo by Lisa Law.)

was cool, and it was on Hubbard's own label. We cut Springsteen's song "Dancing in the Dark" and Ray's "Something About the Night" and "Texas Is a State of Mind." A couple of others were "Dallas After Midnight" and "Rockabilly Rock," all really fun to play night after night.

My little family was back at our place in the hill country, and Iris was taking care of those boys and getting them to school and driving them to Nana and Grandee's house down in San Antonio where they would stay for some days, and Tucker and Trevor would creep into the cupboard late at night and eat those little cake doughnuts covered with white powdered sugar and sometimes even fall asleep on the kitchen floor covered in sugar and milk.

Every so often we'd play a show with Jerry Jeff and his Bandito Band and they were good but it wasn't the Gonzo Band. One festival show when we'd already played and were hanging out in the wings, Jerry Jeff asked me to come out and sing harmonies

The Ray Wylie Hubbard Band at Willie's picnic, 1979. (L–R): Paul Pearcy on drums, Bob Livingston, Ray Wylie Hubbard, John Inmon. It was hot! (Photo by Scott Newton.)

on a couple of songs. After the show in the back room, JJ said that it was fun but then he grabbed me by the lapels of my coat and shook me and shouted, "You *dominate* me!"

"What? What are you talking about?"

And he shouted again right in my face, "You *DOMINATE ME!*" and stormed off. WTF? It was his way of saying something between the lines.

I played with Ray Wylie most of 1980 and 1981. On one of our sojourns, Ray invited a freelance writer named Pete Dexter to travel with us to a gig. Pete was writing an article on Ray for *Esquire* magazine. He came around, got on the bus with us, and away we went. Pete and I started talking and I told him some colorful stories, including one about me beating Jerry Jeff up, just laughing and talking. How was I to know that Pete would include

The chaos of the hotel check-in. (Photo by Gary P. Nunn.)

the Jerry Jeff story in the article about Ray? It took up a lot of room in the piece and I don't think Ray liked it all that much. It was supposed to be an article about him and his music and here was a good slice of it with me talking about wild times with Jerry Jeff. How was I to know? Anyway, more would come of that.

Time passed, with more bus tours and more gigs, but Ray seemed somewhat discouraged. We never thought of ourselves as just a bar band and wanted to go places, *needed* to go places. We were used to going places, and I loved playing with these guys. John and Paul, Ray Wylie, all of us were good friends and it wasn't hard and actually a lot of fun to be out on the road with them. Still . . . I was thinking about a change, and I began throwing some mental lines out into the cosmic waters. And I couldn't help but remember and miss all the fun adrenaline-filled swashbuckling country rockin' Jerry Jeff Gonzo shows.

CHAPTER 38

Jerry Jeff in a Cloud of Dust

1981

It was early morning and a dust cloud was whipping up my dirt road. Jerry Jeff came roaring up in his dirty Cadillac convertible wearing a 13-gallon hat, cowboys boots, and a bathing suit. Horn honking, dusty brakes screeching to a halt, a lot of drama. I went outside to see what this was all about.

Out in the driveway Jerry Jeff said, "Bob Livingston! Bob Livingston. I came out here to find out what you are doing."

"What do you mean, what am I doing?"

"I wanna know what you're doing, what you're up to. Why are you doing what you're doing?"

"I don't understand your question."

"Why are you playing with Ray Hubbard and not with me!" he shouted. Finally it came out.

Jerry Jeff continued, "I got a new record contract. We're going to be playing everywhere, we're going to make a record. You need to come and play with me again. You give me *energy*. You sing on all the songs, the other guys sometimes sing and sometimes don't. You always sing and sing weird harmony parts and I count on that!"

This was a lot to take in. What was the band going to be like? Jerry Jeff said there would be a new record and tour. I'd have to think about it and talk it over with Iris. JJ was insistent: "Come back and play with me—a new record!"

I talked it over with Iris, who said that it sounded good in theory, but she also knew who Jerry Jeff was and she warned me about how it might be. She didn't like me being gone and away from the boys. I hated that part too, but my excuse was that I didn't know how to do anything other than what I was doing. It's a risky life. But I talked her and myself into it. On the surface, it looked like a good opportunity. It meant that I would be leaving Ray Wylie. And Jerry Jeff's offer was opaque—though I wanted it to sound like a good idea. I needed to stay working and progressing and supporting my family. I had two little munchkins running wild and free and they needed food and fuel. That night, I called Jerry Jeff and said I was in.

But . . . the big but . . .

I jumped the gun. Jerry Jeff had made it sound like the new record and tour were happening *now*, so I quit Ray Wylie and the band cold, walking away with nothing but a few vague promises, a gut full of hope, and the mercy of my colorful fate. I gave Hubbard my notice the next day—way too early, as it turned out. Jerry Jeff didn't have anything lined up. The Bandito Band was history, and he was drifting in a dead zone. His new manager, Stu Weintraub, was still sorting things out and chasing a record deal, but there was no tour. Not for weeks. Maybe months.

Somebody should've told me what was real. *He* should have told me. But honestly, I wasn't following Jerry Jeff's situation all that closely. We'd crossed paths at festivals here and there, but I didn't know the whole story. I would come to learn I'd stepped straight into a lull in his career. He was trying to build something new, but didn't quite know what yet. That said, JJ's instincts had always been good, if erratic, and I was already in too deep to back out.

Meanwhile, back at the ranch, I was home on the hill with Iris and Tucker and Trevor. Iris was a great cook and made the best pies in all the three worlds. The boys and I ran with Kitty Dog up and down the hills and ravines and tried to picture life here thousands of years ago. I had a 16-gauge single-shot shotgun and the boys and I would head out to a special place and fire it off from time to time at an old stump. Trevor would hold the three shells and Tucker would take one and hand it to me. I'd load it up and blast away fast as I could. The boys were wide-eyed. We worked on this assembly line until we got it down and could fire off quickly. There were some suspicious folks further up the hill and I'd hear them firing their semiautomatic weapons, so I warned them, letting them know I too was armed.

♪

So I was back playing with Jerry Jeff. It wasn't the Gonzo Band, but hell—I was Gonzo, so close enough. I was carrying the torch. At first, it was a bit of a ragtag outfit. Bobby Rambo was on guitar. I can't for the life of me remember who the drummer was. Jerry Jeff was hustling for gigs but not having much luck—I didn't know why.

Then something finally shook loose: a show at the Cheatham Street Warehouse in San Marcos. No rehearsal. Jerry Jeff just said, "I'll pick you up." He showed up in some fancy Mercedes—600SL or whatever they call those land yachts. I think he was leasing it.

We barreled down I-35 in a full-on Texas toad-strangler, rain slamming the windshield like it had a grudge. We played the gig, packed up, and hit the road back north—still in the same biblical downpour. Cars were crawling along, hazard lights blinking, wipers flailing like crazy. Visibility? Maybe two feet. I was white-knuckling it in the passenger seat, finally blurting, "Let me drive, man!" But Jerry Jeff just kept cruising, cool as ever, grinning into the storm.

"You drive this car?" he said. "Do you realize how much this it's worth? No way are you going to drive my car." We had to stop under a bridge on the interstate. It's a wonder we survived.

On the drive back Jerry Jeff proclaimed, "We're going to a party!" I wanted to head home but this seemed like something I was going to have to do. We went to the party and I remember that there were some Austin underworld people there. It was dim in the room, just candlelight. And I was in a sober period in my life, not indulging at all. I was disgusted and I hated the atmosphere and to me it was just more distorted Fellini faces flickering in the candlelight. I can see it. It's like a painting to me now . . .

Jerry Jeff was unsteady and holding a big blue plastic tumbler of beer and the lights are flickering. It's getting towards 3 a.m. and I am standing in a circle with him and three or four others. I am looking at the uncertain faces and want to leave desperately. I have to get out of there. Bobby Lemons, the road manager, joins the circle. He has a mustache and a soul patch under his bottom lip and a hat that is cocked jauntily on his long braided ponytailed head. Bobby is a great guy with only good intentions but that night, with the candlelight flickering on his face and his eyes twinkling, he looked like the Devil himself, especially when he said to me, "Welcome baaack, Bob. As you can see, *nothing* has changed." It hit me hard. I knew then I had made a mistake. I didn't know how big. Oh my god. Now what?

Up the next morning early with a purpose, I told Iris I had to find out what was really going on. It was a freezing March day. As I drove through the gate into Jerry Jeff's driveway, I noticed the front door and all the windows were wide open, wind blowing through with leaves, twigs, and newspapers scattered around. Not a sign of life, not a light on, not a sound, like it was abandoned. I walked through the front door calling out "Jerry Jeff? Jerry Jeff?" After further investigation, I found him stretched out on his couch in the living room, dead to the world.

"Jerry Jeff, are you okay?"

He woke up. "Oh . . . I was dreaming, I was just dreaming. . . . My head was in Jessie Jane's lap. And she was stroking my head saying, 'It's going to be all right, Daddy, it's going to be all right.' It was such a beautiful dream."

I said, "Jerry Jeff, I just came to find out what's real."

That brought him to attention. "Huh?"

I said, "I came to find out what's real. You've promised me the world, a tour, a record, and in reality there's nothing that I can see. When are we going to do what you said we were going to do?"

Jerry jeff sat bolt upright, suddenly wide awake and ready for bear. "What is real? You wanna know what's real? I'll show you what's real," and he ran out and dove into his swimming pool. It is freezing cold and he shouted, "Woo-hooo! NOW THATS REAL! WOW!" Then he crawled out and padded down the hall dripping water, slipping and sliding, soaking wet and freezing and he comes back still dripping and sliding and he has a copy of that *Esquire* magazine article about Ray Wylie, and he screams "Do you wanna know what's real?"

I said, "I could have still been playing with Ray. We had a good thing going. I could have stayed. We had gigs . . ."

And he yells back, "Don't you know that I tell you what you want to hear?"

I was taken far, far aback. "What? What are you talking about?"

He held up the *Esquire* article and said, "They write an article about Hubbard and it's all about ME! It's all about me! You will be much better off coming back with me. It's gonna happen . . . you've just got to give me some time! I'm getting it together."

He only told me what I wanted to hear!

I was crestfallen. But there was no turning back. "Okay, okay. When will you know something? I just want you to communicate with me." These were the days of no retainer. Nothing.

To pay the bills, I got a gig on a house painting crew and painted a few houses, hanging on just a little bit longer. Jerry Jeff and his new New York manager eventually did get it together—sort of, I guess—and we set off on a tour and started playing a lot. In the absence of the Gonzos, Jerry Jeff had recorded some records with the Bandito Band, but none of those records had the impact of the MCA albums we had recorded in the '70s, all the hits. Most of the songs we did in the shows came from those earlier albums.

So I was back in the wild and woolly saddle again. John Inmon was not back with us yet and there was a guitar player from Florida named Gary Walker who played a mean telly but didn't sing. Freddie Krc from the Bandito Band took the drummer's chair. Bobby Rambo was playing another guitar and Riley Osbourn was on keys. But at least for me it wasn't the old hand-in-glove. These were all great guys, but I had played in the original band and this was different. The Gonzos used to open up at all the shows for Jerry Jeff. And when we played we were all on the front line. But now it was the Jerry Jeff Walker Show with his mic and his monitors way up front, and the rest of the band way back, about ten feet back in another county. "That's the way it is now," Jerry Jeff said.

But I wasn't in one of those Nashville country bands with all the guys relegated to risers and dark corners. Over time I would inch my monitor and microphone up just to dick with Jerry Jeff, which became a thing onstage at sound checks. We'd get to the sound check and he'd have the sound guy put my monitor and mic stand way back there. And I'd slowly inch it up. I didn't want to be looking at his butt! And he'd inch it back. And I'd inch it up and inch it up and as the night wore on I'd get up about a couple of feet further forward. At least not ten feet back. This would always happen, even up to the last gig he ever played. It didn't make a difference where the guitar player was to Jerry Jeff. John, Mitch Watkins, Tommy Nash, all the guys who played with us over the years. They could be in front of him for all he cared, sitting in the audience. But it made a *big* difference where I was. He kept an eye on me. I wasn't your everyday ho-hum bass player in a country band and he knew it. He wanted me there for my energy and drive and I gave it freely.

After I left Ray Wylie, John and Paul stayed on with him for a few more months, but that band broke up and they left Ray too. John joined up with Delbert McClinton and then spent some time on the road with Omar and the Howlers. Paul stuck it out the longest with Ray and inherited the band van, the Butter Dish. So we all went our respective ways, but it wouldn't be long before things came back around and we would be reunited.

John's tour with Delbert wound down and Omar wasn't exactly his cup of tea. I don't remember if I called him or if Jerry Jeff did, but soon we were back together, this time with Freddie "Steady" Krc on drums. Jerry Jeff always preferred Freddie on drums because he played simple and solid.

Riley Osbourn, from the great Antone's house band, joined us on organ from time to time. Riley was probably the best keyboard player in Austin, and that's saying a lot. A true blues aficionado, he could channel the souls of Pine Top Perkins, Professor Longhair, and the voodoo funk of Dr. John.

But Riley wasn't just a wizard on the keys—he was a gourmet interrogator. At truck stops and hole-in-the-wall Chinese joints, he grilled the servers. "Is that brown sauce or white sauce? Are there clams in that? Fresh or canned? Who caught the clams? Who canned the clams?"

And Riley could be grouchy. Get in a car with him behind the wheel and you'd witness road rage as performance art. In fact, Austin songwriter Danny Britt named his band *Grouchy Like Riley* in his honor.

It's hard to believe Riley is gone now. He wasn't just a monster player—he was a great friend, a gifted songwriter and guitarist

On tour in Nome, Alaska. (L–R): Bobby Lemons, Riley Osbourn, and me, 1989. (Photo courtesy of Bob Livingston.)

too. He wrote "Isabella," a beautiful song he played on his classical guitar, for the Gonzo Band's *Hands of Time* album. We miss him deeply

> Hey, Isabella, you put the good old days in your old
> suitcase forever.
> Hey, Isabella, you took the good old days and your old
> suitcase down the road.

CHAPTER 39

The Gonzo Compadres

1990

A couple of years with Jerry Jeff went by and then I was off to a State Department tour where most of my days were taken up either touring or spending time with my family either on this side of the globe or the other. Jerry Jeff had a new band with Lloyd Maines, Paul Pearcy, Roland Denny, Champ Hood, and John Inmon. They recorded *Live at Gruene Hall.* I had wandered off to India to play another tour and wasn't around for the session. In fact, I was homeless. We had sold the house in Oak Hill and at the time I didn't know where I was going to land. Iris and the boys had gone all in and were in India for the long haul. I'd spent almost all of 1989 and 1990 in India looking for the secret of life. And it was not "the wet bird never flies at night" kind of secret either. Back home, I couch-crashed with a friend and his family. They gave me a room and all I had to do for it was sing their kids to sleep every night. They fed me good, but all things considered, these were peculiar and curious times full of widely divergent worlds.

I recorded a cassette called *Signs of Life* that had songs inspired by my Indian sojourns. "Looking for signs of life, scattered 'cross the universe . . ." I was on the road with Jerry jeff and I felt homesick for my family in far-off India and was throwing lines in the water for another tour over *there*. But times were tough. I played a few gigs here and there and recorded a radio commercial or two. I even painted a few houses. I was a freelancer depending on several income streams. There was no clear path forward, so I just kept moving—following my own footsteps and tossing messages into the ether, hoping one might land somewhere. Apparently, one did. Out of the blue, Jerry Jeff called and asked, "What've you been up to? We've kinda lost track of you." I still don't know how he found me—there were no cell phones back then—but there he was, like a voice dropped from the sky.

"Well, I'm just here in Austin. I'm doing some things. I just got back from a tour in India. I'm going to do it again, not sure when."

"You need to come out on the road with me. Be my road manager. You know how to do it."

It was the craziest idea I'd ever heard but the long and short of it was that I actually went to Dallas to road-manage a show for Jerry Jeff and ended up singing most of the set with him. A couple of days after that Jerry Jeff called to tell me that when he had spoken to Susan about me road-managing his California tour she said, "If Bob is going to be out on the road with you why would he do anything else but play bass?" Jerry Jeff said that got him to thinking in a different direction. He told me that if I was back in the band, then he could get Freddie Krc back on drums.

Freddie had played in the Bandito Band and Jerry Jeff liked his sense of rhythm and that he sang harmonies. Freddie was hilarious, always had a joke or a pun, and the tedium of the road was greatly alleviated when Freddie was around. So that's what happened. Freddie and I were back in the band and we all hit the road. Gary Walker from Florida played lead guitar.

With a more comfortable band, Jerry Jeff started talking about doing a new record and was looking for a studio. Back in the '70s and '80s we had played Austin City Limits several times. Even the Gonzo Band had played on ACL, twice. They had world-class

(L–R): Lloyd Maines, me, and Jerry Jeff playing our gonzo out. (Photo courtesy of Bob Livingston.)

equipment in the UT communications building on Guadalupe and though it wasn't a recording studio per se they had a whole soundstage set up. JJ wanted to record the new record there. He had a new song he was messing with by Ian Tyson and Tom Russell called "Navajo Rug." He'd heard Bill and Bonnie Hearne do it on one of their albums so that was the first song we cut for the new album. Lloyd Maines came in to produce and play steel. I was on bass and Freddie on the drums and John Inmon was back on guitar. Brian Piper from Dallas played keys. It felt natural to be back in the saddle with old friends.

We played everything live on the ACL stage. Lloyd Maines was once again behind the knobs when he wasn't playing steel. We cut songs that would become part of Jerry Jeff's shows for the next several years: "Just to Celebrate," "Navajo Rug," "Blue Mood," "All Through Throwin' Good Love After Bad," "Rockin' on the River," and "Nolan Ryan." But—and this is what would drive me crazy about Jerry Jeff—we recorded the Paul Westmoreland song

"Detour (There's a Muddy Road Ahead)." I never understood why JJ would record a song like this that he knew he would never do live. And he didn't. He's done this many times over the years, just put filler in there. He could have recorded one of my songs or we could have written something together or done a Beatles song or a million different others but not "Detour." Made no sense to me, but maybe it did make sense in another realm. Anyway . . . we cut all the tracks and then did some overdubs, including the harmony vocals. Austin singer-songwriter Christine Albert was called in to lend a woman's voice to the blend which was very cool, and we stuck a fork in it and called it done.

Navajo Rug was released in 1991 and we toured hard in support of it. After the *Navajo* project we cut almost an album a year for several of those mid-nineties years with that band: *Hill Country Rain* in '92, *Viva Luckenbach* in '94, *Christmas Gonzo Styl*e also in 1994, *Night After Night* in '95, and *Scamp* in '96. We went down to Jerry Jeff's villa in Belize and recorded *Cowboys Boots & Bathin' Suits* in 1998 and then *Gonzo Stew* in 2000. Whew! All these albums were for Jerry Jeff's own Tried & True Music record label. He was tired of big record companies taking all the money, so in a way he pioneered Texas artists' putting out records on their own labels because everybody started putting their own albums out. We called ourselves the Gonzo Compadres and even wrote a song about it in Santa Cruz. We had played a wild hippie wine and music festival and there was a guy in the audience, a Renaissance-looking man with a parrot on his shoulder, walking around, raving, bumping into folks he knew and dancing with them. Later that night we were staying at a motel on the Santa Cruz River and were down on that river around a campfire passing guitars and drinking some earthy wine that had come from the festival. The owner of the place came down to visit and he had a parrot on *his* shoulder. Different guy, different parrot. He put the parrot on my shoulder and soon the bird began to whisper in my ear. I started playing some chords and suddenly I sang out, "Well they call us the Gonzo, the Gonzo Compadres!" A Spanish friend of Jerry Jeff's was there at the campfire so I asked him how to say "five friends." "Los cinco compañeros." And we were watching the stars so . . . "mirando las estrellas!" That's how the song started. Jerry Jeff had bought a new plane and along with it came the new pilot Layne Bybee. He was from Jackson Hole, Wyoming, and was a cowboy who flew by the seat of his pants who had walked away from several near brushes with death in the cockpit. So we wrote a verse for him too.

"Gonzo Compadres" ended up on *Viva Luckenbach*, the sequel to *¡Viva Terlingua!* Jerry Jeff wanted to get that old-time feeling back and record once again in the old Luckenbach Dance Hall. We even kicked the album off with "Gettin' By" the same way *¡Viva Terlingua!* opens up. It was fun to be back in Luckenbach, but we all missed Hondo. Beautiful Becky Crouch came out and read "Luckenbach Moon." There are some good songs on that record, Gary's "Ask Me What I Like About Texas" and a remake of "I Makes Money."

We recorded *Night After Night* at the original Birchmere in Alexandria, Virginia. It has all the songs from JJ's MCA albums: "Redneck Mother," "London Homesick Blues," "Mr. Bojangles," "Sangria Wine," "Trashy Women," "L.A. Freeway," "Jaded Lover," and on and on, all the ones that people always want to hear. We recorded it with just the four-piece: Jerry Jeff, Freddie, John, and me. There's a lot of energy on it, even though Jerry Jeff mixed the album and to me it's not a great mix. Jerry Jeff said, "I want that guitar fighting to be heard."

In those wild and woolly days, we played a lot of shows with Willie Nelson and his family, picnics and fairs and festivals. At the picnics, Willie would play with everyone and was always onstage. Besides his amazing catalogue of songs and being one of the most celebrated musicians in the world, he's famous for his "Willie

The Gonzo Compadres at Billy Bob's Texas, 1993. (L–R): Bob Livingston, Jerry Jeff Walker, John Inmon, and Freddie Krc. It was a hot band, no doubt about it. (Photo courtesy of Bob Livingston.)

Weed" and pot-smoking. I once asked him why he smoked so much pot. "Otherwise I might kill people," he said. Way back in there I noticed a hardness in his eyes and a bit of darkness mixed with the light. You would never want to cross him.

Everybody and his dog was trying to find a parking place near the load-in as we pulled up backstage at Willie's picnic. I was on Willie's bus sitting a few feet away from him as we glided through the parking lot. We were playing that show in thirty minutes and I was lucky enough to have hitched a ride from the hotel.

Willie's bus was almost as famous as Willie himself. The Honeysuckle Rose. They made a movie about it. If only those walls could talk. I heard that Ray Wylie was kidnapped by Willie's bass player, Bee Spears, and he was taken home from a gig. Late at night, Paul, Willie's drummer, was showing Ray his gun. His gun! Suddenly, Paul grabbed a *Bible* and called out to the bus driver, "I'm gonna shoot!" And Paul shoots into the Bible and the bullet stopped at Luke 3:4. And nobody flinched.

As we rolled up to a clear space for Willie's bus, a woman appeared in the parking space and approached the bus and banged on the side. Willie said, "Oh, god, it's Martha" (not her real name).

David Alexander, his road manager, just turned to him and said, "How much you want to give her""

Willie said, "Aww, five hundred." Martha was the wife of some dear departed family member and would show up at his gigs from time to time and Willie would do what he had to do. No telling how many Marthas were out there along the trail benefiting from Willie's largesse. As we came to a firm stop, Ray Price suddenly climbed aboard and said, "Put another log on the fire, Willie."

Between these albums and tours, I would play some shows for the State Department. But I always came back to the States for a road trip or to cut an album with Jerry Jeff. We recorded *Scamp* in 1996 and then after some global back-and-forth we all met up in Belize where Jerry cut *Cowboy Boots & Bathin' Suits* both at his home and live at the Victoria House on Ambergris Caye.

Jerry Jeff had it good. Fans who would follow him anywhere and pay dearly for the privilege. We would set up some equipment and Charles Ray would bring his mobile recording gear in and we'd hit "record," and there it was: the soundtrack of the coast—waves crashing, gulls squawking, and lobsters howling for mercy in the background.

CHAPTER 40

The Gonzo *Rendezvous*

1991

Most of us Lost Gonzos were still in the game though scattered to the winds. John and I were off with Jerry Jeff, Gary was on his own playing country honky-tonks, Kelly Dunn had moved back to California and played a lot out there including a stint in my brother Don's San Diego band, Timberline. Paul Pearcy was playing with everybody. Gary, John, and I got together and decided it might be a good idea to put out an album on our 20th anniversary in 1992. We knew we probably couldn't get a record deal because those days seemed long gone. Everybody was putting out records on their own labels so we thought we should do that too.

We had a guy who offered to fund the album, but he turned out to be more shady than supportive—kind of scary, actually. So we moved on and reached out to Lloyd Maines to see if he'd be interested in producing. Keep the ball rolling. Lloyd said yes without hesitation, and we got to work—jamming, trading ideas, and shaping up songs.

We had a couple of sessions like this and one day I ran down to Kinko's to copy some lead sheets. As I stepped into the parking lot, a tall, lanky stranger with piercing blue eyes walked up to me and said, "Bob Livingston?" He introduced himself as Mike Niland, a diehard Jerry Jeff and Gonzo fan from Ann Arbor. "You were the *guys*," he said, practically glowing. He told me he'd moved to Austin because of the music we made. Right there in the parking lot, I let it slip that we were thinking about making another record. Without missing a beat, Niland offered to help—and just like that, he became the executive producer. He even formed a label, Vireo Records, to release the album.

We recorded at Cedar Creek, a great studio in the middle of the woods in South Austin, with Lloyd Maines producing and Fred Rimmert engineering. We gathered in friends and other great pickers who had gonzo hearts to record with us: Davis McLarty on drums, and Reese Wynans on keys. Reese would go on to play with Stevie Ray Vaughan and be inducted into the Rock & Roll Hall of Fame, but for now he was a Gonzo. It was our 20th anniversary album, so we called it *Rendezvous* after the great Bobby Bridger song.

Rendezvous kicks off with a Larry Joe Taylor rocker, "Hurricane," then "Silent Dancer," a story of two lovers I wrote. We recut Gary's song about old Austin, "Fool for a Tender Touch," and followed with Rick Fowler's movie of a song about Billy the Kid, "Prairie Madness." Then followed Larry Joe's "Corona con Lima," a Gonzo version of "Geronimo's Cadillac," Bobby's "Rendezvous," and John's beautiful "Everywhere I Go I See Your Face." The last three songs are an instrumental called "Comanche Highway," a song by Reade Wood and me called "Friends," and another Larry Joe song on which Jerry Jeff came out to sing, "Terlingua Sky," to close the album. The record was good and we got some radio airplay.

We had an album release party and a reunion concert at Antone's and played a few other gigs, but not many. John and I were still full time with Jerry Jeff and Gary was otherwise engaged as well. We could never promote the record as it should have been or do an extensive tour, much to the chagrin of Mike Niland and his Vireo Records.

A couple of years later, in 1994, John and I made another CD with Niland and Vireo, but this time Gary was too busy with his own tours and recordings and he wasn't able to make it. Once again Lloyd produced it, getting great sounds and greater performances out of everyone. John Inmon, Paul Pearcy, Lloyd, and I were joined by Riley Osbourn on keys and Layton DePenning and Leeann Atherton singing background vocals. The new record was called *Hands of Time* and the title track was co-written with my main songwriting partner at the time who lived in India, Reade Wood.

The Lost Gonzo Band is like Brigadoon. Once every hundred years we appear out on the moors and play a gig or make a record and then vanish into the mist of time. A new episode is coming soon, so keep on reading . . .

CHAPTER 41

Terry Allen and the Madras Freight Train

1995

I had never met Terry Allen but had heard a lot about him from Lloyd Maines and others who had lived in Lubbock. Joe Ely told me a few stories. The Flatlanders and Terry were running buddies and had known each other a long time and had many of the same West Texas artiste qualities about them. I had moved away from Lubbock in '70 and pretty much had never gone back, so I had never met Terry.

Terry learned I was heading for another India tour and he called about a project he was working on with David Byrne of the Talking Heads. They were going to India together to record a couple of tracks for a new record. For reasons that escape me, Terry wasn't able to line up some Indian musicians so he asked if I could help him out with that.

Such was the extent of the conversation, but once both of us were in India Terry called me through monsoon-soaked telephone lines, told me he was in Madras, and asked me about the musicians. I knew a music impresario in Madras I had met on a tour there. He was a promoter and a manager and a booking agent for musicians and actors, so I gave Terry the man's contact info and he called him right off and then lined up some great South Indian players. A few days later, Terry called back and asked if I could get to Madras in the next couple of days. They had booked a gigantic recording studio that was used to record music for Indian films. He said he wanted me to play bass on some tracks. I was to meet him at the Connemara Hotel as soon as I could get there. I had no bass with me, but Terry said he'd find one.

I took an all-night train, the same one John Inmon and I had ridden years before, the Madras Mail. It takes sixteen hours to get to Madras: all night, freezing on the train, a bumpy, loud, exciting ride. When the train pulled into the big railway station I was a deep-space cadet for lack of sleep. It was 100 degrees outside and I was dressed like Ramar of the Jungle, khakis made from the lightest, thinnest material and wearing leather sandals on my feet. The Connemara is a nice five-star hotel, and when I rang Terry's room he said to meet him in the restaurant.

My table was alongside a partition that you couldn't see through but only went down to about to knee level so when people walked on the other side of the partition all you could see was their feet, sometimes ankles and a little leg. I watched the parade of feet walking past, some wearing chappals like I was and some dark brown feet in shoes without socks and then bare feet with tattoos all over them that probably belonged to Bedouins. I was lost in this exhibition of feet when suddenly there were Western boots walking on the other side of the partition. Black lizard-skin boots, followed by a woman's legs in capri pants with skulls and crossbones printed on the fabric. This must be Terry. Sure enough he comes around the corner all dressed in black to match his lizard-skins with his wife Jo Harvey also in black with the skull-and-crossbones motif, and they were a sight. Me, Ramar, him, all-in-black West Texas cowboy in the Indian summer.

We had breakfast and talked, then went to the studio to suss it out and meet all the musicians. Through the music impresario

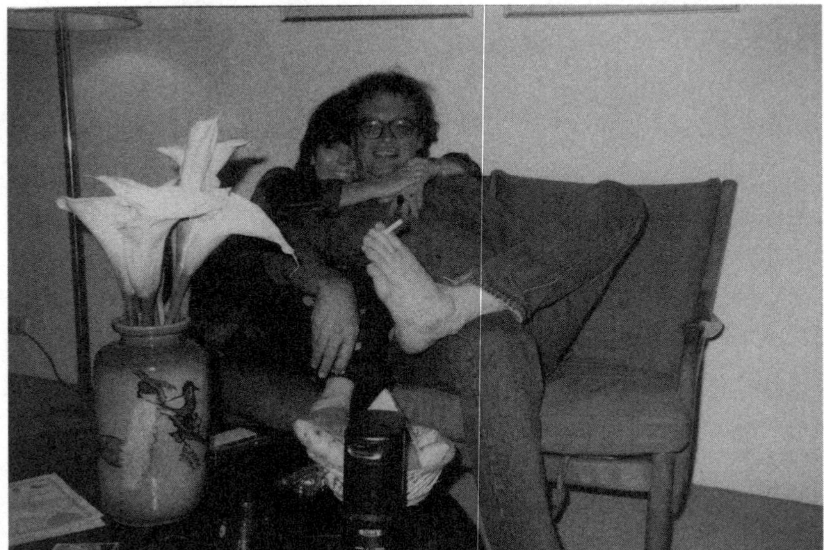

Jo Harvey and Terry Allen in Madras, India, 1992. (Photo by Bob Livingston.)

Terry found some Carnatic-style musicians, including one who played a veena (which is an older instrument than a sitar) and a mridangam player (it's a two-sided drum), and a tabla player too. Plus Vishwishwuran, a musician I knew from Madras, who played the santoor, which is like a hammered dulcimer.

Terry had found me a Steinberger bass somewhere in the wilds of Madras, the kind that doesn't have the tuners up on the headstock but down at the bridge. It's a weird little bass, light as a feather, and it's strange playing it because you think you're not in the right place but are further up the neck than you really are. Very confusing at first without the headstock.

Terry played a small keyboard he had brought with him from Texas. He started off with "New Delhi Freight Train." It had been a hit for Little Feat, but it was Terry's song. And we had the veena, tabla, mridangam, and santoor, and it really sounded great, because they all made it sound like a train. The santoor was really jangly and it goes through the song and at the end the train pulls

With Terry Allen at a recording studio in Madras, India, 1992. (Photo courtesy of Bob Livingston.)

into the station. It's a great cut! We recorded that and three other songs that day, including "Big Ol' White Boys" and "Yo Ho Ho."

The Indian musicians loved it. They just thought it was the most fun thing in the world. Sometimes right in the middle of a song there would be a power outage so we'd break and sit around for a while and someone would bring in big trays loaded down with tea and we'd drink and talk and commiserate and get to know these guys and they'd get to know us. Terry didn't realize he was paying for the tea and for the boy to go get the tea and for the studio and for the musicians' time even when the power was out and the impresario was getting a cut of everything. According to Terry this was the most expensive four songs he'd ever recorded. But listen to the album *The Moral Minority* and hear for yourself if it wasn't worth the money.

I had to catch a train early the next morning but couldn't find my ticket. In the end I had to buy another, a third-class ticket because everything else was sold out. I improvised, telling the conductor I was a US diplomat and should be moved up into the AC compartment. I had a passport that was issued in Bombay and an official document with my name on it, so somehow he fell for it and believed I worked for the US government, which I sometimes did. This maneuver worked a few more times over the years.

Terry never once took off those lizard-skin boots, and he never changed his look: black shirt and pants—not once. He was a true artist willing to experiment, and we rolled putting east and west together. I'll never forget it.

CHAPTER 42

Not Fade Away in the Middle East

2001

A few years after the '98 State Department tour with Tucker, I got a call from Donna Winton, who was now stationed in Bahrain. She was working on a big fling for the Sultan's 25th anniversary of diplomatic relations with the US. Donna issued an invitation I couldn't refuse: a royal performance for the Sultan himself, his extended royal family, a gathering of Bahraini dignitaries. There'd also be a crowd of Foreign Service folks who wanted to party with the Americans. It was to be a night of high diplomacy, desert royalty with a soundtrack called "Bob Livingston's Texas Sounds."

I told Donna that if I was going to go that far I'd like to play all over the Middle East and not just one show. She said she'd work on it and the wheels begin to spin and soon a whole tour was arranged for seven Middle Eastern countries: Yemen, Syria, Bahrain, Oman, Qatar, Jordan, and Kuwait. On that tour, we also played in India and Sri Lanka. All of this was right before 9/11when the shit hit the fan . . .

In the Middle East and India, Buddy Holly's "Not Fade Away" became our theme song. At one point we were in Yemen playing

Tucker and me with the Royal Omani Orchestra in Oman, 2000. (Photo courtesy of Bob Livingston.)

Tucker and me in Bahrain trying to learn the complexities of the beat in Pearl Diver music, 2000. (Photo by Donna Winton.)

In Aden, Yemen, 2000. What a beautiful country! (Photo by Tucker Livingston.)

An impromptu jam with the greatest oud player ever, Kuwait, 2000. This photo ended up in a college anthropology textbook. (Photo courtesy of Bob Livingston.)

for an art school, packed into the biggest room they had, no sound system, no stage. The room was full of art students, young men and women. All the women were wearing burkas, and all you could see was their eyes—it was very mysterious.

I introduced "Not Fade Away" by explaining that it was written by a fellow Texan from my hometown of Lubbock. I said, "His name was Buddy Holly, and his song is about how big and how wonderful and how eternal his love was for a girl in his English class." A young woman, maybe 18, was sitting in the front row, covered from head to toe in black, and all you could see were her dancing eyes. After I said it was written about this young girl and about how big and powerful his love for her was, she suddenly burst out, "Yes!" One beautiful word. Yes! It was rock-and-roll diplomacy.

"Not Fade Away" was a great icebreaker and an open-door bridge-builder when we played with local musicians. Invariably we found that they didn't want to play with us. They were shy and

In Damascus, Syria, playing guitar with some cool cat students, 2000. Where are they now? (Photo by Tucker Livingston.)

Tucker and me with Damascus, Syria, spread out below, 2000. It sure doesn't look like this anymore. (Photo courtesy of Bob Livingston.)

felt certain we were playing a completely different kind of music. One man in India said flat out, "I don't think it'll work, I am not at all comfortable. We play different modes and in different time signatures. No, let me just play my song and you play yours. I'm not at all comfortable to play with you."

But I persisted: "Come on and play this one, here is the beat," and I would start doing that riff, that Bo Diddley riff that "Not Fade Away" is built around, Bop-bop-bop, bop-bop. You know it. And always, the musician I was working with would say, "Oh, you mean *that* beat? Well, I know *that* beat," and would start to play along. It's as if the Bo Diddley / Buddy Holly beat is the primal beat in all cultures and it always broke down barriers and made friends for us wherever we went. After we played "Not Fade Away" they'd play anything with us. It was a blast!

And oh my god, we played in Syria and the people were wonderful. Many friends and musicians we met then may not be there any longer after having been bombed to rubble. I have lost all track of them, with no idea if they are dead or alive or what side they are on. Their world has turned upside-down. Syria is a Mediterranean country where the people eat baba ghanoush and hummus and stuffed grape leaves, and they love to listen to and play music. There were '54 Fords and '67 Chevys being driven around like you saw in Cuba. It was a beautiful country at that time, and we were treated like music kings of the desert. I don't even want to think of how it is now. What is going to happen? How will the regional tensions ever be resolved?

CHAPTER 43

Mahatma Gandhi & Sitting Bull

2003

Up to this point, Jerry Jeff had never wanted to tour in Europe. Back at the Jerry Jeff ranch, John, Freddie, and I were still playing together and Jerry Jeff amazingly accepted a European tour that took us to Finland, Norway, and England. The first shows were in Finland, which is a long haul from Austin. JJ was always grumbling on the tour because the beds were small and there was no ESPN. Once we got rolling we played exciting shows to enthusiastic crowds and got a lot of new fans. The shows in Finland were broadcast live into Russia and for years later I got e-mails from both Russian and Finnish fans.

Back home, I had found the muse, was writing a lot, and really wanted to make a record. Mike Niland of Vireo Records approached me and said he wanted to do a record with me, so we marshaled the forces and commenced to record at Cedar Creek studio. Lloyd Maines was back in the producer's chair, the man who is responsible for getting it all down on tape. Lloyd has golden ears. He can be in the control room engaged in a serious conversation about politics or the worth of taking zinc for your sex life, all the while someone is in the studio laying down a guitar part, and Lloyd would ask me to "wait a second" and hit the talk-back to the earphones in the studio and say, "Hey, man, can you just pull on your B string a little, you're just a hair sharp. Just pull on it."

Lloyd played steel and mandolin and acoustic guitar. Glenn Fukunaga was on bass, Paul Pearcy on drums, Riley Osbourn on keys, and Mitch Watkins on guitar. John Inmon came in for a few things, including a "guitar-sitar" on "Wilderness Song" that sounded just like a sitar.

The record opens with "Original Spirit," followed by a song that Bobby Bridger and I wrote called "Mahatma Gandhi & Sitting Bull." "On a Dream with You"—later recorded by Bill Hearne and by Walt & Tina Wilkins—and then I reached back to the old Gonzo days and grabbed a song that I'd written for our debut record, a bluegrass number called "Take Advantage of Your Chances." Next was a song that Reade Wood and I wrote in India, "I Believe It," followed by another co-write with Bridger, "Cowboys & Indians." A song I co-wrote with my son Trevor and his mother called "Love Cannot Be Broken" was next in line. One night I was putting a three-year-old Trevor to sleep. I said, "You know that I love you, don't you, sonny boy?" And Trevor said, "Yes, Dad.' I said, "How do you know I love you?" And he said, "Because love cannot be broken."

One of my house-painting friends, Steve Martinec, had written some really good songs and one, "Raining for So Long," sounded almost like a James Taylor tune. "Wilderness Song," another Lost Gonzo reprise and the first song I wrote in India, followed, John Inmon playing guitar-sitar, making it sound so raga-esque. We finished-up with "When the Beat Was Young," a song I wrote thinking of Jimmie Vaughan, the blues king of Austin. Sometimes I like to put a few interludes between songs and instrumental things and I'll play some modal unity chord and guitar man Mitch Watkins would take it from there and it was always beautiful what came out. Fourteen songs with instrumental interludes called *Mahatma Gandhi & Sitting Bull.* It was released June 24, 2003.

We had a CD release party at an Indian restaurant downtown called the Clay Pit. It's a big place. The restaurant is downstairs, but upstairs is a significant room of wood floors with a stage at the far end. We had a big band. Tucker and Mitch Watkins were the guitarists. Glenn Fukunaga on bass. Paul Pearcy, on drums and percussion, was trading measures with Oliver Rajamani on tabla. Tomás Ramirez showed up on gonzo sax. There were many guest appearances. Even Jerry Jeff showed up.

When I was thinking about the title for the new album I went through several different ideas—*Original Spirit*, *Brand*—but then looked at *Mahatma Gandhi & Sitting Bull* and thought that was a catchy title, cosmic. So that became the title. I knew I had made a big mistake after the album came out. I was in Lubbock playing a gig and promoting the record. I was on a local country station called KDAV, and the disc jockey Jerry Coleman was just a good old boy. I think he had known Buddy Holly pretty well back in the day. Anyway, he played a song from the CD and then he said, "That was a song by Bob Livingston, who is here in the studio with us, and the name of Bob's record is . . ." And he looks real hard at the title and mispronounces it and says, "Well, the name of the CD is ME HAT MI GAN DA and Sit-ting Bull?" with a question mark at the end. It suddenly hit me that it was a mistake to name the album as I did because there would be plenty of DJs just like him who wouldn't get it. The song tells of a mythical meeting between Mahatma Gandhi and Sitting Bull that Bobby Bridger and I made up, recounting the two Indians talking about the way their lives are and just having a friendly conversation. Later, when we re-released the whole CD plus some bonus tracks, we renamed it *Original Spirit*.

CHAPTER 44

Deep in the Heart of Africa

2005

My foreign touring experiences informed some of my songs and some of my life thereafter. The State Department's Foreign Service officers carry on and attend to hard diplomatic matters. But there is that cultural side in the Public Affairs section and they like to spread American goodwill and they love it when there's a cultural program they can dive into. Music, song, dance, photography. My impression of the State Department folks I met is that they were all smart, really sharp and spot-on. They have a hard row to hoe from administration to administration. Different presidents and mainly different secretaries of state. The politics can be diametrically opposed, but somehow these State Department folks can roll with it. Have to roll with it.

Earlier, Tucker and I had gone into North Africa, to Morocco and Tunisia, but now we headed for Angola, which is on the western coast in Central Africa. There had been a revolution going on there for thirty years and the US had backed the rebels, the wrong guys, and now the United States needed to make nice. We played at the new US Embassy in Luanda with some strangers in the audience claiming that Russian bugs were put in the offices by the builders. Angola's Catholic cardinal was in full regalia beaming and singing along to the "Cowboys & Indians" chorus. There were American flags everywhere, and we sang "This Land Is Your Land" and everybody knew it and sang it out happily.

We did a theater gig and several shows with young African performers and dancers. It was one of the times I got in trouble with the State Department. It started with the airline losing our guitars and bags. The State Department public affairs officer who picked us up at the airport was a 32-year-old, high-powered Black woman. Unflappable competence in the face of any situation. She got right on her cell phone, making arrangements to get us our bags, which wound up taking three days. All the while she's driving us to our quarters, weaving through dense traffic, darting in and out among military trucks full of soldiers, beggars, and hawkers on the street, Tucker and I wide-eyed. Then she's talking to a congressman in Lisbon who has missed his plane: "Look, baby, that's not my problem. You're just going to have to buy your own ticket. We'll refund you when you get here. Take care of yourself now, baby!" Click.

She took us to the nicest hotel in town and as she dropped us off she said, "Okay, don't leave your hotel. There are armed bandits on the streets, so don't leave your hotel, 'cause they will rob you. But if for some reason you *do* leave your hotel, make sure you have some money, 'cause if they get you and you don't have any money, that's going to really piss them off and they are liable to shoot you!" We followed her instructions. We were exhausted but, like they say, "You must rest in the afternoon even if it's on a bed of nails."

It was the most expensive hotel I've ever stayed at in my life, probably because you might die there at any second and they are bleeding you dry first. I am making this sound a lot worse than it was, as our hotel was the only game in town and relatively safe for foreigners. Yet a bottle of water was ten dollars, and while we'd been given per diem, still. . . . We'd arrived there with nothing but the clothes on our backs. I went down to the business center to use the computer. It was the slowest machine on the planet, a dial-up, there was a line to use it, and once you got your turn it might take twenty minutes to formulate an e-mail because it kept crashing.

Once I figured it out, I posted on my website journal something about the streets being "full of hawkers and gawkers and prostitutes" and about when I was in the restaurant downstairs I swear there's a guy "who looks just like Idi Amin sitting next to his wife with jewels and she spit something she didn't like into her plate." I mean it was just this strange, dark, international soldier-of-fortune scene. Then some guys with dark sunglasses on indoors told me, "What are you talking about, Luanda's a great city, it's an international city, a party city, come on! We're going out tonight."

Later we met a troupe of university dancers and singers, and we worked out a great show with them and played to a full house. At rehearsal they wanted to do a song with us, but they couldn't speak a word of English. So I suggested "Blowing in the Wind," but they didn't know it. We decided they'd just do the chorus which they did, singing phonetic English but with the most beautiful voices we'd ever heard. There were about thirty young people in the show, all dressed in white, incredible singing and dancing, both traditional and modern. We ended with our version of Dylan's song which I finished up with an impromptu rendition of "When the Saints Go Marching In," the crowd dancing and singing.

After we got back to the hotel I got a call from the State Department PAO. She said she was working on her final report to be sent to the African Regional Services Paris and declared, "Imagine my complete dismay when I went to your website to see what you had written and saw that you're talking about prostitutes and Idi Amin's wife spitting in the plate and you don't say a word about the wonderful students and their dance." It was a fair assessment. But I tried to explain that it was stream-of-consciousness, late at night, me just being me, that I wasn't thinking and I would fix it. And I did, I changed it, adding all about the students and how we collaborated with them and all the other good things that happened on the trip. I knew I had made a mistake writing all that stuff without thinking, trying to be clever or something. No more of *that*. I wonder how her "final report" turned out?

A couple of years passed, with more Jerry Jeff tours and an occasional Gonzo and some solo shows. My State Department friend Donna Winton was now head of the African Regional Services mentioned above. Donna had booked Tucker and me in Lahore, Pakistan, and in seven countries in the Middle East. In back-and-forth e-mails she began to work on a return tour to Africa and had soon signed up four countries. This time Tucker couldn't make the trip but suggested I get Bradley Kopp instead. I had already played a lot with Bradley, but we had never done one of these foreign tours that take you to the end of the road and back.

♪

More about Bradley Kopp. In 1975, one of the Jerry Jeff tours took us through Santa Fe, where we played one evening at an outside amphitheater designed by the internationally known architect Paolo Soleri. It was on Native American land at what was called an Indian school. They hosted amazing concerts there produced by Tom Campbell, who'd become known by producing "no nukes" fundraisers with the likes of Jackson Browne, Bonnie Raitt, and Bruce Springsteen. The amphitheater is closed to the public now, but it was a special, magical venue with powerful medicine and an eclectic audience of saints, sinners and artists.

Ramblin' Jack was there that night, but what sticks out in my mind is that's where and when I met Bradley Kopp. A guitar player from Wellington in the Texas Panhandle, Bradley was working the show for Tom Campbell. He met everyone backstage and Gary showed him "Pot Can't Call the Kettle Black" on the piano. We sat around a table piled high with foodstuffs and picked till it was time to play. It was years later before I would really get to know Bradley.

Our next meeting was after another Jerry Jeff show, this one at the Galveston Opera House. Jerry Jeff and I went over after the show to see Freddie Krc who was playing the Old Quarter, the famous Galveston club where Townes Van Zandt played all the time, a great little place run by a guy named Wrecks Bell, one of those rare souls who keep songwriters and their songs and music alive no matter what. Freddie Krc had quit Jerry Jeff by then and was out playing his own shows. We walked right onto the low stage and sang background vocals. Freddie's guitar player that night was Bradley, and I noticed he played really well and was in the pocket and he didn't play too loud at all for an electric guitar man.

Years later I ran into Bradley and his wife Lorrie at a gig at Alice's Restaurant in Niederwald, Texas. I asked if he had his guitar with him and invited him to sit in on a few songs and he ended up playing the whole night with me. I thought he sounded great, plus he sang good harmonies. He understood that the song is the important thing.

It's been almost twenty years now and we've been playing together on and off ever since. I do a lot of solo shows, but if it's feasible and the money is there, I get Bradley. He's my go-to guy in whatever configuration I have. We've had a lot of good times traveling and playing, but the problem with Bradley is . . . well, he's so even-tempered and chill there's never any tension between us, no eggshells to walk on. So there are no fistfights or wild nights with whisky and lighting fires in the desert stories to tell. No jails to be bailed out of. No confusing explanations to our families. And Bradley likes to drive.

Bradley plays a Fiesta Red Stratocaster plugged straight into a hot Fender amp, no toys to mess up the sound. He's played with a lot of artists, from Eliza Gilkyson to Jimmie Dale Gilmore and many more in rock bands and country bands. He also has a great recording studio in Buda, Texas, called Red Boot Ranch and I've done a lot of work there. He's a good engineer and producer who can see the whole picture. Like Lloyd Maines, Bradley always demands that you play in tune, which is annoying. What's wrong with those guys, haven't they ever heard of Keith Richards?

♪

Donna Winton told me I could take two more musicians with me on the Africa trip—a trio. I brought in Bradley on guitar and Richard Bowden on fiddle. We geared up for a month-long journey to four posts: Rwanda, Lesotho, Namibia, and Malawi.

But in the end, Bradley couldn't make it. So it was just the two of us—Richard and me—heading out into the unknown.

On the way to Africa, Richard and I stopped for some shows in Switzerland and Paris where we met our State Department service team. In Paris we played at Club 61, which was owned by a guy named Rémy, the foreign editor of *Le Monde* newspaper. It was a hangout for foreign correspondents and media types. There were pictures of naked women all over the walls. We had a good crowd and had a great time and played loud for a folk duo. Richard is a monster player and leapt about the stage as we rocked the club. We had everyone singing and stomping and we left them hanging from the rafters. My correspondent friend Mort Rosenblum brought some artists and writers with him and we schemed on a new French tour during the breaks.

The next morning we met our State Department folks on their own turf so they could give us our charge, meaning the rundown of what we were going to do, including the detailed tour itinerary. It was freezing cold in Europe so we had brought heavy coats and winter gear. But the next day we were off to Africa, and it was *hot* down there! We left all our coats and extraneous gear with Donna, who had it shipped back to my house in Austin. Early the next morning we flew to Kigali, Rwanda's capital, arriving jet-lagged and pretty spaced out at around midnight with the temperature at 90 degrees.

There was no downtime and we were up early for a meeting with US Ambassador Stuart Symington IV. His father had been a Missouri senator and he was smart as a whip. He came over to the brightly colored couch where we were seated and sat opposite us and looked at us intently. He was about to give us our marching orders, which went something like this:

"Gentlemen, you are United States ambassadors. Whatever you do, whatever you say, the way you act is being watched by Rwandan citizens. Fifteen years ago there was a massacre here. It was genocide, nearly a million people killed. This country is still in a state of mass post-traumatic stress. They are stricken and you will see it in their eyes. But they're good people and they're turning this country around and we're trying to help them as much as we can. Everywhere you go people are going to ask you for help and they want you to do something for them. And you see if you can find a way to turn that around and say, 'What can you do for yourself?' The first thing you are going to do today is go to the holocaust museum. You need to find out what made this genocide and try to make some sense of it."

Later that day we did a workshop for college-age musicians. Many of them were very poor. There was one guitar for every five players. There were singers and some dancers. They all had wonderful voices that were soulful in the extreme. They loved western music and were writing songs in that genre and wanted a place to perform them.

We told them that we were from Austin, Texas, the live music capital of the world. It turned out that Austin is a sister city to

Kigali. We met the mayor and he gave us the key to the city and we gave our workshop kids Austin Music lapel pins. But what they needed was guitar strings.

One young man holding an acoustic guitar with only five strings told us, "There's no place for us to play music here. No clubs with live music like we want to play. There's some clubs but they're just hip-hop. It's not live music. Some rock bands play but we want to sing our songs and have people listen."

We told them they could at least play in coffee shops. "Put out a tip jar. Or your hat. Ask for tips."

"Oh, man, we can't work for tips, it's demeaning."

"What are you talking about, dude? *We* play for tips. Musicians in Austin get paid but we also ask for tips. It's always good to have a tip jar somewhere in the room. It's at least gas money."

They promised to give it a try.

We formed a music association on the spot. All these kids exchanged phone numbers and e-mail addresses and they said they were going to do something and keep in touch with each other and think outside the box. It was a real positive meeting—our workshops emphasized that they could do for themselves and with just a little bit of communication with each other they could jumpstart things to find places to perform live. Richard spoke about the music community in Austin, that we embrace all forms of music, we are not elitists. I told them that I wanted to hear their traditional music, and invariably they said, "Oh, you know, that's old school. Traditional music is old school." And every time I'd say, "But it's beautiful. We love African music."

"Well, here's one favorite song," and they began to sing and the whole atmosphere changed as they sang their beautiful ethereal harmonies. I told them they sounded like Ladysmith Black Mambazo and they laughed and said not quite the same, but almost. "Yeah, maybe we could put some of that into our music." It was too old school for them, but these traditional songs were what could help them define something separate from hip-hop. I promised them audiences go for a traditional singalong just every once in a while. And when they sang the old-school traditional songs the place came alive.

They asked for my old guitar strings. They either couldn't get them or didn't have the money. It was sad. I gave them everything I had and when I got back to Austin I connected with a guitar string relief project that collected used strings and sent over cases of used as well as new strings.

The PAOs would schedule five or six events daily. They had us work our asses off. We went from workshop to workshop then immediately to an elementary school to play for a thousand kids sitting on bleachers all laughing and singing along and learning how to yodel. After that there was a radio interview and a television show. We had a spicy local vegetarian lunch as we hurried over to the high school that afternoon. The schedule was bam, bam, bam, all day long, with a driver and a State Department woman. Richard and I were loving it because we're hard travelers and we know how to do it and there was a sense of purpose in what we were doing. The impact we might have on young lives and the care that was taken to present these shows was not lost on us. We played and told stories and jokes and sang and we were quite energetic and had a lot of audience participation numbers with people singing and yodeling along. Hokey but fun. The State Department was loving it because we were easy to work with—a lot of times they will get musicians who are just not that into it and don't find it all that much of an adventure, but a lot of work and exhaustion, not much sleep. But I was road-hardened and could take it. I had played with Jerry Jeff, for Chrissakes. This was a piece of cake.

Richard and I were running on adrenaline and coffee and felt we were doing good work and were representing American music and Texas music. We took pains to be good US ambassadors. We minded our p's and q's.

We played a show at the US Ambassador's residence one night. They'd invited local media people as guests, maybe a news anchorwoman or anchorman, the diplomatic corps, a lot of Foreign Service folks from the US and other countries. There were also local musicians, poets, and artists.

From Rwanda we journeyed to Lesotho, a kingdom surrounded by South Africa. It retained its independence during the Boer War because of its fierce fighters who battled in the mountains. It looked like New Mexico, the most beautiful place you've ever seen. Everything seems to be made of adobe. Round houses with green gardens.

Rwanda was one of the cleanest countries I've ever seen—spotless, really. You wouldn't expect it, but there's no trash on the streets. Every morning, people come out and clean them—no cigarette butts, no plastic blowing around. In fact, plastic bags are outlawed entirely. There's a strong spirit of volunteerism, and it shows.

The highways are pristine. Even the roadside restrooms are immaculate—cleaner than most anywhere I've been. You walk in, there's an attendant, but he doesn't expect a tip.

And the snacks? Wild curry Cheetos—hot, spicy, addictive—and fresh, natural fruit drinks that hit the spot in the heat.

In Namibia we played a radio station and when we walked in the woman DJ just sort of rolled her eyes as if to say, "Look at these crackers." As the interview progressed, she loosened up. "Whoa, so, you're cowboys from Texas? Ha!" Then we did "Original Spirit" and that immediately got her. She danced and was talking to her listeners: "Ah, it's beautiful, this has made my day! It's the original spirit of life in here. We're all coming to your show." And of course Richard burned it up and I was 100 percent sure that they'd never heard anything like it. I had never heard anything like it!

Namibia is bigger than Texas and Louisiana combined and it looks like West Texas and you drive for hours and then you see an ostrich run out of the bush and there are hyenas and lots of monkeys and baboons, all side-by-side along the road. We went to a game park, an all-day trip, and we were tired but we wanted to do it and they were going through a lot of trouble getting the safari together so I knew I'd better buck up. We saw lions and giraffes and rhinos and hippos. The hippos were swimming at us at a great rate of speed, so we had to get out of there fast!

We got to see so much of the countryside and played a lot of shows. Richard and I would come back around 11 in the evening at the end of a hard day's work, ride up the elevator to our rooms, and look at each other and shake our heads. Richard would break into a big smile and say, "I can't believe what just happened." I would try to process it and settle down and go to sleep fast because we were going to have to get up again at 6 in the morning and do it all again. I don't know many musicians, no matter how young, who could handle the pace. Playing music in foreign countries is a hard gig many musicians have turned down. Davin James, a Houston country singer and picker friend of mine, said, "Bob, I don't know how you can go to those places. Aren't you afraid? I'd be scared to death to do it." But to me these foreign tours and just being on the road playing music for a living was always a big adventure. Still is. I can't get enough of it.

CHAPTER 45

You're Fired!

2005–2006

The philosopher Eckhart Tolle said, "Become comfortable with not knowing."

That's the way it's always been in this business. You never know what's up next. I had played with Jerry Jeff on and off for thirty-five years. Then the craziest thing happened. He fired me. This is why and how it went down . . .

In the summer of 2005 a couple of my old pals, Tommy Alverson and Walt Wilkins, called to say they were recording a tribute to *¡Viva Terlingua!* for Palo Duro Records. They wanted to do it live in Luckenbach in the same dance hall where we recorded the original album in 1973. It would feature a lot of young singer-songwriter types and country bands that loved *Viva* and were influenced by it. Tommy and Walt wanted to get as many of the original Gonzo Band members as they could and reconstruct the album song by song. Original *Viva* veterans Gary P. Nunn, Herb Steiner, Craig Hillis, and I joined up. John Inmon, Freddie Krc, and Sam Hendricks joined up for this 2005 version of the Lost Gonzo Band.

Jerry Jeff got wind of what was happening and a couple of weeks before the sessions he called me up and asked what was going on, why was I doing it? I replied that a lot of young musicians who loved *¡Viva Terlingua!* were going to be singing the songs and we were going to back them up. JJ was pissed because he wasn't involved, but he ended the conversation with, "Aww, go ahead and do it, it's not gonna be a big deal, is it?" "No, it's not gonna be a big deal at all. It's just a gig. I need the work." He said again "Aww, go ahead and play it, I don't care." But he did care.

On the day before the recording was to begin everybody showed up, but Luckenbach was deserted. I don't even think the general store was open. I wasn't sure what was up. There was no sound system set up and no recording equipment. I figured there would be an advance guard or something. But the only people there were us pickers.

We met in the middle of the street in front of the dance hall. One lonely little road meanders through the town, hardly any traffic, ever. We pulled out our guitars and I started singing "Hi, buckaroos, it's Gonzo time again . . ." and suddenly we were all singing harmonies and playing, "gettin' by on gettin' by's my stock and trade / living it day to day . . ." We started going into the songs like that, really informal, all in a circle standing in the middle of the street singing out. There was some magic brewing and it felt right.

Suddenly Walt got a call while we were all in the middle of the street. Dirt, the sound guy, had broken down somewhere and was asking someone to send him $100. It was such a crazy thing to hear. I thought to myself, *Oh my god, here we go. This is going to be a clusterfuck.* I don't know if Dirt ever got his money or if he was kidding or whatever but he finally showed up early the next morning and he set up the sound system. Fred Remmert from Cedar Creek studio brought in some mobile recording gear and everything was tied together in a ragtag way in the old dance hall, but it all worked perfectly.

The recording was scheduled over two days. Each of the musicians would come and we'd rehearse the songs two or three times during the day. Other musicians, such as Jimmy LaFave, had been asked to participate, to sing songs not necessarily on the album but that were an important offering in the scheme of things. Two Tons of Steel did "Sangria Wine." The McKay Brothers did a funky version of "Wheel" that brought back psychedelic memories. Tommy Alverson sang "Backslider's Wine" and Walt Wilkins did a stellar rendering of "Little Bird," probably the best version ever. Cory Morrow sang "Redneck Mother." Gary and I kicked the whole thing off with "Gettin' By," and Gary sang his anthem "London Homesick Blues." There was never a technical hitch. The songs were recorded with reverence as a tribute to Jerry Jeff and *¡Viva Terlingua!* There was never a sound failure, never a broken tape or a miscue. The younger musicians really had a lot of feeling for that record, saying things like, "I wouldn't be in country music if it wasn't for *¡Viva Terlingua!*"

The record was mixed and set to come out and it was going to be called *¡Viva Terlingua Nuevo!* The Walkers were furious and believed everybody was trying to rip them off and accused the producers of making it look like it was a sequel to *¡Viva Terlingua!*, which is not what it was intended to be at all, and I don't think anybody but them thought that.

Sometime after the CD was released the Walkers sued Palo Duro Records and got a cease-and-desist order, claiming copyright infringement and misappropriation of his identity. Jerry Jeff sued his own tribute record. Now the rumor mill kicked in and over 100 newspapers carried the story. It eventually went to court and the judge dismissed the case, except he ordered that the record's name be changed to *Luckenbach Compadres*.

With all this drama, I just kept my head down but there was an iciness towards me from both Jerry Jeff and Susan. My last show with him was on November 6, 2006. We flew to Key West in Lowell Liebermann's Learjet to play a Buffett show. It was a kick-ass show, probably the best we'd played in years, but storm clouds were gathering in the Atlantic and followed us all the way back to Austin. A tumbleweed blew down the narrow aisle.

The next day an angry phone ring Bojangled me wide awake. It was Jerry Jeff. He said in a very irritated voice something like, "Bob, this Gonzo thing is over for good. You have showed no loyalty to me at all. And I want it to be over. And I'm gonna let you go right now as of today. I want it to end with us while there are still any good feelings left." I didn't try to argue, though I pointed out that he *had* told me before I could go ahead and play on the record. But when he said he wanted it over with while there were still good feelings left I told him, "Jerry Jeff, there aren't going to be any good feelings left." He began screaming so loud that my cell phone buzzed, shorted out, and went dead. That was it. It was over.

For me, it was simple—this was about free speech and getting paid for playing a gig. Whoever planted the idea that we were trying to pull a fast one had it all wrong. We were just a bunch of friends and musicians playing on a record, having fun. The Gonzos who showed up for the new album had earned their stripes—we played on every track of the original *¡Viva Terlingua!* This new record was a tribute, plain and simple. A celebration. But I was the only one Jerry Jeff could actually fire. The rest of the guys? Maybe their reckoning would come later . . .

CHAPTER 46

Gypsy Alibi, the Album

2007–2011

Now I could accept a gig and know that I could put it on my calendar a year in advance. It was incredible freedom to know that when someone asked me to play on April 14 I could say, "Yeah, sure, I'll be there." It was a big weight off of me, and I started playing a lot. I supported my record and I sold a lot of CDs at a lot of clubs and house concerts. House concerts were a new thing to me, but I was jumping in with both feet.

About a year later I was driving back from a gig in Houston and I started thinking about Jerry Jeff and I thought it was crazy that we had to end like that. So I called him up. "Jerry Jeff, I don't want to walk into Heart of Texas Music and see you over there trying out a guitar and feel weird like I can't go up and say 'Hi.' This town is too small and we'll run into each other at some point. We went through a long road together and it just feels weird." He said he felt the same way and that we should let it go. "Things will come back around," he said. "Things will come back around." And they did.

Meanwhile I was doing some heavy traveling. I made another couple of foreign tours with Tucker to Vietnam and Thailand and was sick most of the time. There was always this vague nausea creeping through my vitals, I think from the food. We ate street

On tour with Tucker in Vietnam, 2004. We were playing in Hanoi with these musicians. (Photo courtesy of Bob Livingston.)

Tucker and me in Ho Chi Minh City playing with the brilliant T'rung player, NS Linh Phi, 2003. (Photo courtesy of Bob Livingston.)

food and felt fine, but the stuff at the hotels did me in. For the last show in Thailand I was so sick I could barely get out of bed, but I still had to play the show. It was for the new American ambassador at his house and there were hundreds of locals and Foreign Service folks invited. I had to play it. I lay on the grass in a quiet part of the lawn until Tucker came to tell me it was time to play. We played with a group of local musicians at one point in the show, but they were clueless and didn't have the same free-wheeling attitude the rest of the musicians we met on these tours had. Maybe it was just me, about to throw up.

Since I had no Jerry Jeff tours in the States, I wound up back in India with Iris and the boys sitting on a veranda and staring into a thousand shades of green, an ancient river flowing. I gave myself permission to stare. I had no agenda at that point but was just looking out and listening to the birds and watching the sunrise and the sunset and getting up early and eating great food. And staring.

I had my guitar with me, so I started playing and writing and singing to the jungle. A new record was brewing. Within a week I was working on six or seven songs *at once* and I would sit on my veranda and I had all the lyrics spread out before me. I had brought my pipe with me and my practice was to get out my pipe, smoke a little bit, have tea, write, have some more tea, work on the chords and the melody I as writing and if I got stuck, which was frequently, I would go to the next song and work on that. I was working on all simultaneously. Andy Wilkinson gave me some songwriting tips and showed me a graph he had made and told me a new way to look at songs if you were stuck. It sounded like he was saying to go through a different door. So I'd write these songs and if I got stuck, I might pick up a book and read a sentence and then turn it around and that might become the first sentence of the next verse. I was jump-starting my imagination, and that's where I wrote "I Can't Sleep Tonight"—still one of my favorite songs I've ever written.

Bradley Kopp and me playing a giant block party in Dallas. (Photo courtesy of Mike Looney.)

After my sojourn in India, I returned to Austin to record new songs. Mike Looney, a fraternity brother from Texas Tech and longtime friend, offered to support a new record. He brought in a few more brothers—Paul Knuckley and Jay Rigby—and their good friend Fred Baker, along with Dr. David Johnson, a Smithsonian ichthyologist and diehard Gonzo fan. My friend and lawyer, Max Addison, joined in too. With their support, we suddenly had a recording budget—and my own label, New Wilderness, was born.

Once again, Lloyd helped me with the production. We recorded at Cedar Creek. The band would set up in one room and I would set up in a different room but still be able to see them. I had my acoustic guitar and a microphone in front of me and I would sing the songs live and the band was in the big room so they could play with me so it all pretty much went down live. We left some holes for leads and stuff like that, but it has much more of a live feel on it. Bill Kirchen, the famous twang telly player of Commander Cody and His Lost Planet Airmen, played the lead on "Middle

Ages Rockabilly Blues." Bradley Kopp added some hot licks here and there, and Chris Gage was also on the session. Dave Sanger from Asleep at the Wheel was on drums, and Glenn Fukunaga and Chris Maresh shared bass duties. What a band!

The album was called *Gypsy Alibi*. The title came from a song that I'd written with Tucker in India on that writing spree. I had started it years before as a piano piece that sounded a little bit like Leon Russell meets George Gershwin. Tucker helped me finish the song and took it in a completely different direction.

Even after I started the record I was still writing songs for it and playing out on the weekends. There was a show in Mineral Wells at a place called the Double J Hacienda and Art Ranch. Mineral Wells had at one time been an internationally famous resort centered around the mineral spas in the basement of the Baker Hotel. Presidents and princesses, Arab potentates and principals, movie stars and millionaires all came out to partake of the healing waters. Outside of town there were several dude ranches, and one of them became the Double J owned by Jimmy and Jane Baldwin. It was right on the banks of the Brazos River. John Wayne, Betty Grable, and Bette Davis used to come and hang out at the swimming pool. The Baldwins filled the pool and made a courtyard out of it. There were guest rooms, and at the four corners there was a massage studio, an art gallery, a yoga studio, and then the Great Room where they had music performances like mine coming up. They served great food, and folks would come from the DFW area and stay the whole weekend.

Jimmy and Jane had a daughter named Ruby. She was a free spirit and everything that came out of her mouth was a song. One afternoon we all went on a drive to town and returned by the back roads. There was a little wooden building on the Baldwins' property that looked like an outhouse. I asked what it was and Jane told me it was the well house. Ruby's ears perked up. "The *well*?" She'd never noticed it before so she had us stop the car so we could all get out to look. When you opened the door to the little structure you saw a pipe in the ground. It was the water well for the property and not much to look at. But Ruby was convinced it was a wishing well and she got all of my change and all of her mother's change and she started wishing and she wished and wished and flung the coins towards the pipe in the ground with each wish. And when she ran out of coins she collected all of them back up and began wishing again. Meanwhile, the sun was dipping low in the sky over the Brazos River. It was a beautiful sight. I turned to Ruby and told her, "Ruby, I hope all your wishes come true, I really do, but I don't want to miss the sunset on the Brazos." Ruby just looked up at me and said, "Take my hand, I'll show you a shortcut to that sunset." It was such a cool thing to say that I forgot about the sunset and wanted to write that song. Back at the ranch, there was a grand piano in the Great Room and I started playing chords and the words came, "Ruby's come up with something new, a shortcut to the sun / If I was standing in Ruby's shoes, I could be anyone . . ." and I had the first verse and the whole melody down. The song is called "Ruby's Shoes" and opens *Gypsy Alibi.*

As I got closer to finishing the new record I reached out to John Hadley to help me finish some of the songs. I had heard of John from my songwriting friend Susan Herndon. She said he'd written some hit songs and was a great "closer." I went up to Norman, Oklahoma, where he lived and we sat around for two or three days and wrote five or six songs. I told him the story of Ruby and I played him that first verse. I also told him that her mother had cut a Band-Aid out in the shape of a lightning bolt to put over a scratch near her eyes and Ruby loved the lightning bolt so much she had her mother do one after another so she had lightning bolts coming out of her eyes when I first met her. Ruby was only six, but she was a great inspiration.

She had thunder, she had lightning
Painted like an Indian around her bright eyes
Her shadow's jumping from cloud to cloud
Spinning in a circle beneath the blue skies . . .

Susan Herndon came over the second night in Norman and we finished a song that we had started almost a year before called "Oklahoma Girl." "She's an Oklahoma Girl, singing songs at midnight / with a lonesome cowboy from the Lone Star State. . . ." There's some great yodeling on the track by Jill Jones, a gal from Wimberley and Santa Fe. She and I do a yodel-off at the end and Jill wins hands down. My favorite line in there is Susan's, "She wrapped him 'round the finger of her tanned and freckled hand."

Gypsy Alibi won Album of the Year at the Texas Music Awards in 2011.

CHAPTER 47

Cowboys & Indians

1995

Another whirlwind State Department tour in India came and went and I returned home excited with a new idea. I wanted to form an Austin group to recreate the sound I was hearing in those foreign shows I'd done with Indian musicians. A few weeks later I chanced to be at a house concert played by Will Taylor and his group. During a conversation with Will afterward he said he'd received funding for his group with a cultural contract grant from the City of Austin. I thought this might be a way I could put my new multicultural project together.

Will directed me to Mario Garza, who oversaw those grants. Mario looked like an American Indian out of a movie, with long hair and wearing cowboy boots. He was at his desk, playing a Native American flute when I came to his office. Mario outlined the process, which entailed writing a grant proposal to describe every aspect of what I was going to do. I pored over it. I would write late into the night. Trying to get ten inches into a two-inch rectangle, whittling a thousand words down to 200. Every word counted. I edited and edited and distilled and distilled. I became *obsessed*. And there was a deadline.

Meanwhile, I needed music—and content—for this still-unnamed new show. So I headed down to Houston, to Bobby

Bridger's place, looking for inspiration and insight. We sat in his living room, surrounded by art and good energy, and in just a day or so, we wrote two songs: "Cowboys & Indians" and "Mahatma Gandhi & Sitting Bull." I also had two songs I'd written with Reade Wood back in India—"I Believe It" and "Village Story Man." Those four songs became the backbone of what I was building. With that, I pulled everything together and turned in the grant request.

A couple of weeks later I found out I had to have a site visit, which meant Austin Arts Commission folks had to come see the show. As I didn't have any shows booked, I asked John Inmon to my house to play the new stuff and I invited the entire Arts Commission over. Iris served Indian chai and samosas. I explained the whole concept, the vision. There would be more musicians involved and some of them would be from India. John and I played purely acoustic and I walked the Arts Commission folks through what the show was going to be like, making it up as I went along. I told them we didn't even have a group yet but "this is the way the tabla will sound" and I made the sound with my mouth for a few bars. And "this is the way a sitar would sound" while John was playing raga style licks, and they got it. The songs and the vibe in my house sold the show. A couple of weeks later they told me I wrote "an A+ grant" and it got funded.

We called the show *Cowboys & Indians: A Wild East Show of the Imagination*. We needed Indian musicians to make it happen. We had plenty of cowboys, Western musicians, but we needed the real Indians, from India. John Inmon was the first guitar player and played a guitar-sitar which sounded great and was evocative of the real thing. These days, the group includes Bradley Kopp on guitar, Oliver Rajamani on tabla, Richard Bowden on fiddle, Nagavalli, a gifted singer from India, on vocals, Steve Schwelling on drums and percussion, David Carroll on upright bass, and Anu Naimpally, a bharatanatyam dancer from India. Anu worked out

The first Cowboys & Indians group, 1994. (L–R): Bob Livingston, John Inmon, Richard Bowden, Alok Dutta, David Heath, Oliver Rajamani, and Paul Pearcy. (Photo by Scott Newton.)

This was my favorite version of Cowboys & Indians 2015. (L–R): Anu Naimpally, Oliver Rajamani, Bob Livingston, Richard Bowden, Tucker Livingston, and Paul Pearcy. (Photo courtesy of Bob Livingston.)

hand gestures with movements that serve to interpret the lyrics. The band and the show are unique and exciting and it's so much fun to play with all those cool cats! Mahatma Gandhi and Sitting Bull meet Buddy Holly and Ravi Shankar!

CHAPTER 48

My Most Popular Rap Song

2004

In the early Lost Gonzo days, Ray Wylie and I would get together every so often. One night in a fever of poker and cigars we wrote "Hold on for Your Life." It was a decent song and the Gonzos recorded it on our ill-fated last Capitol album that never was to be. A few months later the Gonzos were in New York City with Jerry Jeff. Michael Brovsky mentioned he was producing a New York band called McKendree Spring and asked if I had any songs that he might pitch them. I told him about "Hold on for Your Life." He told me to meet him in the bar later that night and bring my guitar. Sitting on a stool in the crowded noisy bar I played the song for the leader of the band, Fran McKendree. He liked it well enough to record it the next day.

McKendree Spring's *Get Me to the Country* came out in 1975 with "Hold on for Your Life" as the first song on the A side. I made a little money on it but it wasn't going to pay many bills, much less get me a new house. Still, it's always nice when someone likes your song enough to record it.

Thirty years or so later I was in my office in the Guadalupe Arts Complex in Austin, a cool little office and studio with all my treasures from my travels, my guitars, my books, and my computer. I would go there and write and hang out with artists and photographers and feel good. One fine day, the phone rang and a woman's voice asked if I was Bob Livingston.

"Yes."

"Did you write a song with Ray Hubbard called 'Hold on for Your Life'"?

"Well, uh . . . yes."

"And do you still own the publishing rights to that song?"

"Well . . . yes. Hey, what's going on? What's all this about?"

She told me that a rapper named Lloyd Banks had just recorded a song called "Warrior" and he had sampled "Hold on for Your Life" from the McKendree Spring album and therefore I own a percentage of the new song. "I'm making sure you have all your publishing together because it's on Interscope Records and Eminem produced it and Lloyd Banks is gonna be the next 50 Cent. It's gonna be big!" Banks had been in G-Unit with 50 Cent and Tony Yayo. This was a rather strange turn of events.

When your song is sampled you can be paid in various ways. If it's just on the bridge you get 10 percent or 15 percent of the proceeds from the song, but if it's used on a verse or the choruses you get a little more. If the whole song is sampled, which was the case on "Warrior," both Hubbard and I became quarter-share songwriters and publishers with Lloyd Banks and his brother Loui V.

Lloyd Banks was known for his hardcore style and gritty, explicit lyrics. Looking back and trying to figure out how it all went down and how he had even heard "Hold On" in the first place, I imagined Banks was probably walking down a dirt road in New York City and ducked into a discount record store, browsed through the 25-cent record bin and came across the McKendree Spring vinyl record. He might have liked the cover and took the record home with a bunch of others that had caught his eye. Lloyd and Loui V listened to the first song, which just happened to be "Hold on for Your Life," and decided right then they liked the groove and sampled it and wrote a song to go with it. It is further than 100 degrees of separation to even know that our song is embedded in his track, but Interscope Records was a big outfit and their lawyers made Lloyd Banks and his team track us down so we could get all legal and everything. They sent Ray Wylie and me contracts and an MP3 of the recording to check it out.

The song was on my computer desktop, but I hadn't really listened to it. I was in a session in Dallas and somehow Ray tracked me down there and called me up in the studio and asked me whether I had listened to the song yet. Hadn't had a chance, I said.

"Well, you and I need to get straight who wrote which line."

I was thinking, *Oh my god, what are you talking about?* I didn't know if there was going to be a fight over lyrics or share of the song or what.

"What are you talking about, Ray Wylie?"

He repeated, "You and I need to get straight who wrote what line. Are you the one that wrote, 'Nigga, ride till I die, the song I sing'? Because I'm pretty sure I wrote 'I'm a grown man, dog, I ain't no bitch!'"

Those were the lyrics from "Warrior," of which each of us now owned 25 percent! It was strong gangsta rap, and to have Ray grill me like that was hilarious. Meanwhile "Warrior" sold almost a million copies the first quarter. Sales fell after that, and Banks was never to be a top-selling rap artist even though that record went platinum and did amazingly well enough for all of us, considering it came out of nowhere.

Later on, I was playing in Lubbock at the Buddy Holly Center and had the occasion to tell Butch Hancock this story. Butch just stared off into the flat angled Lubbock landscape and said wistfully, "Gee, I'm gonna call my new album *Sample Me*."

CHAPTER 49

The Reception Vector

2018

Jerry Jeff and I had always been friends, more like brothers, fighting but occasionally loving each other. He was a hard man to figure out and I was too. But things did come back around. Jerry Jeff was real happy with his new band, Steve Samuel on drums, Brad Fordham on bass, and Chris Gage on guitar, but occasionally Brad couldn't do a show and Jerry would call me. It was the easiest gig in the world: We would usually fly in and play the gig and fly back home so we could spend the night in our own beds. You couldn't do it any easier than Jerry Jeff did it. The only thing easier might have been to send over a hologram of himself so he never had to leave his house. And I think he was seriously looking into that.

So occasionally I would play a one-off gig with Jerry Jeff. He had a big show at Billy Bob's in Fort Worth and asked me to come play. I drove over to the little airport in Georgetown where Jerry Jeff kept his plane. The drive out there is longer than the flight we were about to take. Wheels up at 3:30 p.m. With the adventure of learning how to use the live broadcast feature on Facebook I decided to go live for as long as I could on the flight. I called my new Facebook show Reality Ranch.

I got out of my car at the tiny terminal and immediately went live on Facebook. "Hey, this is Bob Livingston and this is Reality

Ranch and today I'm going to take you on a little ride with me and Jerry Jeff up to Billy Bob's to play a show!" As I was walking into the little terminal I saw Jerry Jeff waiting at the flight desk. We were still broadcasting live. I said, "And here is Jerry Jeff now, folks" and pointed the camera phone at Jacky Jack, who looked deep into the lens and shouted "Fuck you!" then smiled and laughed. We all laughed. That was Jerry Jeff, unexpected but by his very nature totally expected.

We walked out to the plane and all this time I was broadcasting live. We took off and I tried to keep the signal and hundreds of Facebook friends were tuning in, "Hey, it's Jerry Jeff." For 3,500 feet we were still live, and I interviewed him and he told a funny story and I got an inside exclusive until we climbed above "the reception vector" and the screen went dark.

Later that night at the Billy Bob's sound check I went live again and got an interview with Jerry Jeff and some of his friends and the other guys in the band, Chris and Steve. We're all laughing and eating pizza and getting ready for the show. Then it was showtime and I walked on stage still live on Facebook and put my phone on my amp just as Jerry Jeff said, "Hi, buckaroos . . ."

We got off stage about 10 p.m. and were back at the airport in Fort Worth at 10:30. We touched down in Austin about 11:45. A little over seven hours and we'd flown to the venue, had a good meal, sound-checked, played a whole sellout show, and come back safe and sound. I was home just after midnight. You can't do it any easier than that.

CHAPTER 50

Up the Flatland Stairs

2017

Don Richmond has a completely shaved head like a monk and plays in a western folk trio based out of Northern New Mexico and Southern Colorado—The Rifters—who write, play, and sing their western-themed folk songs with authentic harmonies and style. In a way they remind me of my old compadres, Three Faces West. This new trio of compadres—Rod Taylor, Jim Bradley, and Don Richmond—are all longtime friends and much loved by listening audiences and dancers alike.

Don has a record label, Howlin' Dog, an independent singer-songwriter outfit based out of Alamosa, Colorado. They had just released new CDs by Shake Russell, Michael Hearne, and Bill Hearne. I had always respected and admired Don for his songwriting, his musicianship, and his lowkey demeanor. So when he approached me at Michael Hearne's 2017 Big Barn Dance in Taos and asked me about doing a record for Howlin' Dog, I jumped at the chance. The label has a team behind it run by Don's wife, Teri McCartney. Don and Teri are a righteous couple. Best friends. Mindful of the task. Great vegetarian cooks.

We planned to make the record in Don's recording studio in Alamosa where he and Teri worked, played music, recorded albums, sent CDs out to DJs at radio stations, and ate the best vegetarian known to man or beast. The compound is surrounded by the San Juan Mountains. 360 degrees. There is a big recording room, a separate drum booth, and a bass booth. Don has a large and comfortable recording control center with lots of bells and whistles. He uses Logic Pro as a recording program. There's a keyboard in the control booth that sounds like a grand piano or a Hammond B-3, whatever you want. A full band can record live all at the same time and there is enough soundproofing and isolation going on that there is no bleed between rooms. But playing with a full band was not the way Don envisioned making this record.

It seemed that every musical instrument you could imagine was either lined up on guitar stands or hanging on the walls. Just walking into the room you would catch the vibe and want to lay something down. And there are a lot of vibes. There is magic floating through the air supercharged by the San Juans. A whirlwind of energy and creativity. You can't help but be moved by the flow.

The first day of recording Don asked me to play down as many songs as I was considering for this record, twenty-five songs in one day, just me and my guitar. I had done some homework and had it fairly organized, at least for me. Even so there were one or two songs that needed making up on the spot in the energy of the Now. The next day we started at the top of the list and added bass and a little guitar here and there and we plunged in working on the songs, building them from the ground up. I'd never worked this way before for an entire album.

Don is practically a virtuoso on almost any instrument. On *Up the Flatland Stairs* he plays guitars of various persuasions—acoustic and electric and slide and steel—both upright and electric bass, as well as banjo and fiddle.

We got Jimmy Stadler in from Taos to play piano and organ. A cool cat who's a ski instructor-musician-singer-songwriter and killer on keys and guitars. I played one of Don's acoustic guitars that records really well and stays in tune. Intonation is the key with recording a guitar. Playing a G chord might sound in tune but when you go to the D, it may sound out of tune. Most of the time it's the B string's fault. That damn B string. You have to tune it flat, I don't know why nor just how flat. It's always a problem. I played the bass part on "The Usual Thing," a rocker that changes tempos quite often and one that I'd originally written on bass.

At some point, maybe the second trip up to Alamosa, Don snared a drummer passing through the town. He was John Michel, who'd played with John Oates of Hall & Oates. We asked him if he had some time to slow down and throw down some drum tracks on several songs. He said he would be back in a few days on his way to Aspen. He had only five or six hours to do it. "Whatever we can get done in that time will be okay." We had recorded everything with a click track and John ripped through them. He only had trouble with "The Usual Thing," a song I wrote in the '70s that the Lost Gonzo Band had tried to record. It's an unusual tune, which is why I played bass on it and this time got a good high-energy track. There are tempo changes from 4/4 to 3/4 and back. Dropped beats. Tablas and hard rock guitar. Siri even made a special appearance reading a Native American poem.

We recorded Walter Hyatt's retro-country gem, "The Early Days," with Warren Hood adding some sweet fiddle and James Doyle, a professor at nearby Adams State University, adding some steady drum tracks between teaching classes. There were background singers in the office. It was a family! After we had all the rhythm tracks together, Don added everything else. We sent some tracks to Bradley back in Texas to lay some guitar parts down. We got Eric Johnson's drummer Phil Bass to play on "You Got My Goat (You Might as Well Take My Dog)," a rocker that I co-wrote with Oklahoma girl, Susan Herndon.

"Can't Get Enough of It" is a new song dedicated to the house concert hosts of the world and the long, colorful road that never seems to end: "I haven't unpacked in 47 years." And Ramblin' Jack even makes a cameo in the lyric. The album also features several co-writes: The ever-inventive John Hadley and I wrote "A Few Things Right" over the phone. Laurie Turner, a whip-smart Austin singer-songwriter, wrote a line I've always loved in "That's the Way Things Go": "Anything that moves between these parallel lines is true." Eliza Gilkyson brings her own kind of magic with a soulful guest appearance on this one. There's also "It Just Might Be Your Loving," a co-write with my longtime cosmic cowboy friend Michael Murphey, and a sweet appearance from Kelley Mickwee singing "Cowgirl's Lullaby" with me—a song Andy Wilkinson and I wrote and then recorded at Bradley Kopp's studio in Buda, Texas. We flew the vocal tracks up to Alamosa to mix in and finish it off.

Valery Fremin captured the perfect photo, and Dick Reeves brought it all together with his sharp graphic design, giving the album a cover as cool as the songs inside.

Up the Flatland Stairs was released January 15, 2018, on Howlin' Dog Records.

CHAPTER 51

Dispatch from Pakistan

February 2017

I packed up, ready to go on another State Department swing. The itinerary was to tour posts in India, Pakistan, and Sri Lanka. The plans were in place, but Trump had just become president and he was talking about slashing immigration and dismantling Obamacare and he seemed to be anti-Muslim or whatever he was. And I was headed for a Muslim country, maybe the most Muslim country. Pakistan. Into the thick of it. But after the Trump administration's announcements, India and Sri Lanka dropped out mysteriously. They went silent. No answers. Nobody knew what was going to happen with the State Department's cultural programs. It seemed that the various posts saved their money, waited, and watched.

But Pakistan was still on and I was full steam ahead, jumping through hoops, doing the paperwork to become a government vendor, which required my joining Dunn & Bradstreet for some reason. Itineraries, a hundred questions sent via e-mails, packing equipment and then . . . changing musicians! Pakistan wanted a trio and when I offered the gig to Bradley Kopp and Richard Bowden they wouldn›t take the gig. They had their reasons, but the long and short of it was, they didn't want to go.

Cam King lived in Fredericksburg and had been the lead player for the Austin punk band The Explosives. He had played with

Roky Erickson of the 13th Floor Elevators and had played with me on some of my shows around the Hill Country. So I knew he was a good player and a hilarious fellow to boot. Cam joined right up for the trip. Since Richard couldn't go and the State Department was excited about having a fiddle player in the mix, I thought of having a female fiddle player to add a little class to the outfit. I asked my contacts at the State Department if it would be a problem bringing a woman to Pakistan. They said, "Are you kidding? This is exactly what we want to show. This is our mission. Diversity. Women's issues and roles." They said it would be wonderful to bring a woman musician and especially one who played the fiddle.

There was no time to lose. I looked around but a lot of female fiddle players I knew were already booked and the ones who were available didn't have their passports. It got to where the first question I would ask a prospective player was, "Do you have a passport?" And not many did. Finally, I found a young woman in Nashville I had never met before, Maria Kowalski, who'd gone to the Berklee College of Music and was supposed to really be able to bring it. She came to Austin for a couple of days of rehearsal and then we flew out Saturday, February 11.

Our Pakistan tour was physically stressful beyond measure and rewarding in the extreme. It all boiled down to Karachi, one of Pakistan's largest cities with an ancient past. Everything else was cancelled, a portent of things to come. The State Department folks were great and were glad to see us. John Warner and A. J., the public affairs officers, would be our guiding stars for the trip. They put us in a grand hotel and told us not to leave except with an armed guard. We took different routes out of the hotel every day to play the various events they had in store for us. We did a show and a workshop at the Pakistan American Cultural Center with a roomful of young Pakistani college students who turned out to be the greatest singers I'd ever heard. Like so many of the young people in the world, they are going back to their roots and these kids were singing Sufi folk songs and it was beautiful and haunting and goosebump-raising. Cam and Maria and I learned some raga-esque songs from two Pakistani musicians and we played two shows with them. Waqas Hassein played sitar and a fellow named Ifran played tabla at lightning speed. These were great guys—into the music, the experiment, and the wild fusion of East and West. The shows we played were a huge success, and we made a lot of friends.

Unexpectedly and mysteriously, two of the shows that were coming up on the same day got canceled because of what were called unspecified threats. We never found out the specifics. There were ISI, Inter-Services Intelligence agents, nondescript men who worked for the Pakistani secret service, hanging around at the shows and outside and across the street. On the last night in town, we showed up for the main performance of the tour at the US Consulate on National Day, a commemoration of Pakistan's independence. There was a crowd of over 1,500 scattered around the lavish lawn and gardens. An arena stage and world-class sound and lights were set up. We did a sound check with the Pakistani musicians and went over the new ragas we had learned. The guests arrived, which included Pakistani dignitaries but also foreign officers and diplomats from other countries. There were media people, reporters, all the folks the US courts. Actors and musicians. Bankers and industrialists. The USA wanted to have a big party and so far it was going great.

Right before we went on, David Hale, the US Ambassador to Pakistan, walked through the crowd with his security right up to me: "I have some bad news." He said there had been a bombing of a Sufi shrine by extremists. The bombing was far enough away that we weren't in any danger but it wouldn't be the right thing to do to have loud music and possibly dancing in the crowd. We were outside, surrounded by a high wall, but you never could tell who might be on the other side of that wall and pissed to hear "Public Domain" and Texas Swing and laughter. The American parties and receptions are suspect anyway. The Americans have the booze and the parties they throw are lavish affairs. Ironically, the party went on but not with music. People on the other side of the wall didn't know what was happening on the garden lawn.

We were all very, very disappointed. The Pakistani musicians burst into tears of disappointment, and I felt so sorry for them. The fanatics and their terror tactics might at any moment blow you up, which was something they had to deal with on a daily basis. I told the ambassador and A. J. that we could play for them later after the party in the mansion and that's what we did. A house concert. So we played for about fifty highly vetted folks in an ultra-secure facility with Marines just outside the door.

The roughest part of the trip came at the end, when I flew from Karachi to India to visit Tucker and his family. He had married an American woman, and they were raising their young son—my grandson—in India. Iris had just arrived as well, and it was going to be a good reunion. I was still jet-lagged at the start of the trip as we had only been in Pakistan for a week and I hadn't had time to even get over that. Now before me lay a new grueling ordeal of night-long layovers in Abu Dhabi and Bombay and the world's worst five-hour taxi ride over the bumpiest roads with the angriest taxi driver, alternately gunning it and slamming on his brakes. I got major carsick and threw up on the side of the road with cows in a field looking concerned. By the time I got to where I was going, I'd been awake forty-six hours and I was no spring chicken walking down the wild roads of India like I had been before. I ended up losing my cell phone and my belt at the Abu Dhabi airport security screening area, so I was out of touch the whole time and my pants fell down for over a month. But then I don't wear pants when I'm in India anyway.

CHAPTER 52

It's All in the Cards

2019

Jerry Jeff's health began to decline. He wasn't feeling right—something was off. Eventually, doctors discovered the cause: **throat cancer**. It was a heavy blow, not just to him but to all of us who had ridden the wild trails by his side. The voice that had shouted anthems from Austin to Luckenbach, howled from back porches and barrooms, was now under threat. The man who had once been larger than life—charging stages, laughing loud, always one step ahead of the chaos—was suddenly facing the fight of his life. It was surreal. Even legends get sick. Even cowboys have to hang up their spurs, if only for a while.

Various remedies were tried. Sometime in the winter Jerry Jeff was at MD Anderson in Houston for a second operation. As I understand it, the doctors were planning to use a revolutionary new procedure involving immunotherapy and interferon technology whereby the cancer shrinks to an operable state. At least this is the way I understood it. They were prepping Jacky Jack in the hospital as they explained the ins and outs. Meanwhile, way down in the basement, there was a doctor scientist bent over his lab looking through a microscope when someone remarked that Jerry Jeff Walker was up on the fifth floor. Hearing this, the doctor made his way upstairs to Jerry Jeff's room. He said, "I'm

Jim Allison and I'm a big fan and I was at the *¡Viva Terlingua!* recording in Luckenbach. I was in the audience. I've been a fan all my life and I'm in a doctor band and we do all your songs." He continued, "This procedure that you're about to have on your throat, well, I invented it, and I just came up here to tell you how it was going to go down and what we're going to do." Dr. James Allison had just won the Nobel Prize for Medicine for that exact procedure and now he was Jerry Jeff's doctor.

Even after this surgery and with his voice barely above a whisper, Jacky Jack had a couple of dates at Gruene Hall lined up and asked if I was open. At the time I couldn't imagine him doing the shows. His voice was raspy and his tongue was thick. He had been through the wringer. But on September 7 and 8 we played that historic venue, maybe for the last time. The band was Chris Gage, Steve Samuel, Jerry Jeff's son Django, and me. Django played rhythm along with Jerry Jeff the first night, with Bradley Kopp filling that role the next. We sound-checked and then strolled over to the Gristmill overlooking the Guadalupe River to eat before the show. It is an altogether beautiful spot. It was hot and humid with something intangible in the air, and that night and with a packed Gruene Hall it would be even more so. These natural forces would only add to the movie that was about to play out that evening.

Gruene Hall is "the oldest continually operating dance hall in Texas." At least that's what they say. The band was backstage crammed into our tune-up room, which is really only a place to store equipment in front of the men's bathroom where there are cops barring entrance to anybody except those with the most urgent need to pee. The murmuring crowd began to grow louder and louder, suddenly beginning to cheer as Jerry Jeff made his way through the multitudes in the hall fifteen minutes before showtime. I don't know why they didn't use the "Willie Door" for him, the one that cuts straight into the backstage.

When Jacky Jack walked up to us we were startled to see he had a black eye and his hands were bandaged. He looked like he had been in a fight, like the good old days. But in fact he had fallen down in the street in front of his house chasing his dog. Jerry Jeff loved that dog. "The pavement gave me a rude awakening," he said. So here he was, after two bouts of chemo and so beat up that he couldn't even play a G chord. And yet Jerry Jeff took the stage in a good mood. What a trooper!

John Prine had called him and told him to keep on singing, that he would get his voice back. For now it was barely above a whisper. A lot of creaks and cracks. And Jerry Jeff would find out later that he had two fractured bones in his hands from the fall. He wanted me to sing the melodies, not the harmony that I'd always sung. He needed meat in there. Jerry Jeff's audience is typically rowdy, but they were respectful this night, aware that this just might be the last time they ever see him sing "Mr. Bo" again. Jerry Jeff said to the now-quiet crowd—the crowd so silent you could hear a train conductor down the track cleaning his muddy boots on the rails—"I have an agreement with my audience. I come here, I come all the way here, and I tell you stories. And *you* are going to sing the songs. You know the words better than I do." And from the first "Hi, Buckaroos" to "Pick Up the Tempo" the crowd sang every word to every song. It was an emotional show, and I wished I had a video camera. Afterward, someone came up and said, "Tell Jerry Jeff that as long as he keeps coming, we'll keep coming."

CHAPTER 53

Kerrville and the "West Texas Walk of Fame"

2018–2022

The first Kerrville Folk Festival was held in 1972 and the two red-beards showed up for it. A couple of days before, Murphey and I had arrived in the dead of an Austin night and crashed on Segle Fry's couches to dreams of guitars being passed overhead. When I woke up there really *were* guitars being passed overhead. None of the long-haired musicians scattered helter-skelter around the room with guitars in their hands knew what to expect other than they too were here to play the new festival and that just outside Segle's door it was 101 in the shade.

Rod Kennedy, the festival's producer, was a gruff local entrepreneur and folk-music lover who had owned the Chequered Flag, the best folk club in Austin, where he'd booked everyone from Murphey to Jerry Jeff to Steve Fromholz to Willis Ramsey to you name it. Rod had cobbled this new festival together on a wing and a prayer. It was held in the city of Kerrville for a couple of years and then moved down the road in 1974 to the Quiet Valley Ranch at an outdoor amphitheater where it's been ever since. Rod built the festival from scratch with the help of other like-minded souls enduring several phases and stages and through bad weather and financial catastrophes. The first festival was in the high school gym. Murphey and I played all his great songs, "You Can Only Say So Much," "Wildfire," "What Am I Doing Hangin' Round." Lots of singing, harmonies, and energy. Crowd pleasers all. Murphey was fast becoming a folk icon, in Texas and beyond.

As the years rolled by, the Kerrville Folk Festival developed quite a gypsy campfire scene, an all-night cacophony of singing and playing in the outlying hilly terrain and down in the meadow. Retro country to alternative tribal African rhythms to heavy metal played on ukes to French and Irish and Scotts folk music. Guitars, upright basses, banjos, dobros, fiddles, zithers, and finally the miracle three seconds of silence. If you happen to be tired and want a respite from the constant playing and partying you need to get far away from all those colorful camps with the musics all coming together swirling in your brain as you are desperate for sleep amidst the songs, music, laughter, loud talking, and strange stories. It can be pretty nerve-rattling, being totally exhausted and on the edge of dozing off where you stand. So as for me, I head for the Hilton in town. I had lived on the road with Jerry Jeff, so I'm no slouch at hanging out, but Kerrville goes on for eighteen days!

And many hearty folk stay out there for the whole thing. San Antonio blues-man-turned-folkie Butch Morgan has the constitution and preparedness for long hauls and he stays the whole time, roaming the endless all-nighters and campfires and playing with everybody 'til dawn. How does he do it? Butch says because it's so much fun.

♪

Nowadays I'm back to being a folkie most of the time. A singer-songwriter, storyteller, letting my good side show. Layne Lauritzen, of Austin's Texas Accountants and Lawyers for the Arts, told me, "You're a singer-songwriter, so start acting like one. No more bands." He continued, "If you can pull it off, most of

A cool version of the Lost Gonzo Band, both old and new, Kerrville Folk Festival. (L–R): Radoslav Lorković, Gary P. Nunn, Kelly Dunn, Paul Pearcy, Bob Livington, John Inmon, Lloyd Maines. (Photo courtesy of Bob Livingston.)

the house concerts, folk clubs, and festivals want to hear just you and a guitar. It's folk music!" It was good advice and it spurred me onward. I do lots of house concerts and folk clubs where it's so quiet you can hear a pin drop on a down blanket. When I need more ammunition, I take Bradley because he knows the drill and covers a lot of bases. Just the two of us can do it. If it's a good-paying show like Kerrville or New Year's Eve I bring along David Webb on keys, drummer Kevin Hall, and bass man Will Landon. It's a mean five-piece and those guys can really rock—and the best thing is, they love the music.

In September I usually play Michael Hearne's Big Barn Dance, in Kit Carson Park in downtown Taos. Michael is a virtuoso on the guitar and has a pure sweet voice and writes hits like "New Mexico Rain." Michael has put together one of the best music festivals for singer-songwriters there is. His uncle Bill Hearne of Bill and Bonnie fame is always there with his flat-picking magic.

It's a listening crowd like Kerrville with new and old-timers, road warriors all. They love Michael and anything he puts before them.

The wandering minstrel life, complete with endless driving and flying, gets harder every year. The getting there is harder. But I love it. What can I say? There's a line in one of my songs, "I can't get enough of it . . . but I want to go home." It's a vicious two-edged sword. But that's the only answer. I love it. Otherwise, why do it? When I'm on the road I get homesick, but I am into the adventure, the rhythm of the road, the sunset at seventy miles an hour, trying to catch up. There is a special connection and meaning for life out there.

"Bob Livingston is one of us," said Andy Wilkinson at the West Texas Walk of Fame induction ceremony in October 2018. You have to receive the honor in person, otherwise they'll find somebody else, so there I was about to get a nice plaque and sing two songs. I didn't know too much about the Walk of Fame itself. I thought it might be like the Hollywood Walk of Fame where people can actually walk on your star. I had no concept. And for some reason I never checked it out. So I went to Lubbock to get the award blind to what it was. Vicki Key picked me up at the airport. Vicki worked for the Civic Center, was sharp as a tack, and had lived in Lubbock all her life. She knew how to handle all of the complications of the induction ceremony and knew most everything there was to know about the Walk of Fame. Don Caldwell, the Lubbock sax player and big event producer, was at the helm. There were three other inductees, musician Josh Abbott, sculptor Garland Weeks, and the actor-musician-songwriter Donnie Allison. Donnie came along after my time in West Texas, but he had made a big impact on the music and theater scene in Lubbock.

The best thing about the Lubbock trip was seeing the actual Walk of Fame. I wish I had seen it before the awards ceremony because then I would have known the specialness of it. The next

Playing "Original Spirit" in Lubbock at the West Texas Walk of Fame induction, 2018. (Lubbock photographer with the paper unknown.)

day on the way back to the airport, Vicki Key took me to see it. Across the street from the Buddy Holly Center, it's a solemn but nice outdoor space with a larger-than-life statue of Buddy playing his Fender guitar. Behind Buddy is a twelve-foot-plus-high wall in a semicircle with the plaques of former inductees in rows all over it. Buddy was the first to be inducted, followed by others whose plaques now include Waylon Jennings, Delbert McClinton, Joe Ely, Dan Blocker—who played Hoss Cartwright on *Bonanza*—and more than sixty others. Look them up. Many honored there are long gone now. My plaque will be up on Buddy's wall for a long time after I'm gone too. It's kinda cool—and spooky—to think about it.

CHAPTER 54

Reality Ranch Livestream

2020

The past, the present, and the future walk into a bar. It was tense.

The world pandemic of 2020 with all its COVID-19 catastrophes came crashing down. We were in a real-time reality show singing the coronavirus blues. Mother Nature had stricken back as she often does every eon or so and . . . turn me loose, I don't think we'll ever be the same. Only time will tell.

The news of the virus must not have seemed so threatening at first or I wouldn't have been out on the road driving towards Arkansas and a three-state tour. In hindsight, I shouldn't have been there, but it was all a part of the learning experience for me and everyone else in this brave new world. Or maybe I was foolhardy. Or just a fool.

Be that as it may, on Friday the 13th of March I found myself in Fayetteville, Arkansas, scheduled to play a house concert that would kick off a series of shows in Arkansas, Louisiana, and Missouri. Everyone that was connected with the tour including me *or especially me* was concerned and astonished about what they saw and heard on the endless television and PBS radio reports.

Busking in Jackson Square, New Orleans. I always wanted to do it just to say I did it. (Photo by Kim Carson.)

We had all been inundated with the news and weren't thinking about much else. Yet here I was out on the limb of a tour that was growing tenuous. But the show must go on, right?

I had driven into Fayetteville on Thursday before the show and all that night and Friday afternoon we watched the country and much of the world close up shop. Venue after venue in Fayetteville had shut their doors for an undetermined amount of time. Back home I heard that all the Austin clubs and many businesses were closing. This all happened fast, within a few days, or even a few hours, and many of my friends told me that Friday the 13th was their last gig too. Musicians all over the world were suddenly out of work.

My house concert hosts, the Lindleys, asked me if I wanted to cancel the show. Larry said there were still some stalwart fans who wanted to come out and he left it up to me to decide. Well . . . I was already in Fayetteville and I was already at the gig. Let's do the show, I said. That night a decent posse of music lovers came out. Everybody had smiles on their faces, bumping elbows, laughing and talking, eating and drinking, and wanting to be entertained. But an atmosphere of uncertainty was in the air. Worried faces behind the smiles.

To get our minds off all this disturbing news, I opened up the night with "Original Spirit" and the spirit ruled, and we stayed away from current events, any current event, and we all had a grand time. When all else fails, music prevails. The Arkansas folks were good listeners and laughed in all the right places and sang in all the wrong ones and we were transported out of there.

All the other shows on my tour *did* cancel so I headed back to Austin the next morning, almost afraid to breathe any time I stopped for gas and had to go inside. I didn't own a mask yet. It was science fiction out there and it was hard to take it all in. I listened to the somber news as I drove the now-desolate highway.

Back in Austin I hunkered down with Iris and our Austin family and quarantined for weeks on end. There were Skype calls to India where Tucker, Kari, and grandson Arun were safe and sound, so far. KN95 masks became the rule of the day and home deliveries and curbside pickup was a way of life. No one knew what else to do until we all got vaccinated and felt safer. Even as thousands began to die from COVID, idiots came up with conspiracy theories saying it wasn't real.

The future wasn't what it used to be. I needed gigs. Virtual gigs. There had always been livestreams going on. I'd done live broadcasts of Reality Ranch on occasion and a lot of folks had tuned in. But those were spur-of-the-moment sign-ons with no advance notice. On Friday night, exactly one week after coming back from Arkansas, I propped my iPhone on a stepladder in my living room and went live. Just like that. People tuned in and made donations and asked questions in the chat that Iris would hand me so I could answer them as best I could. There was communication going on in real time. There were lots of music fans out there and they wanted to support their favorite musicians because they understood what kind of predicament we were all in. That first night was so successful I thought I'd never go out on the road again. I could make a living like this from the comfort of my office studio and living room. And it went on like that for a few weeks. Reality Ranch was streaming along. And this had been, up to that point, all from my iPhone straight to Facebook.

A week later I drove to Strait Music in Austin where I'd bought my Baldwin piano all those years ago. Just as the doors were about to close I dashed in with resolve and bought a simple Focusrite interface that gave me the pathway to plug my voice and guitar into my computer and into a recording program and then out to the internet and the world. It was a game changer. For years musicians had been recording and sending virtual tracks back and forth but it was all confusing to me and I never followed suit. I couldn't fathom the technology and had no recording equipment. Iris had been telling me I needed to get that interface for at least a year, but the real significance of having it had been lost on me until there was no other option. I could use the technology available to me now to do virtual recording sessions, voiceovers, commercials, and livestreams without ever leaving my house.

I had bought some recording equipment a couple of times before. But after fiddling with all the buttons and levels and

With Woody the dog—outtake from *Up the Flatland Stairs*. (Photo by Valerie Fremin.)

settings and mics and pre-amps my ADHD would kick in and I would become so incredibly bored, for want of a better word, that it was physically painful for me to continue. It sounds like I was crazy but I swore then to never record another song by myself and instead always use a proper studio with a good engineer running everything.

But now I had to learn to broadcast a show virtually. Bradley Kopp and Logic Pro expert Ben Cocke explained the basics of recording to me. Zoom calls became the method of choice to communicate. Soon Bradley and I were recording new songs for a Cowboys & Indians album, sending tracks back and forth, adding parts and video from the others in the group who were also learning how to use these hi-tech contraptions.

There were technical issues. After broadcasting sideways, losing signal, going dark, and with minimal sound and video quality from the iPhone, I decided to upgrade. I got new mics and a new camera. I learned to use software like OBS that helped me broadcast on Facebook, YouTube, and many other platforms all at the same time. There was an immense audience out there to try to corral, but soon every Tom, Dick, Harry, and Jane were also live streaming their music to the four corners of the galaxy. Thousands of singers and bands and artists and dancers and anyone who just wanted to rant were all over Facebook and all at once. Everyone was using a different angle and a different way to get into the jetstream on the internet waves. The bandwidth required was immense, the competition fierce and to various degrees of success. All the musicians who made their living by playing live shows had changed course and set out to become tech savvy. Without this new way to reach our fans, we were sunk.

It was a lot of work and a disconcerting performing experience. I was alone in my office, singing to a cold unblinking camera eye. Noncommittal. No feedback, no crowd reaction. No vibes good or bad. Weird. But the chat was there, and I had to pay attention to it.

Reality Ranch continued to be a weekly livestream event and I stretched out and made videos to play at a blue-plate special part of the program. There was a digital waiting room and background music with my own commercials about PayPal and Venmo donations. There was background music while the audience was tuning in and meanwhile I was freaking out over something or other about to go live. It was a two-camera shoot. I used my new high-resolution webcam as the main stage cam. My computer camera was used when I sat down to commiserate with the Facebook audience. The OBS software let me switch back and forth between cameras but occasionally I would forget to hit the switch back to my main camera and unbeknownst to me I would be singing and the audience would see only a profile view instead of the main camera straight on. But the audience would write me in the chat and tell me what was going wrong. It was like I had a hundred engineers and sound technicians out there giving me feedback and they told me the sound and quality was better than most. Who's to say?

I became bogged down in the process and the music was secondary in a way. I made it work on the fly and sometimes making mistakes was part of the show's charm. Or so I was told. The fans liked to see me mess up and leap just as the net didn't appear. Anyway, in spite of any technical mishaps, I kept charging.

My most watched programs had themes like "The Cosmic Cowboy Years, Part 1" and "The West Texas Revue." I produced videos for every show with relevant photos and movie clips. There were wild beginnings and endings, sometimes with rocket ships blasting off from Earth saying, "Tune in next week." I sang and played and told road stories about Murphey, Jerry Jeff, and Ray Wylie with my bird's-eye view of history. Sporadically I read from the eternal memoir I was writing and still am right now.

Producing the show was a considerable and complicated chore and a vast learning experience. I was having fun putting such a newfangled presentation together, but it drove me crazy at the same time. It was a lot of work. I would become so exasperated with what I had to go through to get the show up and running that I would say out loud, "I'm not going to do the show this week!" and this would be just a few moments before showtime. Most times I would come around, decide to go live after all and make it red: "Live and in person from Austin, Texas, it's Reality Ranch."

But sometimes even if I pressed the "Go Live" button nothing happened. Darkness at the edge of town. No signal beaming out from Bob. As the appointed hour of the show had come and gone, I would be trying to track down the problem, every button and switch made sure of, every connection rebooted, every frame rate locked in, every setting set. Then . . . voilà, I was live!

It was a mystery and a surprise when everything actually worked and we were broadcasting and scattering seeds. There were folks in Finland and India and Lubbock watching. But I was gun-shy from all the miscues and lost connections and going dark and I couldn't trust that everything was in gear and functioning. Like Tolkien said, I was "thin, sort of stretched, like butter scraped over too much bread." I would ask the audience if they could hear and see me, and sometimes they couldn't. Soon the chat with the audience became part of the show, as if I didn't already have enough responsibilities. I was the producer, editor, camera operator, and video guy first then I was singing and playing guitar and harmonica trying to remember lyrics while monitoring meters for signal output. At the same time I had to pay attention to the computer screen and to the chat. I was always distracted by the eccentric moment of doubt from the uncertainty and wondered if I was really broadcasting or not. One time, I had played and sang my heart out for twenty powerful minutes before I learned from the chat screaming at me that I was not sending an audio signal to anyone but Iris and the dog outside.

Then came the spring and the fight with COVID seemed to ease up a bit, so much so that I accepted a live gig. It was raining cats and dogs as I pulled around back of the Remedy Room in Aledo, Texas, for my first live audience in fourteen months. It's a great listening venue just west of Fort Worth, part house concert, part folk club. My old friend Steve Long met me out back wearing a mask and told me to leave everything in my black SUV until the rain stopped. Steve is a longtime Fort Worth schoolteacher, baseball and football umpire, and fellow songster who was as hungry for live music as anyone. "Bob-o, in twenty minutes, this line of thunderstorms is going to pass right by us and it will be a beautiful night from then on out." Steve was right as rain and the sun came out with a fanfare and everything had been washed clean and purified and the air was fresh as a daisy. It was a new start and great to be back in the saddle again playing for a live audience in this delightful garden dripping with sunlit raindrops from the flowers. It was like a fairy tale . . . and there was no chat room to fool with. And for now, being outdoors and all, there were no masks.

CHAPTER 55

Jerry Jeff Leaves the Building

2020

The winds of change continued to blow and by the time the pandemic hit like a hurricane on the Gulf Coast Jerry Jeff had lost most of his voice to the cancer. He was still as crusty and resilient as ever and wanted to play and talk guitars and said he was going to do a show. He had called me to play with him for a private party at Dartmouth College in Hanover, New Hampshire. There was a fraternity there, Theta Delta Chi, more popularly known as the Boom Boom Lodge. The rumor was they'd modeled the movie *Animal House* on these wild and crazy guys. Hundreds of them were descending on Hanover in their private jets to see their hero Jerry Jeff play at their 50th anniversary. We had played the Boom Boom Lodge many times over the years, and always after the show Jerry Jeff would hold court and hang out with the boys in the fraternity house basement. He could drink toe-to-toe with these guys and stay up all night until everyone but him and a few hearty lads were still going through the motions of being awake.

Now the Boom Boom boys wanted Jerry Jeff one more time even though he was literally a year away from death's door; they made an offer Susan and Jerry Jeff couldn't refuse. So Jerry Jeff, along with his son Django, guitar virtuoso Chris Gage, drummer Steve Samuel, and me—Cosmic Bob—met at a private terminal in Austin for the flight to Dartmouth in Hanover. Unbeknownst to anyone at the time it would be Jerry Jeff's last full public performance. Everyone had their guitars and I was still lugging my '67 Fender P bass around. While we were waiting for our plane ride, Jerry Jeff took out an old Gibson acoustic and I videotaped him singing Paul Williams's "Rainbow Connection" in a raspy whisper. The reaction to the cancer chemicals coursing through his veins had caused his fingers and especially his thumb to dry and crack. He couldn't hold a pick. He brushed the strings with the backs of his nails very softly and he had a smile on his face: "Someday we'll find it, the Rainbow Connection / The lovers, the dreamers, and me." He seemed happy and he looked straight into the camera and through all his pain and weariness, I could see the old Jerry Jeff. I could see him with his youth restored, singing and looking at me as if to say, "Isn't this a beautiful song? I know you can appreciate it too, Bob." It was all there in his smile.

One of the grown-up Boom Boom boys and his grown-up New York model girlfriend came to fetch us for the Dartmouth show in a very large and grown-up Gulfstream II or perhaps a Falcon jet. I forget which. It was lightning fast and came equipped with a pilot and a co-pilot and a stewardess who gave us delicious sandwiches and filled our champagne glasses—except that since I didn't drink, I missed out. Our Boom Boom boy host explained how much Jerry Jeff meant to the fraternity. Several classes over the years had sung "Trashy Women" and "Pissin' in the Wind" out loud with their arms around each other. This was a serious bonding ritual and all those late-night basement bullshit sessions with Jerry Jeff were the stuff of legend and folklore.

The plan was to fly in, check in to the hotel, have a nice dinner, go to bed early, and do the show the next afternoon. When we arrived for the sound check at 2 p.m. the Boom Boom boys were waiting. They knew Jerry Jeff couldn't even talk above a whisper, much less sing, but they didn't care. They wanted him there for one last time. They wanted to touch him and be touched by him. There was a camaraderie and brotherhood in the big tent erected for the show, the big moment was at hand. Jerry Jeff came onstage holding a staff in his hand to help him balance when he walked and he looked like Gandalf from *The Lord of the Rings* and he stamped his staff on the stage in three-quarter time to the music as the whole room sang "Mr. Bojangles, Mr. Bojangles, Mr. Bojangles . . . Dance!"

Before the show, I had helped Jerry Jeff get to a meet-and-greet in an ornate room in the fraternity house. The room had a lot of gold and red velvet and was probably used for secret rituals and blood sacrifices. He sat on a red velvet couch holding his staff in his hands as one by one the VIPs of the Boom Boom Lodge came in to pay their respects, older gentlemen who were movers and shakers. It reminded me of a scene in *The Godfather* until they whipped out their CDs and Jerry Jeff good-naturally signed them and reminisced about the good times gone by.

His health continued to fade, and soon thereafter I didn't see him or talk to him much anymore. The COVID crisis was still going on but we would text back and forth. He was still writing songs but couldn't sing them. Jerry Jeff was inducted into the Texas Heritage Songwriters Hall of Fame on February 22, 2020, at the Paramount Theatre in Austin. He had a hard time at the show, but he was there and he was honored by his friends both live and in a video tribute.

Jerry Jeff passed away on October 23, 2020, at the too-young age of 78. Scamp—rascal, troubadour, wild-eyed poet with an ironclad constitution—had finally checked out. People say it all the time, but in his case, it was true: there was no one else like him. One of a kind, all the way.

CHAPTER 56

"The Return of the Lost Gonzo Band"

2021

Townes Van Zandt had a joke about betting on the seventh horse in the seventh race and the horse came in seventh. The Gonzos hadn't played together for seven years. Since our dissolution in 1979, we had played a few reunion shows, but only a few, and if truth be known they weren't much fun. The last show was in Nocona, Texas, at a festival run by W. R. Tucker, a crusty Texas Music lover if there ever was one. It was a quartet with Gary Nunn, John Inmon, Paul Pearcy, and me. We did a decent show, but our hearts and minds were out of kilter. The feng shui just wasn't right. There was too much baggage under the bridge. But as Mr. Rogers once said, "Often when you think you are at the end of something, you are at the beginning of something else."

Gary and I had hooked up for a couple of duo shows in 2017, one at Poor David's Pub and the other at the Heights in Houston—both great listening rooms. We had never played as a duo before. It was new territory for both of us, but it was smooth as glass. We told stories and sang anything we wanted, the songs stretching all the way back to Lubbock, back to the Sparkles and the Livingston Brothers, back to Red River days and Roy Orbison nights.

Gary's manager, D Foster, launched a full court press for the Poor David's show with radio interviews and early morning television. *The Dallas Morning News* put us on the cover of their *Guide* magazine with lots of photos and a significant story across a five-page spread penned by SMU professor Brentney Hamilton, well written and the biggest fanfare either of us had received in quite a time. It was as if Gary and I had taken a turn down a side street full of color and jive. There were radio DJs and anchormen and women, some with beards, some without, beckoning to us while the jugglers juggled. It didn't make much sense to me either, but let's just say it was a whirlwind of a day. Then, as fast as a wink we were driving down Mockingbird Lane on the way to the Poor David's show in the back of a 1970 Cadillac convertible with longhorns fixed to the front, iPhone cameras snapping away. The day's events pointed to some far-off cosmic happening that had not yet been realized. Pieces of a puzzle not quite fitting together. Yet.

Four years passed and the Gonzos were still scattered to the winds without a notion of ever playing together again as a band. We were removed far from that, hard-wired and hard at work all by ourselves alone. We'd been through the pandemic in various stages of isolation. The lockdown had taken its toll, but I was back in the saddle again, or thought so, now on the road in various incarnations: solo, duos, and trios. I didn't really need a band for most occasions. I'd go to the Barn Dance in Taos as a solo and have a six-piece band onstage by the end of the show. Bradley Kopp and I together sound like a band. But the most focused, stream of consciousness, on the edge, connected moments have been in my solo shows, and thank God for 'em.

John was busy all the time recording in his home studio, and he had put together a band that played residencies at El Mercado and the One-2-One Bar. Gary was Gary P. Nunn after all, and he was busy starring in the dance halls of Texas and writing a book. Paul Pearcy had moved to Santa Fe and was out of reach in a kayak down a canyon somewhere on the Rio Grande.

And now, Jerry Jeff "Mr. Bojangles" Walker, the man who had meant so much to us Gonzo guys amidst all the ups and downs, bittersweet truths and musical beginnings, was gone. Even though we knew it was coming, it was thunderbolt lightning. It made us all take stock and reflect. Gary and I had already taken to singing a few Jerry Jeff classics in our own shows. Audiences still loved those songs and would sing out and whoop it up. The songs were a big part of our lives, and they were still out there somewhere, begging to be sung.

D Foster is a fast-talking idea guy. He's a veteran of down-and-dirty Arkansas politics and he'd decided that if he could handle that kind of stress and drama he could handle anything. So he turned into a music manager, agent, promoter, and bullshitter, and he was doing all of that for Gary P. Nunn. D had an idea for a Jerry Jeff tribute show of some sort and was talking about "making lemons into lemonade," and D and his partner Richard Sutton set up a meeting with us in a downtown Austin law office. We sat close together around a table, looking into each other's eyes and talking all things Gonzo, past, present, and future. D had done a great job for Gary the past few years, so we listened to what the man said. We all wanted to do *something* for Jerry Jeff and celebrate the music we had made with him. It would be all-encompassing, singing the songs and telling stories about Jerry Jeff and the Cosmic Cowboy years, the Gonzo era. This was our story too, and I for one wanted a chance to sing all that great stuff again and send out my good wishes and "happy trails" to 'ol Jacky Jack. It wouldn't be a Gonzo "reunion" like before but instead would be called "The Return of the Lost Gonzo Band." The first show would be at Gruene Hall and, depending on how it went, we'd go on from there.

The Return of the Lost Gonzo Band, 2021. (L–R): John Inmon, Bob Livingston, Gary P. Nunn, and Freddie Krc. (Photo courtesy of Bob Livingston.)

We asked Freddie "Steady" Krc to join us on drums. Though Freddie wasn't in the original Gonzo band and hadn't played on the records we put out in the '70s or '90s, he had major Jerry Jeff credentials. He was in Jerry Jeff's wild Bandito Band with Bobby Rambo, Tomás Ramirez, and Ron Cobb and he had roamed far and wide with John and me as a Gonzo Compadre. Freddie had serious Jerry duty that lasted a hundred years or so. And they don't call him Freddie Steady for nothin'.

The four of us met at Freddie's house and crowded in his music room for a few initial get-togethers and rehearsals. "Somebody start a list!" There were songs to go over, "Railroad Man," "Public Domain," and "Rock Me, Roll Me" mixed in with Jerry Jeff and Murphey hits like "Hill Country Rain," "Cosmic Cowboy," "Getting By," and "Geronimo's Cadillac." There were songs of ours that Jerry Jeff had recorded: John Inmon's "Easy Street," my "It's a Good Night for Singin,'" and Gary's classic Texas music anthem, "London Homesick Blues." Gary P. played electric guitar and piano and the four of us were tight as a drum. And it felt good.

And, lo and behold, I was playing bass again. I dusted off my old '67 Fender P bass and dove right in. With the exception of playing in Bill Oliver's Otter Space Band and some recording sessions here and there, I hadn't played bass guitar in a band for a good long while. It was a challenge and I had to get back in shape, playing scales, getting power back into my fingers. Bass is a driving force in a band and you can't hold back. Boom!

CHAPTER 57

The Day the Book Ended

2021

On October 22, the Lost Gonzo Band sold out world-famous Gruene Hall. And I mean world-famous. And I mean sold out. With big-ticket VIP seats and standing room only for everyone else. John Burris, Gary's former road manager and all-around good guy, texted us, "If you are going to do this thing it needs to be big. And I mean really big. And one more thing. B.I.G." A big sound like the Gonzos of old with a sound like Kelly Dunn's organ ripping and swelling over John's otherworldly leads. So we brought in a couple of fellows who could help with that. David Webb, one of Austin's go-to keyboard guys, brought out a keyboard that could sound like anything in the universe, whether it be organ, piano, or the Mormon Tabernacle Choir. We got Steve Layne who had played upright bass with Junior Brown and was in Gary's band for years. Gary wanted him along for the ride and that was fine with the rest of us. Steve brought out a unique nine-stringed acoustic baritone guitar and he many times doubled my bass lines and the bottom was fat. Yes it was.

David and Steve were icing on the Gonzo cake we were whipping up. The sound *was* big and everybody sang with Beatlesque harmonies and played like there was no tomorrow or the next day. The audience was all ears. We told stories about playing and recording with Jerry Jeff and the start of so-called "progressive country music" with Michael Murphey. We played everything with our fun-rockin', slam-bang, Cosmic Gonzo attitude. There was electricity in the air and the audience's love stretched a million miles.

On the day the Gruene Hall show dawned there was a whole lot of shakin' going on. A three-camera crew was filming everything from start to finish for future consideration. They were shooting the load-in of the sound system, our amps and drums. The roadies and helpers, or lack thereof. The ice man, the Lone Star Beer guy. Freddie setting up his drums. The security guys practicing headlocks. Me sweating bullets about my bass amp crackle. Gary fussing with his in-ear monitors that never were to work right. Everybody had an opinion and everybody was talking at once and everybody was in the movie.

Richard Sutton was running the merchandise and had hired some pretty girls to wear the new Lost Gonzo Band T-shirts at the merch booth. Morgan Avery, a San Marcos graphic artist, had designed a cool poster with that same long-horned Cadillac convertible with armadillos crawling out, Hondo riding a rocket guitar over the moon, and cactus and smoke rising. I had to hand it to D Foster's team for the rollout.

There were two different sound checks that day. One for real, getting all the vocals, instrument and drum levels, fixing the crackle in my amp, running wires and cables and working on monitor mixes. "Testing, testing, testing." The second sound check was for the 150 VIPs, who were the only folks in the joint that got to sit down. Their tickets included a ringside seat, the cool poster, a T-shirt, and a personal sound check. We played "Backslider's Wine," "Roll on Down the Road," and a couple more that didn't make it into that night's setlist. Everything was wrung out for the second time and the pre-show energy and excitement were infectious.

After the sound checks, we had a couple of hours to kill, but not really. It was interesting and exciting watching it all go down, with the cameras filming the hustle and bustle everywhere you looked. We were already tired from an early call and the long day's work. And we still had to rock the house. I needed to get prone, flat off my feet for a while. I don't take naps often, but I felt one was needed then.

There was a nice B&B apartment behind Gruene Hall overlooking the Guadalupe River that was set aside for the band as a base of operations, including a tune-up room, a shower, and snacks. It was stocked with hors d'oeuvres, alkaline water, English Breakfast tea, coffee, and beer if anybody cared, but nobody did. There were also some fancy whisky and vodka bottles that disappeared like greased lightning, spirited away (pardon the pun) off to some secret after-party that was already in full swing at an undisclosed location. Camera operators wandered in and out, filming and interviewing.

Friends and well-wishers dropped by to say hello: Bill Hearne, who would sing "London Homesick Blues" with us that night, San Antonio songwriter Bill Lewis, Dr. Robert Mingea—one of Jerry Jeff's guitar-playing doctor friends—and Doyle Jeter, who booked Jerry Jeff and the Gonzos at Enoch's Pub back in the day. Armadillo artists Jim Franklin and Danny Garrett compared notes with Bobby Bridger and talked about Sioux Indian Sundance rituals and whether they could be painted accurately. Becky Crouch Patterson was decked out to cowgirls' heaven adding flair, history, and fashion in one stroke. D Foster was directing traffic as T-shirts, guitars, and 150 posters were passed around the room for signatures, us signing our names over and over. And over.

There was a bed in our backstage clubhouse all made up Western-like with big pillows and a nice comforter with wagon wheels embroidered there. It all looked so inviting that I crawled in with my boots on and closed my eyes for a few minutes.

Considering there were guitars and posters all over the bed, it was quite a feat getting settled in. It was a beautiful October night, and the door was wide open with a cool breeze from the river wafting in. The roar of the murmuring crowd in the dance hall next door sounded like white noise and I dozed off dreaming of a Moroccan highway from Casablanca to Marrakesh and all that happened afterwards. I came to the surface with band members, technicians, and onlookers standing in the doorway not sure of whether they were coming or going. A cameramen walked through filming anything remotely interesting or not.

I could hear animated talking with sarcastic quips, punch-lines, and laughter on the deck outside as the other guys were interviewed and filmed. For now I was content to lie back, half in and half out of consciousness, eyes closed, taking stock of it all. So far, it had been a good ride and an adventurous life. I had a sweet family with three—count 'em, three—grandkids whose exploits are famous in our circles. In the hardest of days and the coldest of nights Iris had been a trooper and hung in there and I love her for it.

The surprising Return of the Lost Gonzo Band was definitely a cosmic turn of events if there ever was one. There was a sold-out show to do and it was only minutes away. There was no other option but to kill it, rock 'n' roll, super country loud. I don't usually get butterflies before a show, but that night a whole colony of monarchs had settled in my guts as this Lost Gonzo reality show descended on me. Full circle. Saying goodbye and then hello again. Going into fifth gear, no cruising allowed.

I lay on the bed breathing deep with the rhythm of the moment. Relax, Bob. Like Jerry Jeff said: "Do it like you know what you're doing." I opened my eyes, stretching out my arms wide, reaching for my bass leaning against the end table. I lay back with the bass on my chest feeling the notes in my core. Tuning me up for the night.

Songs and stories at Anderson Fair in Houston. (Photo courtesy of Max Addison.)

Across the alleyway in the dance hall I could hear TV personality and Luckenbach compadre Guich Koock making an announcement onstage. The sound system was playing some redneck rock anthem or another. There was a lot of hooting and hollering and singing along. Excitement and expectation were building. It was fifteen minutes to showtime.

Just outside the door, out on the landing overlooking the Guadalupe, I heard John Inmon shouting, "Hey, Bob, where are you? Bob! We're talking to the TV out here. The documentary people. We don't have much time. You need to come out, tell your story, and get your point across."

Coda

2024

It's been a long, winding road getting this cosmic memoir out the door and into your hands. Call it divine delay or just professional procrastination—but in my defense, the music never stopped for me. My so-called career has kept rolling along with events and shows and I didn't want to leave anything out. So here, before we bring it all in for a landing, I'm shining a light on a few noteworthy events that happened after the last chapter was written. These final notes—however brief—are necessary to tie up some loose ends and give the story its proper sendoff.

My song "Can't Get Enough of It" has a line that goes, "It all happened way too fast / Isn't it strange how the die was cast?" Faces flashing by, old characters reappearing like ghosts in the rearview. Memories, once asleep, now rising to the surface. The endless tours, the longer nights. The songs behind the songs—the ones only we know. Moments of being in exactly the right place at the right time . . . and then missing the train by inches. Rehearsals on a bumpy bus bound for New Orleans, Nashville, or Des Moines. Wrestling with that one ridiculous chord I never could play. Lessons you can't put into words—and sometimes, no lesson at all. And that transcendent trail to India . . . some journeys are better left between the lines. And all of that is beneath the surface.

Somehow, half a century of musical mayhem and milestones has flown by. In 2022, the Lost Gonzo Band marked its 50th

Back in the day. (L–R): Jerry Jeff (back to camera), Bob Livingston, Willie Nelson, and Jody Payne. Nashville, Country Music Hall of Fame show. (Photo courtesy of Bob Livingston.)

anniversary the only way we knew how: on stage, under the Texas sky, at Willie Nelson's Luck Reunion. That's Luck, Texas—Willie's own hand-built Wild West town tucked into the Hill Country, just northwest of Austin. Picture sun-bleached storefronts, dust swirling in the wind, and the same dirt streets where *Red Headed Stranger* was filmed. These days, Luck opens its wooden gates for concerts, cosmic gatherings, and high-rolling hillbilly soirées. And there we were, playing through the ghosts, the legends, and the laughter—fifty years later, still riding the wild Gonzo wave.

There was a great crowd in Luck that day. Lukas Nelson was standing by the gate when we arrived and he directed us where to store our gear. I had just seen him in the film *A Star Is Born* and it was cool to meet him. We opened the show with "It's a Good Night for Singin'" and that's what it was. There was a buzz of excitement in the air for the Gonzos' return. I swaggered a bit when I walked into the outrageous fenced-in Luck back-stage area full of long-haired musicians with tattoos and VIP ticketholders and their significant others. Movie stars held court for small groups of gawking, goggle-eyed groupies. There was a lot of gate-crashing going on and soon there were at least 350 people in the corral, chomping at the bit. Everyone was dressed cowboy and Western, high style. There were several gourmet foodstuffs offered, including vegetarian. Local tequilas and whiskies were being promoted and offered to the already over-served. There was a hipster hat shop backstage selling outlandish hats like hotcakes. Everybody had a hat. With a feather.

Yes, this was Willie World in all its glory, but I didn't feel altogether comfortable. It's the same for me in any festival backstage. Everybody is talking at once and no one can hear a word. They're introducing everybody to everybody else. And nobody is listening to any of it. They're in their own heads looking at cell phones, their eyes darting around looking for someone to appear, someone to sweep them off their feet, or at least take them into the inner sanctum to get high with Willie. It's taxing on a body. Over the years I've avoided most backstage scenes. I can't figger out what I'm there for. I didn't stay for Willie's set. It would have been an hours-long wait, and I wasn't into just hanging out. Besides, I'd seen Willie earlier in the day when they drove him up in a ranch Mercedes to sit in with Tami Neilson. So I ducked out early and went home and watched *Young Sheldon* on Netflix. Safe!

The Gonzos lit up the stage at the Paramount Theatre in Austin for Turk and Christy Pipkin's Feed the Peace Awards—a night that felt part concert, part revival. Turk and Christy are longtime friends, brilliant creatives with hearts as big as Texas and a mission to match. Ray Wylie swaggered onstage for a few tunes, decked out in black-on-black—black guitar, black bandana, black boots—like a cosmic outlaw preacher. And sure enough, after all these years, the crowd still lost its collective mind rolling around in the aisles and pouring beer on their heads howling "Redneck Mother" at the top of their lungs . . . even in the plush confines of the Paramount.

A show in Luckenbach followed close on those chrome heels, like a time machine rumbling down a dusty backroad. Becky Crouch Patterson stood tall and recited Hondo's poem "Luckenbach Moon," casting a spell that pulled us right back to those electric, homespun days of fifty years before. We played Lost Gonzo songs like "Give Me Some Money," "It's a Good Night for Singing" and "Relief." Then there was a lot of Jerry Jeff: "Sangria Wine," "Gettin' By," "Redneck Mother," and of course "London Homesick Blues."

As of this writing, the Lost Gonzo Band's final show (so far) was at Michael Hearne's Big Barn Dance in Taos, 2022. I've got to give a heartfelt shout-out to Michael—he's had me on that bill thirteen years running and I love that man. The Barn Dance takes me back to my Taos and Red River roots, to the wide skies and blue spruce dreams, the romantic sweep of it all drifting through "Life in the Pines'" endless stream.

Rick Fowler, from Three Faces West, hovered at the edge of the crowd—dry-witted, soft-spoken, and that day carrying a faint deer-in-the-headlights gleam in his eyes. Bobby Bridger showed up with none other than Academy Award–winner Wes Studi, and they jumped in on the chorus of "London Homesick Blues," adding their voices to the lore.

More 50s to think about. Michael Martin Murphey's *Geronimo's Cadillac* and Willis Alan Ramsey's 1972 debut record both celebrated 50th anniversaries on May 5—Cinco de Mayo! The 50th anniversary of the Kerrville Folk Festival landed a couple of months later. It was also my 50th anniversary at the festival because I played that first one with Murphey in 1972—all those action-packed years ago. This time around I played with a great band of Original Spirits: Bradley Kopp, Kevin Hall, Will Landon, and David Webb. Murph asked me up to sing on his set, some of the songs that opened doors and most certainly helped create the musical vision quest that led Austin to become the Live Music

Capital of the World. "Geronimo's Cadillac," "Alleys of Austin," "Wildfire," and "Backslider's Wine." "Cosmic Cowboy" was in there too, the audience singing, "I just want to be a cosmic cowboy / I just want to ride and rope and hoot, hoot, hoot!"

The year 2023 marked the 50th anniversary of Murphey's *Cosmic Cowboy Souvenir* and the Jerry Jeff/Gonzo landmark MCA album, *¡Viva Terlingua¡* A special concert was held in Luckenbach, the scene of the crime, fifty years to the day. I played bass in the band with Steve Samuels, Chris Gage, Herb Steiner, Craig Hillis, and Brendon Anthony, who heads the Texas Music Office but who is also a mean fiddler. A few young Jerry Jeff acolytes like Todd Schindler, Robert Earl Keen, and Jack Ingram sang their favorite songs from the record. Murphey did his song "Backslider's Wine." Ray Wylie sang "Redneck Mother" . . . again. A surprise was the inclusion of Dennis Quaid, the actor. He was there to sing, too. He told me, "When I was 18 or 19 years old I was in high school in Houston and when *¡Viva Terlingua¡* came out, I bought it and all my friends bought it and we got guitars and learned every song and played them over and over at parties. It was our *Sgt. Pepper*." Jerry Jeff's son, Django, put it all together and did a pretty good job wrangling the whole shebang.

And I'm not just blowing smoke when I say the Wittliff Collections at Texas State University in San Marcos put together an outstanding exhibit on *¡Viva Terlingua!*. It tells the whole origin story—the real deal: the birth of the band, Jerry Jeff riding herd, the songs, the raw rehearsals, the heady times, and the larger cultural moment that gave it all context.

A few years back, Jerry Jeff donated his entire personal archive to the Wittliff: not just *¡Viva Terlingua!* but everything he owned and controlled—original 2-inch master tapes, quarter-inch mixes, handwritten lyrics, and hours of unseen video footage. Hector Saldaña, the center's curator of the exhibit, put it plain: "Forget

Gonzo Compadres at The Birchmere in Alexandria, Virginia, 2023. (Photo courtesy of The Birchmere.)

Tribute concert for the 50th anniversary of *¡Viva Terlingua!* in Luckenbach, 2023. (L–R): Brendon Anthony (partly obscured, on fiddle), Jack Ingram, Craig Hillis, Bob Livingston, Lucas Hubbard, Ray Wylie Hubbard, Dennis Quaid, Django Walker, and Herb Steiner (on steel). (Obscured, on drums: Steve Samuel; Chris Gage, on keys.) (Photo by Robbyn Dodd.)

Willie. Forget Waylon. *¡Viva Terlingua!* was the first Texas Outlaw Country album." So there you have it. History, myth, and music—all under one roof.

Many of the original instruments that were played on the album are in the exhibit, including my Baldwin piano used on Gary P.'s "London Homesick Blues" and on everything else. There are Scott Newton photos blown up big with stories in the sidebars. And when you walk in, there is a soundtrack playing outtakes and alternate takes of many of the songs, some better than what made it on the record. It's gonzo, it's cosmic, it's fascinating Texas music history. Hector added, "One thing I realized by looking through and listening to the recordings and rehearsals is that the *band* was in the middle of everything. You guys were working up the songs together. Working parts out. There was no tension; there was a lot of creativity going down on those recordings and a lot of laughter. It just sounded like so much fun. And the passage of time has only emboldened the reputation of the album."

In the final say-so, your family is everything. It's a cliché, but of course it's true. Iris and the boys and their sweet wives and our grandkids are a big part of my life. Precious and amazing. Ask anyone. Tucker came back to Texas with his wife and son after sixteen years of living abroad at the end of an unpaved road. He's getting back in the swing of things and playing gigs. He's the ultimate starving artist poet, and his songs are spellbinding and heartbreaking—listen to "City of Gold." My youngest son Trevor and his wife and kids, my grandkids, are full of love, brightness, and creativity and being around them is an inspiration. Trevor is the calm Livingston of the bunch, and he looks at life in a Zen-like way.

My cosmic flower Iris and I just celebrated our 50th wedding anniversary! This is an astonishing and exhilarating feat. Through the good times and the hard times we have stuck together like Super Glue, like ivy on stone, and will stick forever. There's no

On the tarmac with Iris. I'm about to take off for parts unknown—somewhere out west. (Photo by Gary P. Nunn.)

doubt: Iris has hung in there, bearing witness to many of the wild tales scattered through this book, so I send her Great Big Love for being there.

My sister Judy's living the good life up in Plano with her crew. She's always been one of my biggest cheerleaders—and one of the last who still calls me Robert (though now and then it comes out as "Donald Robert" to get things rolling). Whenever I'm playing around Dallas—at Poor David's Pub or a private thing—I'll oftentimes stay with Judy and her husband Benny, who, fun fact, used to be a federal agent. Somebody tell my big sister it's time for a family reunion. I'll bring the music—let's head to Port Aransas, chase the shadows of our younger selves running wild on the beach, sunburned as lobsters, then gather 'round that night for the "sentence prayer" before supper.

Sadly, my big brother Donald passed on to that great listening room in the sky in February of 2024. He was my mentor and first musical influence—the one who showed me the chords and

A 50th wedding anniversary walk with Iris, 2023. (Photo courtesy of Bob Livingston.)

how to play the cross harp. I miss him and the long talks we had during the pandemic and well after that. During my walks in the woods I'd call him and he'd be working on a hat and we'd talk about Lubbock bands or who his closest friends were back then and where did they go at night and on Sunday morning. And he'd fill me in on what *his* life on the road was like. And I thought *my* shenanigans were wild and colorful. I love you, big brother Don.

A selfie with my mad hatter brother, Don. (Photo courtesy of Bob Livingston.)

Bradley Kopp and me at Michael Hearne's Big Barn Dance, c. 2018. (Photo by Dave Hensley.)

Fly safe in your Hawaiian shirt with your Gibson guitar slung over your shoulder, a glass of white wine in one hand and your cellphone in the other, and as the dealer hands you the jack of clubs the giant-screen TV that takes up the whole wall is tuned into TCM and showing *Blazing Saddles* followed after dinner by *Casablanca* and *Young Frankenstein* at midnight. I think about you every day. Send me a sign . . .

These days, I still love driving the open road before me, with music waiting at every turn. I've been playing out—solo, duo, and with a full band when it fits. Like I heard someone say, "Get the gig first, then the band." Bradley and I play a lot of these shows together and we can get a crowd going with just the two of us. We just played Poor David's Pub in Dallas. Most nights, the crowd leans in, quiet as a mouse, listening to the songs and soaking up the stories. Sometimes we even play dances, got one coming up this week. And now that Tucker's back in town, he and I have been teaming up again—father & son style, like on the old State Department tours. He'll be here in a bit to run through a couple of new songs. I'll tell him you said "hey."

Thanks for taking this ride with me and keeping me company on this long, cosmic trip. Here's hoping the trail winds into your neck of the woods soon—so I can share a few of these tales with you, face to face. Now . . . let's stick a fork in it and call it done.

For the time being . . .

Acknowledgments and Last Thoughts

2003

It's a hot Austin night and I'm running through the dark on Town Lake with my younger son Trevor and his friend, Sean. In those days I could run wild at full gallop, and did, quite often. It was exhilarating not seeing where you were going, feet pounding on the trail, pulled along by instinct and a faint faraway streetlight reflecting off the lake. As we ran up a hill on the south side Trevor said, "Dad, tell Sean the story about when you were in a cabin in California with Michael Murphey and Craig Hillis made an apple pie and Murphey hit his head on a cabinet and nearly . . ." So as we ran, I told Sean the story with embellishments, some true. With a little egging on, I told another story about the early days, then another: the riot of the road with Jerry Jeff; a streaker at a concert at Carnegie Hall; hanging out backstage with Bill and Hillary, Al and Tipper; Ray Wylie devising a plot to destroy my mind; and so on and so many forths. Sean and Trevor were running wide eyed and laughing. "Dad, you need to write a book!"

My wife, Iris, some of my close friends, and even band members had encouraged me to do this for years. My son, Tucker, a big storyteller himself, always liked my stories and told me to write it down. But with Trevor saying it right then and there and with

Big night at The Birchmere. Backstage with President Bill Clinton, Jerry Jeff, and Vice President Al Gore, 1993. (Photo by Joe Harris.)

the moon at that angle, a mysterious chord was struck and writing it all down suddenly had a significance. Cosmic cogs clicked, wheels turned, and worlds aligned.

"Write one page a day. Just one page. And you will have a book in a year," Trevor said.

Best laid plans. . . . I never managed to write one page a day, or even one page a week. Instead I began to write in spurts, sometimes in my office in the Guadalupe Arts Complex, hard work for a guy with ADHD. Based on writing samples and my friend and songwriter Crow Johnson's endorsement, I was given a ten-day residency at the Writers' Colony at Dairy Hollow in Eureka Springs, Arkansas. I got serious and almost deliberate. I had jumpstarted the process.

The COVID-19 pandemic came in 2020 and I didn't write more than a few sentences. But in 2021 I got a lot of work done after Michael Hearne's Barn Dance in Taos at a wonderful B&B called Casa Benavides owned by Tom McCarthy and his daughter

Ruthann. I also wrote and edited in a creatively charged hunting cabin tucked deep in the woods owned by my friends, Randy and Leslie Collier, a place of silence without a TV, where long walks along the fence line cleared me out and recharged me for another go at it. I finished up here in Austin at home in my office. Thanks and big hugs to Iris for letting me write late into the moonlit night when she would rather have been walking under it.

Besides Dairy Hollow, I'd like to thank a few friends and supporters who have opened up spaces for me to work. Robert Lotito and his wife, Cydney Donnell, in Fredericksburg, Texas, let me camp out in their historic B&B to write and, as Hemingway said, "to bleed." It poured out. Jim Urban in Port Aransas put me up in his writers' condo, and between paragraphs I'd clear my head with walks on the beach. I got a few stories down at a B&B owned by my old friend, Gwynn Juett, also in Fredericksburg.

Endless thanks and deep gratitude to my great friend and fellow Lubbockite, Andy Wilkinson, who first encouraged me to publish this twisty-turny memoir with Texas Tech University Press. Andy has been more than a friend—he's been my editor, my creative compass, and a steady hand through the whole wild ride. His calm insight, unwavering encouragement, and deep well of *knowing* kept me grounded and moving forward. I'm truly blessed to have taken this journey with him by my side.

Special thanks to everyone at Texas Tech University Press for making this book a reality. Thank you for rolling with me—especially when I wasn't always sure where the road was leading. It's been a joy to work with such a dedicated and talented team. Big shout-out to Travis Snyder, Joanna Conrad, Christie Perlmutter, Hannah Gaskamp, John Brock, and all the behind-the-scenes editorial and production heroes. Your craftsmanship and care brought these pages to life, and I'm truly grateful.

♪

My old pal Bobby Bridger told me that when you write, whether it's a song, a play, or a book, there needs to be a spine, a spine you can hang everything on. No matter how far you think I might be straying from the subject at hand, eventually I'll come back around and hang the story on the spine. In these pages there are journeys within journeys, all the parts fitting into the right grooves.

As I wrote this memoir, long-dormant memories began to stir—what I call *sleeping memories*—rising from their subconscious graves. Faces, places, and moments I'd long forgotten came rushing back in full-blown Technicolor. Writing a memoir is a kind of therapy: you re-walk the roads, re-run the tapes, and wonder why you did what you did—or didn't. Most of all, it's a chance to set the record straight… at least as I saw it. If you don't write it down someone is going to write it for you or not it at all.

Back in 1974, I wrote in a song:

You can take charge of your history.
It's all in the way that you're writing it down.
It's by and large just the way that you see.
And you can make waves without making a sound.
Write It All Down.

Index

Note: Page numbers in italics refer to images and their captions.

About the Author

Bob Livingston is a Texas troubadour, globe-trotting musician, writer, and storyteller whose lifelong journey in music has taken him from honky-tonks and folk clubs to concert halls and stages across the world. A founding member of the legendary Lost Gonzo Band, he played a pivotal role in the rise of progressive country and outlaw music scenes of the 1970s and beyond. With six acclaimed studio albums and performances throughout the US and in more than twenty-five countries as a cultural ambassador for the US State Department, Livingston has built a career grounded in curiosity, creativity, and connection. *Gypsy Alibi: A Gonzo Memoir* is his first book.
(AUTHOR PHOTO BY NICOLA GELL)